# Beyond the Family

For the Stangers and the Moffatts

# Beyond the Family

*The Social Organization of
Human Reproduction*

## A. F. ROBERTSON

University of California Press
Berkeley   Los Angeles

University of California Press
Berkeley and Los Angeles, California

Copyright © A. F. Robertson 1991

Robertson, A. F.
  Beyond the family: the social organization of human reproduction / A. F. Robertson.
    p.     cm.
  Includes bibliographical references (p.    ) and index.
  ISBN 0–520–07518–8 (cloth)
  1. Family.   2. Marriage.   3. Human reproduction–Social aspects.
4. Fertility, Human–Social aspects.   I. Title.
HQ503.R59   1991
340.6'32—dc20     91–9381     CIP

Typeset in 10 on 12 pt Plantin
by Times Graphics
Printed in Great Britain by Billings & Sons Ltd, Worcester

# Contents

# Figures

# Acknowledgements

I have been contemplating this topic all my life, and am aware of the extent to which my ideas have been culled from my own family, teachers, colleagues and students. I am profoundly grateful to them all. In the more immediate process of writing this book I have been given particular help and assistance by John Barnes, Denise Bielby, Bill Bielby, Ann Bone, Francesca Bray, Don Brown, Roger Friedland, Juan Gamella, Jack Goody, Esther Goody, Tamara Hareven, Keith Hart, Elvin Hatch, Bill Hyder, Jean La Fontaine, Don Symons and Michael Whyte. To them, my sincere thanks. I have also been greatly helped by airing the main arguments with members of the Economy and Society group, and successive 'Anthro 120' classes, here in Santa Barbara.

A couple of minor stylistic points: throughout the text I have used the expression 'our own societies' as shorthand for those western industrial countries which seem likely to provide the main readership for this book. I have tried to be gender neutral, but have occasionally resorted to male pronouns. I hope this will not be mistaken for a lack of good intentions.

# 1

# Introduction

Reproduction is the process in which mature organisms exercise their physical capacity to produce other organisms, thereby regenerating their species. In our societies we tend to take a rather narrow view of this activity. We think of reproduction as a strictly private affair, which begins with the fertilization of a woman by a man and ends with the birth of a child: an entry into and an exit from the woman's vagina. Doing these things is an adult capacity to be exercised in domestic privacy, and knowing about them is an adult privilege. Moreover, we do not normally associate the reproductive process with old people, tending to assume that they have neither the physical capacity for nor any interest in such pursuits. However, the melancholy truth is that life is fatal: aging and death are as essential to the process of human regeneration as birth – why else would we speak of *re*production?

No less obviously, human reproduction transcends the lifespan of a single individual: the process involves a minimum of three persons, and exponentially larger numbers as one cycle of regeneration follows another. Organizing reproduction involves lifetimes of complicated relationships among many people. If sex often seems an irresistible animal force within us, the reproduction of people is something over which we can, and do, exert a great deal of control. Sex may be secretive, and even a pregnancy may be concealed, but reproducing people is inescapably public. It is, after all, the process by which society itself is recreated. Organizing it demands extensive cooperation, not just among family members but in the wider contexts of community and state. Our national laws still express a keen interest in these supposedly 'private' affairs: who has a right to have sex with whom, or who should be regarded as the son or daughter of whom.

Surely, if the social organization of reproduction is such an important force in our lives, social scientists must already have said everything that is worth saying about it? Unfortunately not. There are two basic reasons for their neglect of reproduction. The first is that they have been very much more interested in the social significance of *other* processes, especially economic production and exchange. Social science was born nearly two centuries ago during the period of dramatic global change which we call the Industrial Revolution. Seeking to make some sense of this, the founding fathers of social science could hardly ignore the fact that material forces – new inventions, industrial techniques, manufacturing processes, etc. – were transforming society. Those who took any interest in reproduction were inclined to see it as responding, like everything else, to the material forces reshaping our world. Its purpose was tacitly obvious; without this human raw material there could be no social world to reshape.

The second reason is that our view of reproduction has been obscured by our obsession with one particular social institution: 'the family'. Family: the word is loaded with emotional ambivalence. Parents strive to keep it together, adolescents struggle to escape from it. Politicians and clergymen aver that it is the bedrock of civilized society, while social scientists have been saying for decades that it has lost virtually all its influence on society, that it has become 'almost completely functionless' (Parsons and Bales 1955: 16–17). The problem is that while we still make the prim assumption that organizing reproduction is properly and exclusively a family affair, it is very evident that in the kinds of society in which we now live, 'families' have much less to do with the social organization of reproduction than they ever did in the past. Social scientists have explained how the institutions of industrial society, driven by economic forces, have been encroaching relentlessly on the sacred rights and duties of 'the family', reducing it to its most elementary 'nuclear' form. Compressed and fragmented in this way spouses, parents and children are at grave risk of alienation from one another and from the wider community.[1] Here is the double bind: we assume that reproduction is strictly a family affair, but at the same time we believe that families are being put out of business by the expansion of industrial society. Immersed within our understanding of 'the family', reproduction is lost to sight as an active force in society and history. Worse: in social science our conception of reproduction is draining away with the bathwater of the western industrial family.

Here I argue that unless we comprehend our emotional prejudices, dismantle our conception of what families are and do, and assemble new interpretations of the social organization of reproduction, we will certainly fail in our efforts to understand and perhaps influence vital forces in our rapidly changing lives. The moral dilemmas of reproduction are as old as society itself, witness the endless war of the sexes and of the generations. But technical innovations like artificial insemination and *in vitro* fertilization, or the medical means to prolong life, are now presenting serious challenges to the way we think about and evaluate human reproduction. These issues are complicated because they are not simply a 'family affair', but have farreaching implications for modern social organization.

The inadequacy of the old rubric of family studies has become an embarrassment to anthropology and sociology.[2] The questions which other social scientists have been asking about how life processes affect economic or political behaviour betray a mounting uneasiness with conventional notions of 'family' and 'household': a sense that these are weak analytical categories, social epiphenomena with a great diversity of empirically observable forms.[3] In urging the need to think within these categories to the processes which constitute them, feminist scholars in particular have been obliged to come to terms with the basics of human reproduction. 'I was outraged', says Mary O'Brien of her introduction to social science, 'that none of the works I had read paid any attention to the historical and philosophical aspects of human reproduction, the meaning of the event, the necessity for woman's labor to reproduce the species in history' (1989: 22). Again, Rossi has complained that 'neither Marxism nor feminism, to say nothing of mainstream social science, has yet taken up the challenge of the biological component to human behavior, despite the fact that sexual dimorphism is central to both production and reproduction. An ideology that does not confront this basic issue is an exercise in wishful thinking, and a social science that does not confront it is sterile' (1985: 186).

While the biological sciences have appropriated serious discussion of reproduction, in social science it has been reduced to a metaphor for continuity in relationships and institutions. But there are more general problems in perceiving the wider social and historical significance of reproduction. It is very difficult to observe objectively a process in which we are all so personally involved, which extends through and beyond our own limited lifespan, and which involves the private activities of masses of individuals. As a result, our view of reproduction tends to be both very subjective and very inert. To understand its role in the making of history we must extend our knowledge of it in time and space, seeing it as an active and manipulable force in our individual and collective lives. This goes against our own emotional distaste for old age and mortality, which are as much a part of the organization of reproduction as the joys of birth and youth.

Our understanding of the history of reproduction has been coloured by nostalgia for an epoch when there were few other institutions to rival the family. If sociologists talk at great length about 'the family', anthropologists have punished generations of students with the complexities of 'kinship and marriage' in tribal and peasant communities. In the classic ethnographies these fundamental relationships have been seen as ramifying out into the political structures of tribal government, shaping the religions of ancestor worship, and controlling economic activities. Indeed, the family in this larger sense *was* society. Like other social scientists, anthropologists have been very ready to admit that these 'kinship' structures crumble before the onslaught of industrial institutions. They have *not* been able to tell us what then happens to the social organization of reproduction. Does it disappear? Does it somehow become less important than it used to be?

This is plainly absurd. Our problem is that we have simply lost the means of understanding the many ways in which reproduction is now organized in our societies. In this book I try to begin afresh, putting our (mis)understanding of 'the family' into context, and developing a view of reproduction as a vital process which must be controlled and manipulated, and which therefore remains a basic determinant of the way our societies have developed. One effect of focusing on reproduction is to challenge the conventional view that industrial institutions have been displacing the family. Instead, we might say that 'the family' has successfully dumped a great many of the costs and burdens of reproduction on the institutions of industrial society. Today, a wide array of organizations – banks and schools, factories and clinics, mortgages and retirement communities, even governments and political parties – are all involved in various ways in the vital tasks of reproduction, producing new individuals, rearing them to adult maturity, caring for the aged, and replacing the dead. We are simply not accustomed to thinking about these 'economic' or 'political' activities from the perspective of reproductive organization.

In this book I want to put the political-economic and reproductive processes back together, to show how each is influenced by the other. I shall argue that reproduction is not simply a family affair, but has helped to shape all aspects of our modern societies, including such things as salaries and mortgages, suburbs and social classes, which might be thought of as determined by strictly material interests. My purpose is to reveal something of the theoretical importance of reproduction to other social scientists: that there are things about banks or factories or political parties which can *only* be explained by understanding the influence of reproductive processes, and which even the most elaborate economic and political analyses will fail to reveal.

In the first part of the book I begin by clarifying the relationship between the physical processes of reproduction and such basic social groupings as 'family' and 'household'. I consider how reproductive relations become economic and political relations, and the ways in which these are construed and regulated in human cultures. Chapters 4 and 5 examine more closely the interdependence of political-economic and reproductive processes. First, I discuss how people come to grips economically and politically with mating, child-rearing and death; and then, turning the coin, I explain how economic processes respond to the need to organize reproduction. In the sixth chapter I shall show how these considerations help us to understand the social and historical significance of broader relations of class, gender and generation.

In the second part of the book I treat reproduction as an active force in the making of the modern world, tracing the expansion of reproductive organization from households and local communities out into the institutions of modern industrial states. Chapter 8 shows how this analysis can help us to understand the ways in which labour is rewarded in industrial economies, by explaining important differences between *wages* and *salaries*. The concluding chapters focus on our *ideas* about the organization of reproduction, especially about how it has changed and how we think it ought to change. I finally return to the perplexing issues of how we, as social scientists, should interpret reproduction as a socal and historical force.

# 2

# The social dynamics of reproduction

Organizing reproduction is a strategic challenge. Unless we are very young, extremely privileged or extraordinarily lucky we must recognize that our own families demand a great deal of effort to keep them running smoothly. Nevertheless, we tend to think of reproduction, and consequently of family life, as 'simply natural', not something over which we can exercise much control.[1] For most of us, family membership is a fact of birth rather than a matter of choice. The way we reproduce seems to make the family a logical necessity, but the enormous variation in family patterns around the world is a reminder that these elementary relations of reproduction may be organized in many different ways. Nature has dictated to us the basic terms of human reproduction and although we often romanticize it, the process is messy and complicated. We must thank nature for also giving us brains and an interest in social cooperation to help us to deal with some of the greater inconveniences of reproduction.

## Basic relations of reproduction: family and household

We give birth to infants who are chronically dependent on their mothers and require a good many years of care before they can fend for themselves. As mammals we are locked into a very close dependence on our mothers, an intimate relationship which must endure through pregnancy, parturition, lactation and weaning, and then through several years of childhood.[2] This is undoubtedly the central *relation of reproduction*, upon which all others are contingent.[3] Why our mothers should be so concerned about *us* is rather more mysterious. The best they can hope for is that we will take care of them at some stage in the distant future, when they are old and incapacitated. But children do not repay the debts of maternity *directly and in kind*; instead they raise children of their own, extending the reproductive credit to the next generation.

Finding a substitute for either the mother or the child can be very difficult. On the other hand, *mating* may be a much briefer relation of reproduction, and may require regular sexual reinforcement if it is to persist. With the phenomena of conjugal and paternal bonding, nature seems to have given us halfhearted assurance that the man will stick around long enough to establish the relationships we call 'husband' and 'father'. Long-term attachments may be unimportant if his interests are purely genetic, but if he is at all concerned about who will care for him when he himself is incapacitated by old age, he may take a more lasting interest in his progeny. If we extend the relations of reproduction a little further we could include brothers and sisters who are dependent on the same mother.

Because we are each so deeply involved in this network of responsibilities and dependencies, a clear objective view of 'the family' is very elusive. It is a thoroughly egocentric notion, a reckoning of relationships outward from ourselves. Each of us draws irregular, concentric rings around the network of people we think of as 'family', cutting out quite close relatives we dislike or seldom see, and counting in people who might not, strictly speaking, be relatives at all.[4] Families, in other words, are not mutually exclusive, objectively definable groups of people out there in society. They are overlapping components of a huge network of relationships which is created through time out of the basic process of reproduction.

The fact that the network is not static, but is continually being rewoven, raises further conceptual difficulties. It should be entirely obvious that the relations of reproduction are by their very nature always in flux: your family today is not the same as your family five years ago or five years hence. Nevertheless, we seem to cling stubbornly to the idea of the family as durable and stable, perhaps because we are uncomfortably aware of our transience as individuals. Family life, especially the arrival of children, affords a sense of continuity. However, aging and mortality are as much part of the reproductive process as birth and maturation. In our lifetime we may enjoy quite a long period of adult maturity in which both our reproductive capacities and our responsibility for dependants are at their height. During the same period our strategic knowledge about life and material survival usually improves. The older we get the more dependent we become, once again, on other people, whether they are family members, pension companies or nurses in geriatric wards. All of this makes up the distinctively human process of *regeneration*, the transmission of life and the material and intellectual resources needed to sustain it through long periods of history. This process is so slow and extensive, that it largely eludes individual perception, however keenly we may feel the immediate shocks of family gains and losses.

The dynamism of family life is also obscured by the differential timing of human reproduction. In normal circumstances, each family produces children in its own time, and families within the wider community are all producing children at different times. As a result, family development is socially less conspicuous than it might have been if we synchronized our breeding like other creatures. If we did have rutting and birthing seasons, perhaps producing all our children in the space of a month or so every five years, the effects of the reproductive process would become strikingly evident. Maternity clinics and schools, for example, would have to deal with the periodic tidal waves, which would ripple through history creating noticeable rush hours in marriage chapels and funeral parlours.[5] Occasionally, social organization throws an age cohort together and the effects are immediately obvious. A familiar example is the newly built street or housing tract which is colonized by young couples, and after a few years the place is swarming with kids. When the children grow up and leave home, the street is full of old folks, and the 'for sale' signs start popping up, heralding a new wave of youthful colonization. We would describe this as a new *generation*, an egocentric and relativistic notion akin to that of 'the family', by which individuals seek to identify age mates in the cycle of reproduction.

If we are to understand 'the family' we must take care to distinguish its subjective image as a natural, durable and stable group of people surrounding each individual, from the objective idea of dynamic, overlapping social networks. 'The family' is *objectively* identifiable by what its members *do* rather than what they think. While reproduction must be central to any definition of 'the family', it is virtually impossible to disengage this from all the other activities which constitute family life, and which in turn make reproduction practicable. It is the great diversity of these activities which make it extremely difficult to find an objective and universally valid definition of 'the family'.[6] Probably the most conspicuous 'family activity' is *residence*, for the simple reason that a house brings people together in one physical space for long enough to allow us to think of them as separate from other similar groups of people. For this reason people making censuses and surveys have treated a houseful of people as a 'primary social group' synonymous with 'the family'.[7] However, a *household* is not the same as a family: people who regard themselves as members of one family are often scattered through many households, and if it were large enough a single household might contain several distinct families. Moreover, 'households' in other parts of the world may not comprehend many other activities which *we* would normally associate with 'family life': the people who sleep under the same roof do not necessarily eat at the same table or from the same pot, nor do they work in the same fields, or share the same wage packet. Faced with such apparent confusion, census-takers in other countries have resorted to alternative pragmatic definitions of 'the family', for example, 'all those people who sleep behind a single locked door' or, focusing on the activity of consumption, 'all those people who eat from one pot'.

Nevertheless, social scientists have persevered with the concept of the *household* or *domestic group* in their efforts to define, compare and analyse family life.[8] Jack Goody has narrowed it down to four fundamental activities: 'Domestic groups are those basic units which in preindustrial societies revolve around the hearth and the roof, the bed and the farm, that is, around the processes of production and reproduction, of shelter and consumption' (Goody 1972: 4). Although households are seldom neatly constituted by a single reproductive unit, a single roof, a single hearth and a single farm or wage-packet, these activities convey a concreteness which is lacking in the messy notion of 'the family'. However there are costs: analyses of the household tend to focus on residence and the economic activities of production and consumption, rather than on the less visible organization of reproduction – the one activity which remains unequivocally at the heart of family life.[9] Study of the household has tended to circumvent rather than solve the problems which have made study of 'the family' difficult in the first place. If reproduction is formally included within the portfolio of domestic activities and then effectively ignored, its social significance is lost. Concealing the influence of reproduction within 'the household' robs us of the opportunity to understand its influence on social institutions far beyond the range of the domestic group and the bonds of kinship.

As individuals, our own reproductive interests are clearly not confined within the household, but extend to any economic, political, religious or other institution which helps or hinders us in these vital tasks. Indeed, the household itself is an agent of the reproductive process in society at large, a front-line institution for dealing with the complexities and hazards of reproducing whole populations. Its internal activities are geared to the external task of moving a new generation out into households of their own. If we ignore their reproductive dynamism, households appear like social bricks, static and durable, each brick pretty much like any other in the social edifice. Social science has been victim to this static image, defining modal households as the unit of comparative social analysis: the 'Hindu joint family', the 'African polygynous household' or the 'urban nuclear family'. Analytically, this is a soft option: it is so much easier to describe the Jones family as we see it today than to trace the history of the Joneses over several generations, keeping track of the various entrances and exits, and how the separate lives intertwine and separate over time. Whether we choose to describe the Jones family as big or small, poor or prosperous, happy or unhappy, depends very much on *when*, in its history, we happen to look at it. To argue that all these differences even each other out in a population over time is simply to deny that reproductive changes have any aggregate significance.

## The reproductive dynamism of households

The point may be made by comparing the conventional static representation of the 'elementary' or 'nuclear' family (figure 2.1) with a more dynamic rendering of relationships among the same group of people (figure 2.2).[10] Here, their lives are arranged along the horizontal axis, and the basic reproductive events which link them are represented by vertical lines. These *qualify* the relationships among the people involved: we could say, for example, that the line linking A and B turns lovers or an engaged couple into *husband* and *wife*. The next vertical line signals not just the creation of a *son*, but the qualification of the wife as *mother*, and the husband as *father*. The next reproductive step which brings a *daughter* to A and B also creates a significant family change for C, who becomes *brother* to D. But let us note that these categories are not universal, they are qualities organized in particular cultures in specific ways.

Nevertheless, anthropologists have found it useful for comparative purposes to break this sequence of events up into typical stages marking the growth and decline of the domestic group (see figure 2.3).[11] The first is *establishment*, the 'home-making' stage in which a couple set up house

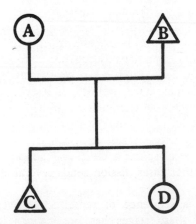

**Figure 2.1**  Conventional representation of the 'elementary' or 'nuclear' family

together, sharing income and food and getting down to the task of procreation. The birth of children initiates the phase of *expansion* and a new pattern of relationships. When the children are mature and create pressure

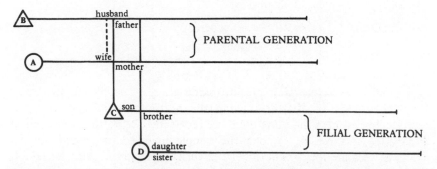

**Figure 2.2**  Family development: intersecting life-lines of two generations in the 'elementary' or 'nuclear' family

to quit and start their own households, the stage of *fission* begins. Finally, as the original couple get old the household goes into *decline*, dissolving when the last person dies or moves out to live with another relative or in a retirement home.

Different domestic activities come into play at different stages. Residence is plainly important in understanding the *establishment* of a new household. But whether and when a couple can set themselves up independently may be determined by such economic factors as the availability of land or housing, which in turn affects their readiness to have children. Many young couples have to start their own households as a dependent subunit of his or her parents' household, perhaps occupying a room in their house or building a hut in their compound. Establishment can thus be a painful and lengthy quest for independence, working and saving and putting up with in-law pressures. Residential arrangements provide very visible (but therefore potentially misleading) evidence of the process of domestic *replacement*. In some cases one household will replace another almost imperceptibly within the same physical space: a child may simply take over his or her parent's house. In other cases, fission sends several children out to build, rent or buy.

While describing a sequence of reproductive events within a single household, each of these stages has implications for the reproductive relationships *between* households. In the repetitive *cycle of domestic development*, fission provides the most obvious link (see figure 2.4). What Fortes (1958: 4–5) has called the process of 'replacement' coincides with the stage of decline in the parental household and establishment in the offspring's household. According to Fortes, patterns of domestic develop-

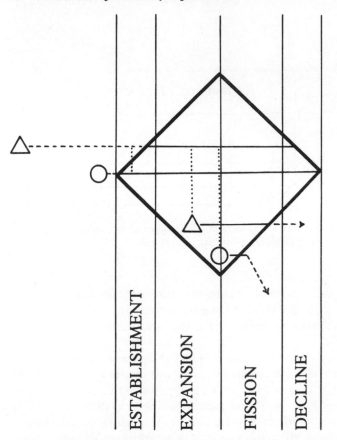

**Figure 2.3** Stages in development of one compact household

ment around the world are variations on this basic theme. Jack Goody (1972: 19) has pointed out that a household can grow along two axes: it can *extend* vertically, to include more generations, or *expand* horizontally to include more people of the same generation. The pattern represented in figure 2.3, common enough in reality, is relatively easy to describe because growth within and between generations is kept to a minimum, the children move out promptly to set up households of their own, and each household lasts only as long as the surviving partner of one marriage. For reference I shall call this particular version of domestic development the *compact* pattern.

The wide range of possibilities for expansion accounts for much of the observable differences in households around the world. They often expand to include lodgers, foster-children, cousins, apprentices, maids, slaves and other personnel beyond the range of the immediate family. Polygamy brings

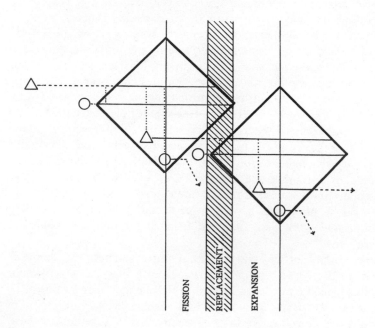

**Figure 2.4** Phases in the replacement of compact household

in extra people in the parental generation and significantly increases the number of children. Thus, expansion and extension tend to go together. The most distinctive feature of what I shall call the *extended* pattern of domestic development is that each household grows to include more than two generations (the compact pattern has no more than two). The household which includes three or four generations has almost certainly kept tight control of the process of *fission*, holding together married siblings and their offspring.[12] The household typically splits up on the death of the most senior man, an aged grandfather or great-grandfather. He may be the last of a group of brothers who have kept their children, grandchildren and great-grandchildren together as a single big household. The units which 'hive off' to set up new households are often quite large, usually consisting of at least two generations.[13] It is very probable that one or more conjugal units will take over the homestead of a parent, thus enhancing the appearance of continuity of the household over successive generations.[14] But the fact that fission may spin off quite small 'nuclear' family groups is a reminder that sheer size is not the defining feature of the extended domestic development process. As Hajnal (1983: 82) has pointed out, at *certain stages* in their development households in the compact pattern may actually be larger than households at certain stages in the extended pattern.[15]

The extended type of household structure works well where a large workforce is needed for farming, herding, trading or similar activities, and where alternative economic and political institutions are lacking. It was common in the ancient agricultural communities of Europe, and many versions of it have been found by anthropologists and historians in rural societies around the world, including America. The nineteenth-century French social philosopher Frédéric Le Play admired the respect for custom and patriarchal authority which made this relatively stable and cooperative pattern of family life possible. Holding several generations together in a big household means restraining the 'natural' desire of young people to move out and set up independent units of their own. Such a 'patriarchal' household was a miniature paradigm of 'good government', settling disputes, allocating work and food and balancing group cohesion with individual rewards.[16]

The same could not be said of the compact pattern of domestic development in the context of modern society. Le Play had a very poor opinion of this type of family organization, which he identified by one of its most striking characteristics, *instability*: 'It establishes itself by the union of two free adults, grows with the birth of children, shrinks with the successive departure of the members of the new generation, and dissolves finally, without leaving a trace, with the early death of the abandoned parents.'[17] It is interesting that he saw it as characteristic both of the hunting bands of ancient times and the emerging industrial working classes of nineteenth-century Europe. Unlike the stolid patriarchal family, it produced short lived households and encouraged a hectic, irresponsible opportunism. It was more suited to allowing individuals to make their way in the wider social world than providing internal domestic security. 'In this system,' he observed glumly, 'a single or married individual is no longer responsible for the needs of his relatives and rapidly rises to a higher situation if he possesses outstanding aptitudes. But in contrast, if he is unskilled or morally delinquent, he falls even faster to a wretched condition, unable to claim any assistance.'[18]

Reckoning that the patriarchal (extended) family was too large and unwieldy for the modern world, but disapproving of the instable (compact) pattern, Le Play seized on a third model of domestic development which, he argued, had neither the clumsiness of the first nor the vices of the second. This he called the *stem* family, which combines some of the features of the other two patterns. A model of restraint and good housekeeping, the stem household sought its own internal adaptations to the problems of reproductive instability, while releasing a restrained flow of personnel to develop the institutions of the wider world. In fact, the stem pattern has been associated historically with scarcity rather than developmental opportunity. Living space and economic resources are typically so limited that there are tight constraints on reproduction, and thus on both the expansion and fission of households. The only reasonable way one household can *replace* another is by one reproductive unit taking over the residential space and economic assets of its predecessor. This means that only one child is able to start a family, and must usually wait quite a long time before the parents are prepared to hand over the household. Thus, the stem pattern is 'compact' in that it is organized around a married couple and their children, but 'extended' in that it reincorporates the grandparents.

The example of the stem family pattern in Ireland is well known through the work of Arensberg and Kimball (1968).[19] Aware of the economic dangers of reducing farms in this crowded region to tiny useless fragments, the people of County Clare sought to ensure that only one married couple had managerial responsibility for the whole farm. This meant that one son (failing whom a daughter) lived on with his parents until they were ready to hand over the farm to him. Even at the age of forty he would still be called 'the boy' – a constant reminder of his dependent status. In an elaborate contract called 'the writings', centred on 'the match' of the son and a suitable bride, the whole family went through a painful process of adjustment. His brothers and sisters were given some financial compensation for moving out, often from the dowry which the new bride brought in. Many joined the church or the army, or migrated overseas. The old couple retired to the 'west room' of the house and were supposed to allow the son and his wife to run the household and raise a family of their own.

In the stem pattern of development, people enter and exit, by birth, migration or death, but the main interest is to keep the household stable as an economic unit. Let us therefore be clear that the pursuit of economic and residential stability does not mean that reproductive dynamism is less important in the stem pattern than in any other. All households in any pattern of development expand and contract; however, as a general rule, this movement is most extreme in the compact pattern, less so in the extended, and quite explicitly least in the stem pattern. Le Play was much enthused by the planning, strategizing and careful husbandry which this involved: being prevented from marrying, or being squeezed out of home and community was hardly 'natural' or painless, but he saw the stem pattern as an intelligent balance of tradition and inventiveness, the best sort of arrangement for the industrializing world, and a restrained way of making progress in our crowded cities. Children who could not be accommodated at home could join the army or go and develop the colonies. The stem pattern 'gives firm guarantees of public order,' he declared grandly. 'It reconciles public interest with individual well-being' (Le Play 1895: 152). In fact, Le Play's 'vigorous and admirable' stem pattern has rarely if ever found a niche in the industrial world. Instead, it is the 'frail shrub' of the compact pattern which has flourished everywhere (Silver 1982: 80).

As Le Play acknowledged, the compact pattern of domestic development is nothing new. The historian Peter Laslett (1969) has been particularly insistent about this, challenging our assumption that large, extended households prevailed in the human past. Indeed, if the latter are more elaborate economic and social constructions, then the compact pattern has at least a logical priority in the organization of human affairs. Is it not 'more natural' for parents to give in as early as possible to pressure from their children to leave home and set up on their own? The cost of prompt fission, as Le Play made clear, is greater exposure to the destabilizing effects of the process: households expand rapidly when children are born and break up when they mature. One round of the cycle involves several new residences and much change in economic activities. Households are more numerous per head of population, much smaller, and much less self-contained than with the extended or stem patterns.

There is a corollary of great importance, to which I shall often return in the following chapters. The compact pattern of domestic development is generally feasible only because there is some well-established wider network of social relations to support it. There is, in other words, a vital connection between the organization of reproduction in this minimal form of the household in our societies, and the complexity of the social world around us. Schools, banks, clinics and all the other apparatus of industrial society have assumed much of the burden of organizing reproduction. My intention is to explain how and why this has happened.

## Reproductive ideals

These issues return our attention to a second basic theme of this book: the unreliability of our understandings about the social organization of reproduction. The strength of our feelings about 'the family' is not only a wonderful source of confusion, it is also a measure of the importance of reproductive organization, both to us as individuals and to the social order on which we depend. Reproduction is a relentless force in our lives, adding to and subtracting from the people around us, and obliging us to change our relationships with each other and with the wider world. It is a persistent strategic challenge, the outcome of which is as important for society as for the persons in each household. Reproduction is simply too important to be left to the whims and fancies of individuals. If each of us is to make a success of reproduction, and if we are to be prevented from allowing our own reproductive adventures to wreck other people's lives, we must take heed of the wisdom which preceding generations have laid down in the form of cultural norms and values. It is a measure of the wideranging implications of reproduction that these ideas and ideals reach out into every corner of our lives, bombarding us with advice about how the game should be played.

We learn these ideas 'on the job': knowing what is right and what is best (not necessarily the same thing) is all part of our emotional conditioning in the intimate circle of the household. We absorb these meanings through our own changing identities as son, sister or parent, by our experience of relationships with others, or by taking different roles in the social dramas of baptism, marriage and funeral. Our mothers and fathers give us an idea of what it means to be husband and wife, and as children we act out permutations of these relationships in play. When it comes to creating real relations of reproduction we may have to struggle to reconcile personal desires with the practical wisdom and the social rules we have learned. For example, we may be constrained to postpone the pleasures of sex until we have the material resources to get married 'properly'.

The social rules which tell us how we should set about the business of reproduction come to us with the full weight of long-established social custom: they are the result of numerous generations trying to make sense of the task of creating new life in a particular environment, and they have force today because they affect a large number of people. Some of these ideas are so rigid (for example, 'don't have sex with a sibling') that they are not often discussed. Others which indicate the latitude for choice ('it's best to marry within your own ethnic group') are often the subject of heated discussion. Some ideals are very explicit ('get married before you have a baby') while others have a more subtle expression (the celebration of a long and respectable marriage in a Golden Wedding). Norms about reproduction are embodied in laws and rituals, names and proverbs, dress and deportment, poetry and gossip. But living up to these ideals is also a struggle in which some people very evidently hold a strategic advantage. And periodically the norms themselves go out of fashion – new experiences force a change in shared ideals.

The institutions of domestic life are a mixture of practical guidelines, goals for ambitious individuals and notions about what society in general or certain powerful people within it regard as tolerable behaviour. Subjectively, we rarely if ever get a well-rounded view of the reproductive cycle as '*an* institution', even though it is so heavily laden with meanings.[20] As individuals we perceive all these ideas, rules and customs in a very piecemeal way, because a different set of norms bears down on us at each stage in our personal experience of the reproductive process. Graduating from the dependence of childhood to the responsibilities of adulthood and parenthood, and thence to the dependence of old age, changes our judgements about the relations of reproduction. Adolescent boys probably have a very partial view of the norms of parenthood. Old folks complain about the loose morals of the young, and young folks complain of parental intolerance. Our ideas about choosing a spouse, when to get married or how many children we should have alter significantly as we proceed through the domestic cycle. Parents tend to be more enthusiastic about children when they are little than when they are teenagers, and teenagers themselves tend to take a dim view of parenthood while they are embroiled in the processes of domestic fission. Everyone says 'times are changing' whereas in fact it is mostly just people who are changing.

The distinct experiences of men and women are no less important in understanding reproductive ideals. Men may be encouraged to look forward to the political status of paterfamilias, to that standing in the community which comes with running a prosperous and independent household. Women, so much at the heart of domestic affairs, may be expected to aspire to the more internal statuses of wife and mother, and may take a more acute interest than men in the history and proper development of their families. They may accordingly be better informants about such things than men, who generally have more to say about the structure of community relations than what goes on day by day, and year by year, within the household. Interviewing the paterfamilias about such things may be relatively uninformative.

I would suggest that norms about domestic development impinge on our individual consciousness in two distinct ways. I have found that when I ask people about these ideals they offer an essentially static image of the household at the peak of its achievements, a little portrait of the happy, fulfilled family at its most expanded and extended stage. This serves as a target for growth which I call the *apical norm*.[21] People do not idealize earlier or later stages of the domestic cycle in this way: newly-weds or retired couples are not the main focus of reproductive aspirations. People generally get more pleasure out of building up their households than from seeing them break up.[22] In the stages of establishment and expansion a household has strong inward emotional orientations – gathering people together around the hearth. Fission creates centrifugal interests, and parents increasingly look outwards from their declining household to those of their children and grandchildren. Building a household up may be an exciting strategic struggle, but holding an established household together can become a lot like warfare. The pressures for fission bring serious conflicts of interest, with the children challenging the managerial authority of their parents. We could say that in the stage of fission the parental generation is trying to hang on to the apical norm for as long as possible, while the offspring are trying to get out and pursue the apical norm for themselves. Parents with adolescent children in our society know how hectic this intergenerational power struggle can be (after that, fission and decline can come as blessed relief).

Such parents may well wonder how the patriarch in the *extended* model of domestic development has the stamina to hold such a large household together for so long. On the other hand, we should not allow our ethnocentrism to obscure the gratifications of a large household. As each new member is *added* to a household, the relationships within it *multiply*. A father, mother and two children have six dyadic relationships among them, but there are thirty-six relationships in a household of nine persons, allowing a degree of choice much appreciated by people with many brothers and sisters, or with resident grandparents. The small 'nuclear family' may pose fewer managerial problems, but is it any wonder that it is often regarded as emotionally claustrophobic?[23]

Just as household organization varies from one society to another, so the apical norms differ. From the 1950s to the 1970s the family which was used to sell everything from insurance to cornflakes in our societies consisted of a thirtyish father and an attractive but domesticated wife, with a boy of eight or ten, and his younger sister. The parents look confident and prosperous, free of the grey hair and worldly cares which come with middle age. The children are delightfully prepubescent; teenage armageddon and domestic fission are still mercifully distant.[24] In 1965–7 I discovered that people in southern Uganda were well aware of our pattern, but still favoured their own much more expansive apical norm. Polygyny is central to the Ganda notion of the *amaka amakukutivu*, the 'well-established' household (see figure 2.5). In this heyday the household will also attract other temporary residents such as unmarried brothers or the children of relatives. The ideal is expressed in many ways, ranging from architecture to terminology. For example, the master of such a household is described as *Ssemaka*, which consists of the word for household with the honorific prefix '*Sse-*'. The parallel term for the mistress of the household is *Nnamaka*. She may also be referred to tellingly as '*Nnakafuga*', 'she-who-rules', or as '*Nnalugongo*', 'the backbone'.

Significant changes in the lives and relationships of household members provide a key to what I call the *procedural norms* of domestic development. They measure off a household's progress through the stages of expansion, fission and decline, and they exert strong social pressure urging individuals along in their domestic careers. People make households, households define social persons, and both change relentlessly. Parenthood, siblingship, marriage and all other domestic relationships are not states but processes; they change us, and the way we perceive them changes as our own lives progress.[25] *Who* we are in society at large, our identity and the kinds of activity in which we become involved, are therefore very largely determined by our position at a particular time in a particular household. As Hobsbawm shrewdly observes, the reproductive cycle also modulates political attitudes,

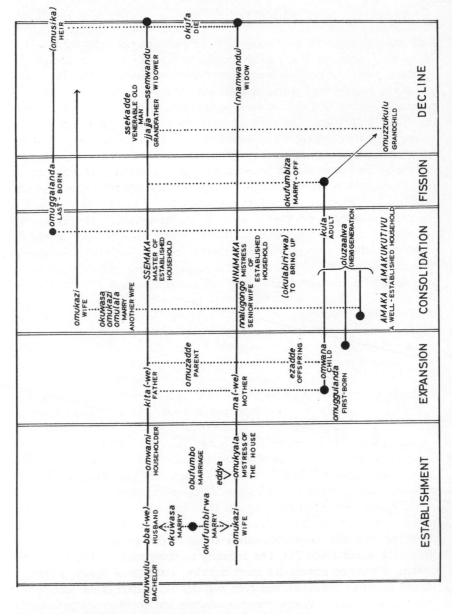

**Figure 2.5**  The Ganda ideals of domestic development

teenage rebels maturing into middle-aged conservatives: 'It is much harder for a man to revolt against the apparatus of power once he has family responsibilities' (1959: 18).

Procedural norms are preeminently concerned with matters of *good timing*: people lose esteem for not doing things promptly (getting married and having a baby) and for doing them in the wrong order (having a baby and getting married). Most societies have some pretty tough ideas about such things as how you get to be a 'mother': they may insist that you ought to be a 'wife' first, otherwise you are a 'loose woman' or a 'whore', and your child a 'bastard'. Chronological age presents a rough guide as to where we should be in our life and domestic cycles. At fifteen a girl in our society may be too young for marriage, at thirty-five she may be 'on the shelf'. Culture punctuates our domestic careers with ceremonial markers of our progress, extending from baptisms to funerals. In so many societies, *marriage* is the basic threshold, a major step which changes a boy and girl into a man and woman.[26] In Buganda, when they get married and set up their own home, they are addressed politely as *omwami* and *omukyala*, the master and mistress of the household.[27] By contrast, the person who does not get married at the proper time faces mounting social disapproval. The Ganda woman who defers marriage too long is *ow'obusa*, 'the purposeless one'.[28] In the *Song of Lawino* by East African writer Okot P'Bitek (1972: 107), the heroine declares:

> You may be a giant
> Of a man,
> You may begin
> To grow grey hair
> You may be [bald]
> And toothless with age,
> But if you are unmarried
> You are nothing.

At worst, spinsters, homosexuals and other reproductive deviants have been hounded as witches and criminals. Wilful failure to have children can be no less sternly sanctioned. A Church of England handbook on marriage warns: 'To refuse to have children is not only wrong in itself, it means that husband and wife deny themselves some of the greatest joys on earth' (General Synod 1965: 21). The *inability* to have children despite diligent efforts is a major tragedy for most couples, a source of agony, acrimony, costly quests for remedies, and even suicide. The arrival of the first-born is celebrated in many communities as the validation of marriage and the inauguration of a new set of family relationships: mother, father, son, daughter. This first child is often given a special title (*omuggulanda* in Buganda), perhaps indicative of special family rights and duties.[29] The institution of *teknonymy*, whereby a parent is referred to by the child's name ('father-of-John') is a conspicuous signal of reproductive progress. In Bali: 'A man who has never had a child remains all his life a child terminologically. When all of his age-mates have become "father of" and "grandfather of" he retains his childhood name, and the shame of this is often very deeply felt' (Geertz and Geertz 1975: 90). Bali also has an elaborate set of birth-order names for each subsequent child. New household members are counted in, relationships are rearranged, and pecking orders established.[30]

Other aspects of household growth, less familiar to us, are also marked by formal titles and changes of status. In many East African societies a man is not 'really' married until he has two or more wives. *Kaddulubaale* is the usual title for a senior Ganda wife, although she may also be called *Ssabadu*, 'second-in-command'. It is often she who takes the initiative in choosing a new bride, taking careful account of her aptitudes and family background. The second wife she 'marries' is usually called *Kabejja*, 'little princess', and the third *Nnasaza*, 'administrator'. These titles are a reminder that plural marriages do not only concern husband and wives, they multiply relationships among the women and children of the household, building up that little society which is the apical norm. A child has particular ways of addressing the junior wife of his father, such as 'little mother'.

Procedural norms, in all their complexity, do not simply tell people how to build up the ideal household, they also programme the stages of fission and replacement. As we shall see in later chapters, rules of inheritance not only dictate the proper sequence of events surrounding the dissolution of one household and the transfer of property to others, but presume an orderly sequence of earlier developments in which prospective heirs were born and raised. The Ganda regard it as a great abomination (*ekivve*) for children to have sexual relations while living in their parents' house. This not only prevents children from settling with their parents after marriage (this would involve *obuko*, the peril of close contact between in-laws), it forces young people to set up independent households when they are still quite young. A striking implication of this is that three-generation households are virtually unknown in Buganda, and the domestic cycle is short, fast and furious – rather like our own, but with the added pressure of polygynous expansion. However we may choose to explain this situation, economically, ecologically, psychologically, Ganda culture is adamant: fission must occur *before* marriage and child-rearing, not after. It is not the third generation itself which poses the problem (children are warmly welcomed in their grandparents' houses). It is the conjugal relationship of sons and daughters, the *danger* of having in-laws living too close together, which breaks up the parental household and obliges young couples to set up on their own.

Divorce is an increasingly significant feature of domestic fission in our societies. In Buganda, too, a high incidence of divorce persistently erodes the 'well-established household'. When her children have grown up and left home, a Ganda wife may return to live with her own kinsfolk or, if she has managed to accumulate some resources, set up an independent household of her own. The woman householder (*nnakyeyombekedde*, 'she who has built for herself') has her place in the proper sequence of reproductive organization, but for material as well as moral reasons, she simply cannot set up a home of her own if she has never been married.

Procedural norms elaborate the respectable ways of dealing with the sad but inevitable process of decline. The plight of the widow may be unenviable, but if she has behind her a successful domestic life (betokened mainly by grandparenthood) she will be treated with affectionate respect. In Buganda the honorific prefix appears again in terms of address: *ssemwandu*, *nnamwandu*. But there are also many unkind ways of referring to old people who have not lived up to the reproductive ideals (for example *nkejje*, dried fish). At this stage in a person's life, well beyond the critical stage of domestic fission, the *obuko* prohibition seems to lose its force, and old people may find accommodation with a child. Nevertheless, isolation in old age is still a dire and generalized consequence of the Ganda pattern of fission.[31]

'Rites of passage' – baptisms, bar mitzvahs, weddings, funerals – mark out our progress through the reproductive cycle. Religious beliefs and practices, in so far as they conceptualize and dramatize values of the greatest importance to us, are profoundly concerned with reproductive organization. Although churches may give the appearance of 'pure spirituality', denying the flesh in favour of chastity and celibacy, their public intervention in the reproductive process has been boundless: authorizing births and marriages, prohibiting or sanctioning divorces, prescribing and proscribing contraceptives. They have also taken a special role in the care of children and of the aged – accumulating sizeable endowments for these purposes.[32] The concern of religious institutions with transitions from life to afterlife is an expression of the values of social continuity which circumscribe the organization of reproduction. We have the poetic notion that 'the child is father of the man', while Ganda proverbs say 'the children and the elders go round and around' and 'the parent never dies.' Many African people see the circle of life closing every *alternate* generation in the relationship between grandfather and grandchild. Not only may they take the same name, there is a very real fusion of identity, an affective bond unlike that of the father–son relationship which has to bear the brunt of domestic fission and other Oedipal burdens.

In Bali, the reproductive circle is closed one generation further back. According to Clifford Geertz: 'The term for "great-grandparent" and "great-grandchild" is the same: *kumpi*. The two generations, and the individuals who comprise them, are culturally identified. Symbolically, a man is equated upwardly with the most distant ascendant, downwardly with the most distant descendant, he is ever likely to interact with as a living person' (1973: 374). Balinese studiously ignore relatives beyond this level: 'They are all, assuming they have been cremated, merged into the general category of "the gods," and it is ritually forbidden to use their names.' Unlike other people who are so concerned about their family trees, Balinese 'regard it as mildly improper even to want to know' the identity of an ancestor (Geertz and Geertz 1975: 85). Here we can see a fusion of the notions of regeneration, reincarnation and immortality. By such cultural devices time is, so to speak, looped back on itself: birth and death are elided, and social structure is given an appearance of timelessness which defies reproductive reality.

## Norm and reality

All these reproductive ideals bear very heavily on individuals in society. Social values would have no cutting edge if they did not claim to measure absolute truth, but society in which everyone *did* adhere rigorously to the rules is very hard to imagine. At best, the norms are our signposts as we thread our way through life, but against each ideal there are innumerable makeshift realities.[33] This is mainly because the processes and values of reproduction are inextricably tied up with the processes and values of economic production and political control. Many Ganda proverbs recognize this, for example: 'He has suffered on both sides – like a man who marries a woman who is barren and is too weak to work on the farm.' Ideas about reproduction are powerladen, expressive of the political and economic differences within a population.[34] If you are wealthy, you can almost guarantee success by buying your way out of difficulties and setbacks, but if you are poor you may have to suffer the stigma of 'immorality'. The rich may actually have strong opinions about 'proper' domestic development for the poor, making a virtue of a pattern which may actually increase the latter's dependence on the rich. Some moral standards may be so widely unattainable that poorer people pay little heed to them, and make do with a sort of second-order morality of their own: they do not regard themselves as particularly stigmatized by bastardy, or premature household fission, or dependency on others in old age. A corollary of this is that when times change and fewer people have a chance of fulfilling the ideals, the ideals themselves will have to yield. It may become respectable to marry later in life, to have cheaper weddings or raise fewer children. These moral adjustments tend to lag behind material change, often pitching one generation into fierce arguments with the next.

This raises the old chicken-and-egg conundrum: which came first, the ideals of domestic development or the economic behaviour? Does the fear of ritual pollution force early fission among the Ganda, or is *obuko* just a convenient pretext in the modern world for getting youngsters out of the parental household to make their own living? The absurdity of this sort of question should be clear if we think back to the realities of the reproductive process. 'Cultural ideal' and 'economic action' do not face-off against each other in a single contest for causal priority. They are locked in continuous strategic interplay, as thousands of households throughout Buganda, over many decades, respond both to their established knowledge and beliefs and to changing economic opportunities.

One reason why complex, large-scale social processes of the sort we call *culture* have been considered 'non-rational' or 'irrational' is because their logic extends far beyond the economist's habitual frame of reference: short-term transactions in markets. The moral logic of the reproductive process – embodied in ideas like *obuko* in Uganda (or, as we shall see later, in apartheid in South Africa) – is a fundamental example of this, extending through the lives of individual people and the structure of whole populations.[35] If we swept time aside altogether we might actually have to admit that it is the relations of reproduction which have priority over the relations of production: if we did not produce people we would have no reason to produce food, shelter and clothes. In reality this sense of priority is lost in the relentless round of daily life. Organizing subsistence claims a much larger share of our attention day by day than organizing reproduction. We are certainly obliged to make decisions about food or work more frequently and more urgently than decisions about marriage or what to do about an aged parent. But it would be a mistake to conclude that economic choices and actions are necessarily more important than reproductive strategies, or that the latter are merely a byproduct of economic decisions. We should not even take it for granted that we can say *anything* very significant about reproductive tactics in the language of economics. But perhaps the most serious mistake of all would be to assume that reproduction is inherently 'irrational', devoid of any kind of calculation or strategizing, and therefore with no constructive role to play in the making of human history.

# 3

# Economic and political relations
# of reproduction

The process of reproduction is a thoroughgoing source of disturbance in our lives, placing us here as defenceless infants, raising us to creative maturity, and eventually crippling us with age and killing us. Nature seduces us with the pleasures of sex but leaves the ensuing burdens of reproduction to our powers of organization and invention. To prosper one must be lucky as well as obedient, one must be physically able to reproduce and, above all, one must be able to muster the material resources to raise the children and secure the welfare of the household as a whole.

It takes several years (commonly more than twenty in our industrial societies) for each of us to acquire the knowledge, skills and physical strength to secure adequate subsistence for ourselves. Until then we are in varying degrees dependent on others. The progression from birth to death takes us from complete incapacity to adult capability and back to complete incapacity. As with other species the human relations of reproduction are nicely *timed* so that an incapable infant is placed in the hands of a capable adult – its mother.[1] When she ages, she in turn may expect to benefit from the adult capacities of her child. By overlapping in this relationship, the two curves describing each person's degree of dependence mitigate one another. The picture is complicated by the birth of a second child. The additional need stretches the mother's capacities, but if the group remains intact their cumulative *dependency ratio* will be favourable later, as she approaches death.[2] If the father of these children remains with the group, his own needs and capacities likewise influence the balance of material dependency. He can alleviate the period of demand when the children are young, but he adds very heavily to their responsibilities as he ages and can no longer produce as much as he needs to consume. At this stage his offspring may have children of their own to support, and if he is older than his mate, she too will feel the pressure of his dependence. The gratifications of conjugality and paternity should not be underrated, but it is probably their involvement in the domestic processes of production and consumption which give men *long-term* interests in the privileges of attachment to the reproductive nucleus.

Human reproduction both generates and drains economic resources, by creating and extinguishing people who produce and consume. The managerial skill is in finding the best balance over time. One strategy is to extend collaboration among more family members for longer periods, thus flattening out the emphatic 'U' shape of each individual's lifetime dependency curve. To survive, the small household has to call on *external* support to deal with the periodic internal pressure: it may draw assistance from the wider network of family and community, or from welfare programmes organized by the state. If it can set aside savings in the fat periods it will be able to buy its way out of trouble in the lean periods. Otherwise it must respond by squeezing more effort from its own able-bodied members. By corollary, poverty is a symptom of the inability to cope with the ups and downs of the reproductive cycle – in any society, peasant or industrial, primitive or modern. As Macfarlane (1978a: 107) has observed, hunger and poverty break up a household, ultimately reducing it to its component individuals.[3]

The 'matrifocal' households of the Caribbean illustrate the material instability and fragility of the reproductive nucleus. Davenport has explained how poverty restricts the expansion of Jamaican households towards the ideal of a legally married husband and wife living together with their children. He notes that the truncated households of the poor are relatively instable (cf. Le Play) – in personnel, income and residence. Statistically 'the size of households increases as a function of greater economic wealth and stability, and this also correlates with the rate of frequency of legal marriage' (Davenport 1968: 275). 'Only socio-economic security enables a man to head his own household group and to achieve a stable marriage' (p. 264). 'Common law' unions provide very little material assurance, and children stay with their mothers through a variety of makeshift living arrangements, forming an 'intense emotional and physical dependence' which is 'expressed by an overt adulation and idealization of the mother' (p. 251). A man who can hold together his own conjugal household will also want to accommodate his mother. Indeed, prosperous households become a magnet for the less fortunate – conspicuously those little matrifocal units which have no secure domestic base of their own. Economic viability is accordingly under persistent threat, and the wealthier classes have become skilled at balancing prosperity and numbers.

Faced with this instability at the reproductive nucleus, it is fortunate that human beings have the capacity, of great importance in the development of our species, to form larger, durable associations: households, corporations, communities, states. The way these reproductive relations ramify is profoundly affected by the means which people have at their disposal for making a living. It has become fashionable (at least among anthropologists) to regard hunter-gatherers as living in aboriginal affluence rather than primitive poverty.[4] Although their lives have been tougher, shorter and very much less secure than ours, they have an admirable understanding of their environment and an ability to manage themselves and the available natural resources. Their adaptation, including the organization of reproduction, is preoccupied with minimizing disturbance of those natural processes which afford subsistence: vegetal growth, the breeding of game, and so on. According to Richard Lee, the !Kung of the Kalahari take an appropriately pragmatic approach to the extension of family ties. The viable !Kung 'camp' consists of ten to thirty people of different ages and sexes. It

> consists of kinspeople and affines who have found that they can live and work well together. Under this flexible principle of organization, brothers may be united or divided and fathers and sons may live together or apart. Further-more, through the visiting network an individual may, during the course of his life, live for varying times at many water holes, as establishing residence at one camp does not require one to relinquish claim to any other. (Lee 1979: 550)

Investing in mobility, hunter-gatherers like the !Kung have a transient construction of 'family' relations. Marriage, for example, is a contingent affair, not supported by any long-term investment in productive property. Nor is there much emphasis on the social rituals of the life and family cycles – weddings, baptisms, funerals.[5]

The !Kung way of life is in marked contrast to that of settled agricultural populations, who work to change what nature offers, manipulating the land, water, animals and even the climate in much more direct and elaborate ways. In this sedentary economic regime, on which by far the largest proportion of humanity still depends, household organization really comes into its own. Farming demands continuity from year to year, planning harvests and transferring seed from one season to the next.[6] The need for a group of producers to ensure that they have undisturbed access to land which they have cleared and cultivated, especially where they are growing perennial tree or shrub crops, means that farming populations have a material interest in *exclusive* group membership, typically family corpora-tions. By contrast, Lee notes that !Kung San organization is much more *inclusive*, the openness of living groups being highly valued. Farmers are also much concerned with orderly political association, both between and *within* households, while the !Kung have little need for the mediation of patriarchs or chiefs – '"each one of us is headman over himself" they say'

(Lee 1979: 457). Even if the price is heavy, farmers know that efficient police and magistrates, lawcourts and armies, can be economically justifiable. They may actually prefer the extortionate protection of a feudal lord to the anarchy which might otherwise prevail.[7]

Agriculture makes a managerial issue of the relationship between labour and food. The reproductive process continually alters the ratio of hands to mouths, increasing the technical demands of making a living from the land. The interests of greater efficiency and security are served by extending the relations of reproduction into larger and more durable domestic corporations.[8] When several reproductive units are merged into a single domestic frame, the instability within each unit is evened out somewhat. In other words, advantage can be taken of the differential development of reproductive units, the weaker and the stronger providing security for each other at different stages in their cycle of growth and decline. While the extended pattern offers scale economies and leaves people less exposed to cyclical pressure, its principal cost is the managerial effort required to resist fission, which can turn one prosperous household into two or three which are much less viable. The prompt fission which characterizes the *compact* pattern of domestic development trades youthful preferences for the hazards of economic independence off against the more conservative security of extended family solidarity.

Europe offers an interesting pattern of historical and geographical contrast between these two sorts of domestic development. Extended households were very common in the semi-feudal eastern and central regions, but are virtually unknown in the west and in England. In the nineteenth-century Russian community studied by Czap (1983), the mean household size varied between 8.0 and 9.7 persons. 'Households of 1 or 2 persons were ... rare and invariably a fleeting phenomenon' (p. 123). Czap quotes a German commentator of the period: '"Nowhere is a large family a greater blessing than among the Russian peasants. Sons always mean additional shares of land for the head of the family ... In western Europe a large family is an immense burden and nuisance for the lower classes; in Russia a large family represents the peasant's greatest wealth."' (p. 105). However, Czap notes that big families were not necessarily happy families: '"Constant fighting" was the explanation given to six of the nine household fissions in Mishino between 1812 and 1816' (p. 136). Large households were sustained by something more than the enthusiasm of the peasants themselves. 'It became commonplace at the end of the eighteenth and the beginning of the nineteenth century for Russian seigneurs to issue instructions forbidding, or at least controlling, household fission among their peasants' (p. 122). 'From a landlord's perspective, one reproducing couple in a farmstead signified a precarious economic unit, for precisely such households were the most likely to become extinct' (p. 145). Large households were not simply more self-sufficient or more viable, they were more durable and dependable for the outsiders who preyed on them.

## Viability and extension: a pastoral case

The material logic of the extension of reproductive relations can be seen with particular clarity in the case of pastoral peoples. Mobile, self-reliant, and in often tenuous contact with the wider economic and political world, they have made their own reproductive processes closely interdependent with those of other creatures. Among the pastoral Fulani of the Sahel region of Africa, 'both the human social unit and the means of subsistence associated with it are breeding concurrently, each within well-defined though different limits of fertility; the fertility of each affecting, indirectly, the fertility of the other' (Stenning 1958: 100). The connection between man and cattle is established at birth. The Fulani boy is given a calf which remains with the family herd but which will be the nucleus of his own herd when he becomes an independent householder. His reproductive career also has an early start when, at around seven years of age, he is circumcised and betrothed to a girl who may be little more than an infant. When she menstruates, she goes to live with her husband and his family. Through him she gets access to a herd and she will bear his children.

When the couple's first child is born, what will be a lengthy process of domestic fission begins with their establishment of a separate hearth in the family compound. At the same time the sexual division of labour is asserted by the 'calf rope' which is strung out across the corral to keep the younger animals apart. This divides the domestic space into his world and hers, but both productive and reproductive life involves the persistent transgression of men and women back and forth across this line, he to sleep with her, she to milk his cows. 'The congress of husband and wife in the wife's shelter will concern children; the congress of husband and wife in the corral will concern calves' (Stenning 1958: 97).

At this stage, the man can speak up in political gatherings and can dispose of his own animals if he wishes, but until such time as the couple has both enough children and enough cattle to be economically independent, they must remain part of his father's household. Stenning tells us: 'In one range of cases, non-viability is a condition in which there are not enough humans to cope with the reproductive cattle assigned to them. In another there are not enough reproductive cattle to feed the humans associated with them' (1958: 101). The Fulani have clear ideas of what this viability entails: at least one prime stock-bull and around twenty-five other cattle – cows, heifers, calves, oxen, etc. Tending this stock requires a commensurate amount of labour, always with gender distinctions attached: men and boys to herd, women and girls to milk and look after the calves. Domestic fission, the division of the family and the herd, thus involves a tension between father and son, the old man seeking to keep the cattle and his sons' families together for as long as possible, while the sons wish to devote their energies to expansion of their own households and livestock.[9]

At all stages, the household depends on external relationships, for the loans and trading of breeding stock which will build the herd and for the exchange of women which will build the household. The size of herd and household distinguishes the senior men in a lineage who, in pursuit of the apical norm of domestic development, are as interested in accumulating wives as they are in building up livestock. This is a complex and competitive business, since dealings in women must be balanced by the payment of cattle to the family of the bride. Marriages can raise political tensions to fever pitch. Networks of kinship are put to work to muster the necessary cattle, and much of the excitement of a wedding is the reckoning of who owes what to whom.

Cattle, as property, are thus often on the move from one corral to another; and women as the providers of labour and progeny for the kin groups are likewise continually on the move, throughout their lives, from household to household. Typically, a woman begins in her father's compound, goes to live with her husband on his father's compound, moves again to start an independent household with her husband, and finally in old age she goes to live with one of her sons. (Old men who have divested themselves of their property also become dependants of their offspring, which is considered a just return for their productive and reproductive endowments.) The movement of women is accelerated by the high frequency of divorce, which says something of the opportunity women have to express their discontent with the productive and reproductive processes which men organize for them. By threatening to quit they can assert their influence over the viability of both family and herd.

## Enterprise and expansion: an agricultural case

The Ganda, whose reproductive ideals I sketched in chapter 2, have for long been sedentary farmers, but have been much more involved than the pastoral Fulani in the political economy of the wider world. Since early this century, the Ganda have been producing large amounts of coffee and cotton for world markets and routinely hiring additional labour from the less developed regions around them. However, the growth of other social institutions, from medical facilities and banking to the apparatus of government, has proved much slower and more capricious than in our societies. Indeed, local self-reliance seems to have been the key to survival since the breakdown of civil order and the collapse of the Ugandan state in the infamous regime of Idi Amin Dada.

The intricate interdependence of Ganda agriculture with their relations of reproduction became very evident in a study I carried out in the 1960s with two economist colleagues.[10] The emphatic pattern of household growth and decline, attributable mainly to polygyny and prompt fission, was matched by the pronounced expansion and contraction of the farm as a domestic enterprise. The effectiveness of the _obuko_ taboo, preventing more than two consecutive generations from living together, was expressed in our censuses and surveys, which failed to reveal a single Ganda household which included parents, married children and their offspring. Economic prosperity has eroded Ganda tradition in one notable way: by the 1960s 'liberated' women (invariably divorcees or widows) accounted for up to 17 per cent of household heads in any rural community. I have distinguished these in figure 3.1 below, dividing them into two groups corresponding to the two post-fission stages of the domestic cycle.

The effect of these norms of expansion and fission is to put most Ganda households through a very marked pattern of growth and decline, in terms both of personnel and economic performance. We discovered that newly established households had 73 per cent _less_ land than the average for all households in our sample (see figure 3.1). In the 1960s a young couple had to build up their farm by acquiring small parcels of land here and there, by purchase, inheritance, or by gift from their parents. The fully established households which correspond to the apical norm of Ganda domestic development had nearly 50 per cent _more_ land than the average. Indeed, as figure 3.1 indicates, they had more of pretty well everything – good material evidence of why this sort of household should be the focus of aspirations. A large, consolidated Ganda household can generate considerable wealth, since such a large proportion of its members are able-bodied producers. But its days are numbered: the moral as well as the economic pressure from the children to quit and get married means that the household can break up very rapidly. Accordingly, in the stages of fission and decline, the economic figures dropped steeply again below the average, particularly in the value of farm assets and the amount invested in farming.

We found that in the initial stages of domestic development there was a strong emphasis on establishing the food crops essential for family growth. These households grew a lot of cotton, an annual crop which was known as a fast fundraiser but which demands a lot of effort. Before they had children a young couple had the time and energy to spare on this crop. However, coffee is the favoured long-term investment in southern Uganda. Although it is less labour-intensive it can be as long as seven years before new trees bear properly. For the established household, pinched for both cash and labour, coffee provides a relatively steady source of income, and can be harvested several times in the year. We found that in the later stages of domestic development coffee was the mainstay, but that as the trees aged along with their owners, yields began to drop off. Eventually the emphasis in production shifted back to annual food crops. A positive aspect of declining productivity, easily overlooked, is that the farms of older people are effectively being rested or fallowed for a new cycle of intensive exploitation by the rising generation.

It is striking that the households which used their *own* labour most intensively were the couples with young children in the second group – a clear indication of how consumer demand exerts pressure on the available producers. Although the 'consolidated' polygynous households worked their farms most intensively and most profitably, they *hired* the most labour. Accordingly, their cash investments in farming were very much higher than households in the other stages. They spent a lot of money on cattle, which few others could afford because in this region it meant turning over valuable crop land to pasture.

At different stages of domestic development, therefore, the Ganda operate *different kinds of farm*. The Ganda are aware of cyclical reproductive pressures and, in discussing the need to work, save and invest, they refer to the immediate welfare of their children, and their own longer term security in old age.[11] This has many interesting implications, especially for those concerned with organizing agricultural development. For example, from a Ganda point of view there is no single best way to run a farm, because different choices of crop and different patterns of investment correspond to the peculiar needs and capacities of households as they move through the cycle. Likewise, there can be no uniform response to opportunities for innovation. Development specialists very often make their appeal to senior people in the community whose households are declining and whose farms are approaching dereliction. On the other hand, farmers in the early stages of domestic development were too poor and too absorbed in establishing their households to afford the risks of innovation. Nor, for example, did they have enough land to offer as collateral for farm improvement loans. Having less in the way of experience and assets they were not the 'big farmers' to whom development specialists like to pay attention. We found that it was the prosperous households in groups 3 and 4 who were most prepared to experiment: they had the cash, labour and equipment to take the entrepreneurial risks. However, these are the households which are beginning to divest their property to their children and run down their farms. The agricultural officials who had made friends with them were typically disappointed when, after a year or two, their 'model farmers' started to perform poorly.

Although external assistance has often been misdirected, there has been a long and intimate connection between the economic success of the Ganda

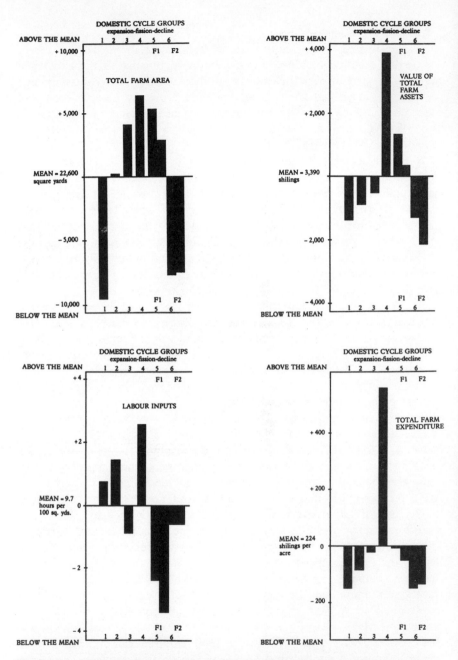

The 352 farming households surveyed by Dr Malcolm Hall in Buganda in 1965–7 have been arranged into six groups, defined according to the ideal pattern of domestic development described in chapter 2 (see figure 2.5). Group 1 corresponds to the stage of Establishment; households in the stage of Expansion were very numerous, so we divided them according to whether they included up to three (group 2) or more than three children (group 3). Group 4 is the stage of Consolidation, 5 is Fission, and 6 is Decline. As explained in the text, the two groups of households led by women, F1 and F2, are placed in parallel with the stages of Fission and Decline, appearing immediately after groups 5 and 6 respectively. The diagrams show the

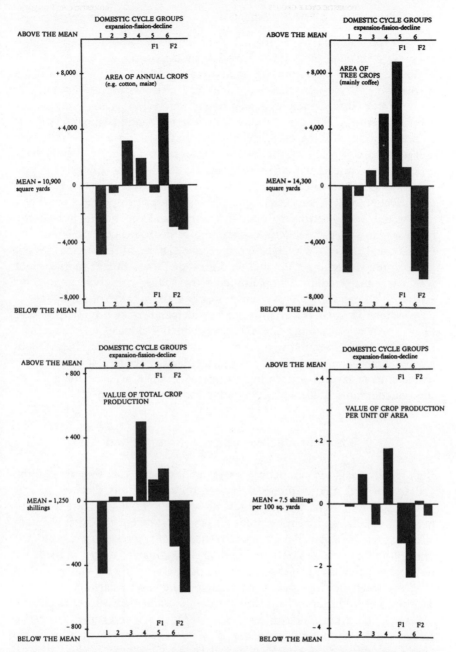

extent to which the mean for each domestic cycle group deviates from the mean for all the households. In other words, in the first diagram the central line indicates that all the households in the survey held on average 22,600 square yards of land; and the first vertical bar shows that the households in group 1 held on average 9,000 square yards *less* than that. A fuller account of this experiment can be found in A. F. Robertson and G. A. Hughes, 'The family farm in Buganda', *Development and Change* 9(3), 1978, pp. 415–38.

**Figure 3.1** Farm inputs and outputs in Buganda, by domestic cycle groups

and the pronounced dynamism of their domestic structure. Of all the peoples of Uganda, they were in closest contact with the British colonial regime, benefited first from the roads and railways, and quickly became involved in cash crop production.[12] They had special opportunities, but it is no less true that Ganda domestic organization has been a motor for economic growth, producing industrious, ambitious and adaptable farmers. In the early stages of the cycle, people are obliged to move out to new land and work hard to lay down the foundations of farm and family. This reflects an early stage in economic *history* when the rapid, labour intensive cotton crop was greatly favoured. Coffee was a later investment, expressing the consolidation of both the cash crop economy and the prosperous household.

It would be interesting to hear the Ganda and the Fulani discuss the relative merits of each other's programme of domestic development. The Ganda could argue for a lively and progressive pattern, full of insecurities but obliging the young to get out and fend for themselves. Fulani youths might well envy this freedom, complaining of the selfish conservatism of their elders. The latter, however, would probably make a virtue of strong family corporations in what is certainly a more demanding environment. Older Ganda men might admire the skill with which Fulani elders manipulate family and herd to secure wealth, wives and prestige for themselves. Fulani women might have good reason to envy the relative freedom of Ganda wives to accumulate savings (increasingly in personal bank accounts) and set up independent households when they are divorced or widowed.

## The reproductive squeeze in our societies

Reproductive and economic processes among both the Fulani and the Ganda are more tightly interlocked than they are in our societies. It is a commonplace in social science to say that we differ fundamentally from our hunting, pastoral and farming predecessors in the extent to which industrialization has distanced our basic relations of reproduction from the organization of production. We tend to view this from the individual's perspective: moving to towns and cities, people typically become detached from the wider network of family, domestic and residential relationships – 'kinship' and 'community' – as well as from the immediate resources of land, herds or game with which to respond to reproductive pressures. Access to capital (land, machinery, expertise etc.) necessary for production is no longer tied up within households, and industrial labour markets deal in able-bodied, mobile, unencumbered individuals, not family corporations. However, in thinking about the gap between family and factory, it would be wrong to imagine that the relationship between reproductive and productive organization has been *broken*. What we lack is an understanding of how this relationship has been greatly *diffused* and is now mediated by a vast range of social institutions which we do not conventionally associate with human reproductive activities.

Unfortunately, questions about how reproduction is organized in modern society have been distracted by a very different sort of presupposition: that modern society has been squeezing 'the family' out of business. We have the nostalgic notion of a past in which big households and family corporations were forced to yield to small fragile households and minimal family networks. However, there is nothing exclusively modern about the compact pattern of domestic development: it is not confined to any particular phase in the human evolutionary story, nor can it be understood simply as a *response to* a particular set of ecological or material circumstances.[13] Very significantly, historians have exposed as a modern fiction the notion that industrialization deprived the English of a heritage of large, self-reliant households. It is becoming clear that the English people have been coping with small, instable households for a very long time, and that the upheavals of industrialization may actually have brought some long-term relief. As we shall see, the solution, so important for social history, has been the proliferation of institutions far beyond the range of the household, which have absorbed much of the stress of the reproductive process, and which have thereby helped to make industrial expansion possible.

Economists and demographers speak of the 'family life cycle squeeze' in our societies.[14] Domestic development is marked by a sense of urgency: a couple has only a few fleeting years to overcome the consumer demands placed on them by their children, and to insulate themselves from the effects of their own physical decline. In their prime they must take a grip on productive processes, save and invest, take innovative risks, and pin their faith on any institution which can help to guarantee their long-term security. Margaret Wynn's illustration of the changing relationship between income and needs in a 'family of modest means' (figure 3.2) shows the 'coincidence of maximum stress in the typical family with the adolescence of the children' (Wynn 1970: 139). While they contribute little or nothing to earnings, their education, housing, clothing and personal allowances are a heavy charge on the domestic budget until their late teens. Thereafter, the 'relative prosperity' of the household recovers, only to lose ground again as the parents retire and age.

The wider social implications of cyclical stress in the compact pattern of domestic development were revealed in the pioneering social investigations of Seebohm Rowntree.[15] Himself a member of a wealthy manufacturing family, Rowntree was acutely interested in the causes and effects of industrial poverty in England at the end of the nineteenth century. His concern about the precarious circumstances of working-class families in the city of York led him to try to define a 'primary poverty line', a reckoning of

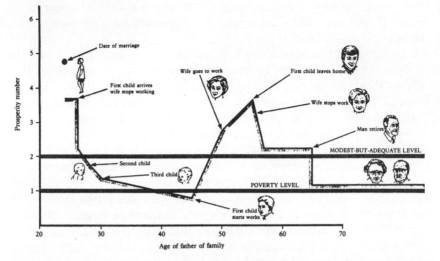

**Figure 3.2** Prosperity numbers [or 'welfare ratio'] in the life-cycle of a family of modest means (*Source*: Margaret Wynn, *Family Policy*, Michael Joseph Ltd, London, 1970, p. 168)

the very basic requirements of food, clothes and shelter. He costed everything from groceries and rent to boots and bus fares, and compared this with the earnings of many hundreds of families in York. Seeking to explain why a significant minority of them fell below this basic poverty line, Rowntree examined very closely the composition of each family. He then made the inspired deduction that poverty was not so much the *permanent* plight of a *few* families, as a *periodic* predicament of almost *all* the households he studied. Rowntree illustrated this with a simple diagram (see figure 3.3), remarking 'We thus see that the 7230 persons shown by this enquiry to be in a state of "primary" poverty, *represent merely that section who happened to be in one of these periods at the time the enquiry was made*' (1922: 171 – emphasis in the original).

Rowntree's discovery has had great impact on welfare policies around the world.[16] With the 'scientific' precision of the social survey he showed how the welfare of individuals was qualified by changes in their domestic circumstances, but also how working-class households in places like York are not, and cannot be, 'self-sufficient'. There is a public responsibility, a need for government action to prevent *all* families falling below the threshold of poverty. Alas, his observations have also encouraged the irresponsible attitude that households deal with their own problems and that, given time rather than constructive aid, all but the most wretched families will eventually struggle back across the poverty line. Rowntree could explain how and when the most useful assistance could be delivered.

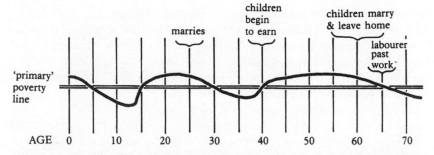

'The life of a labourer is marked by five alternating periods of want and comparative plenty. During early childhood, unless his father is a skilled worker, he will probably be in poverty; this will last until he, or some of his brothers or sisters, begin to earn money and thus augment their father's wage sufficiently to raise the family above the poverty line. Then follows the period during which he is earning money and living under his parents' roof; for some portion of this period he will be earning more money than is required for lodging, food and clothes. This is his chance to save money. If he has saved enough to pay for furnishing a cottage, this period of comparative prosperity may continue after marriage until he has two or three children, when poverty will again overtake him. This period of poverty will last perhaps for ten years, *i.e.* until the first child is fourteen years old and begins to earn wages; but if there are more than three children it may last longer. While the children are earning, and before they leave home to marry, the man enjoys another period of prosperity – possibly, however, only to sink back into poverty when his children have married and left him, and he himself is too old to work, for his income has never permitted his saving enough for him and his wife to live upon for more than a very short time.

'The labourer is thus in poverty, and therefore underfed –
(a) In childhood – when his constitution is being built up.
(b) In early middle life – when he should be in his prime.
(c) In old age.'

**Figure 3.3** Seebohm Rowntree's diagram and description of the phases of poverty in the life course of working-class people in York, England in the early twentieth century (*Source*: B. Seebohm Rowntree, *Poverty: A Study of Town Life*, Howard Fertig, New York, 1922, pp. 169–71 – originally published in 1901)

He could see, for example, that 'women are in poverty for the greater part of the period that they are bearing children' (1922: 171) and that poverty is exacerbated by the fact that the periods of productive and reproductive stress tend to coincide. Although now well known, such considerations still play a disappointingly small role in social welfare policies.[17]

Without wider social institutions to support it, the compact pattern of domestic development offers little insulation from the pressures of the reproductive process. However, the converse is no less true: if people know that they can count on external assistance in dealing with reproductive instability, there is less need for the effort involved in managing and sustaining a large household. Factories, banks, land registries, livestock markets and computer dating services reduce the need for large family corporations. People are evidently willing to transfer the costs of reproduction to other social institutions rather than bearing them within the organization of their own households. Socially efficient means of dealing with the material pressures of reproduction are not simply a historical accident, a happy byproduct of industrial processes. People have laboured to *create* those institutions, with much the same strategic zeal that our predecessors applied to the management of complex extended family households.

This helps to explain why Le Play's gloomy view of the 'instable' households of industrializing Europe was in the long run unwarranted. Although he doubted that a healthy society could be built on these continually shifting sands, he recognized that the compact pattern connotes a go-getting individualism – a vital ingredient in the making of the modern world. The more self-contained 'patriarchal' household was much less likely to provide the recurrent stimulus to economic growth. As Cain remarks, apropos of India, 'the very notion of *individual* fortunes as distinct from *family* fortunes is foreign to joint-family cultures' (1985: 150).

## The micropolitics of reproduction

Rowntree did much to dramatize the importance of wider political relationships in the organization of reproduction. In social science the politics of reproduction *within* households is a much more recent concern, attributable largely to modern feminist initiatives. The historical prevalence of 'patriarchy' remains puzzling: if women are at the core of the relations of reproduction around which domestic groups form, why should they so generally be subordinate? Men may come and go, but the fabric of domestic continuity owes much more to the presence of women, and to the material and moral responsibilities which they shoulder.[18] It was this sort of logic which inspired nineteenth-century social philosophers to propose an epoch of 'matriarchy' in human evolution.[19] But if women have been the main agents in the domestication of mankind, why and when did they cede control to men?

Human reproduction deals inequitably with women in two fundamental ways. Firstly, they are intimately encumbered with children. Being producers of food and producers of people puts them in a double bind. Even in those 'original affluent' hunter-gatherer societies women do a disproportionate amount of work: they produce about two-thirds of the food consumed in a !Kung San camp in addition to bearing very literally the burden of children.[20] Through the processes of gestation and parturition it is women who are left 'holding the baby'. The need to secure food and shelter for long enough to bear and raise their children reduces their bargaining power with men; the threat to abandon their offspring to the care of their fathers has never been very credible.[21]

But a primary commitment to offspring does not in itself explain bias in the division of labour and the allocation of power between the sexes. This raises the second fundamental inequity in reproduction: the fertility of women is scarcer than that of men. Compared with women's capacity to have babies, men's capacity to inseminate is superabundant. While women can get the reproductive services of men at the drop of a hat, gestation is a long and laborious business, and the menopause cuts short their reproductive years. Meillassoux (1981) points out that this puts men in competition with each other for the scarce reproductive (as well as sexual and productive) services of their womenfolk – sisters and daughters as well as wives. Controlling reproduction means that women must be dominated, which is probably why male ideology tends to derogate both the social status of women and the reproductive process itself.[22] Men must at least *appear* to rule the roost, even though it may generally be suspected that their womenfolk 'wear the pants'. The idea that women have no proper roles or influence outside the household is part of this male ideology (although female networks are of course no less vital to the fabric of any community). The lengths to which men go to 'domesticate' women is a measure not of the natural weakness of women but of their political importance in the reproductive process.[23] However, men in our industrial societies who continue to insist that 'woman's place is in the home', and are perplexed by feminist politics, have failed to recognize the extent to which the social organization of reproduction and production has outgrown the boundaries of the household, taking women's interests with it.

Although the bonds of reproduction and of interdependent cohabitation generate powerful emotions of unity among household members,[24] it is the (usually male) household head who has a particular interest in representing the household as a little corporation, protecting and advancing the interests of its members in competition with other households in the community. This integral view of the household has been shared by (predominantly male) social scientists, who have persistently treated households as undifferentiated units of analysis, its interests represented adequately by one spokesman. Feminists have stressed that the household has not one mind but several, and is a pattern of differentiated sentiments and internal schisms.[25] It is a 'knot of individual interests' (Laslett 1984) whose collective behaviour is a complex of internal transactions.[26] In its methods of dealing with these internal differences and making necessary decisions the household can look less like a little democratic republic than a little despotic state.[27] Its members have different powers and privileges, with little children as the most disenfranchised subjects. However, at the stage of fission the interests of the younger generation will prevail, the children passing out of one domestic domain to construct their own in the community. In the final stage of decline the bastion of the parental household crumbles, with the aging parents themselves perhaps seeking refuge as dependents in the home of a mature son or daughter.

## The macropolitics of reproduction

Good breeding is ambiguously a private and public affair: it involves transactions among the individual lives which comprise a household, between the households of parents and offspring engendered over time, and among unrelated families in the wider community. The reproductive cycle forces each domestic unit into political association with others. For men, this is most fundamentally a question of securing a mate. The marvellously varied institutions of marriage are the sociable alternative to the persistent male violence which reproductive transactions might otherwise entail.

In this wider social domain the relations of reproduction are themselves the fundamental basis for reckoning who has obligations to whom. Blood, we say, is thicker than water. Family relationships form slowly and intimately, and tend to define our most serious, long-term responsibilities to one another, no matter how well we may get on with our other friends and neighbours on a day-to-day basis.[28] An extended idea of the family has therefore been very important in defining who individuals are in the wider community, and what activities they should properly engage in with each other. In the social guise of kinship and affinity, reproductive relations become instrumental in the organization of such matters as the resolution of disputes without recourse to violence; the protection of people's claims to land and other resources; mustering the labour needed to harvest a crop or help build a house; economizing in child-care; assembling a really good orchestra; or throwing a truly memorable party. Corporate kin groups have been especially important in the lives of pastoral and farming people. They are a means of 'locking up' access to labour and other resources, 'embedding' them in political extensions of reproductive relations and specifying who can get labour or food or land or equipment from whom.[29] Kin groups strike marriage bargains with each other, making elaborate arrangements to move people and productive property around. But even for nomadic hunter-gatherers, kinship provides a pragmatically useful, farreaching system of identities. For people who are continually on the move and thinly distributed over their territory there are advantages in being able to distinguish friend from foe during chance encounters, and to make snap decisions about who may join the chase or share a kill.

The *reckoning* of kinship is determined not by some internal logic in the relations of reproduction, but cultural rationales about the uses to which these relations are put (transmitting property, selecting mates, etc.)[30] As we saw in chapter 2, the problem with family relationships is that they proliferate exponentially into ramifying networks of relatedness – they are simply *too* inclusive. Distinct corporations based on kinship depend on the concerted application of a code for teasing out single lines of descent, the most prevalent version of which is 'patrilinearity'. The remarkable feature of such a 'unilineal' system is that it depends on everyone in the population knowing and using one very simple rule: 'reckon that you are the offspring not of both parents, but of only *one*.' A genealogy becomes the subjective key to identifying discrete family segments such as lineages or clans, large-scale social units with a temporal span far beyond the compass of individual lives. These serve as the basis of many sorts of transaction, conspicuously the exchange of mates. The reproductive relations of the past, teased out by cultural rules into distinct family groups, become a means of organizing the reproductive relations of the future.[31]

Anthropologists have often remarked on the *work* involved in sustaining genealogies and the groupings which derive from them: resolving inconsistencies, discarding irrelevances and affirming solidarities.[32] The larger the population, the more laborious becomes the process of using genealogical keys to sort out the ramifying reproductive relationships. In his classic account, Evans-Pritchard (1940) explained how being a Nuer depends very fundamentally on the idiom of descent, the idea that the largest group with whom one can expect to live peaceably is comprehended by the relations of reproduction. Dinka, Shilluk and people from other neighbouring tribes neither include the Nuer ancestors in their genealogies nor encourage intermarriage. They are beyond the reach of Nuer 'law' and if they intrude on Nuer pastures or injure a Nuer herdsboy it is an act of war, with physical violence the only remedy. The Nuer are, in a word, a *nation*, a single political unit, membership of which is a *birthright* of several hundred thousand Nuer.

In our societies, the wider political significance of the relations of reproduction have become fraught with ambivalence. While on the one hand politicians assure us passionately that 'the family' is the bedrock of our modern nations, they also insist on the right of individuals to define themselves and make their own way in society. Although our compact pattern of domestic development accentuates our dependence on external association, we have lost the knack of tracing relations of reproduction out beyond a generation or two. While it cannot be argued that the organization of reproduction has lost its importance in the perpetuation of humankind, our understanding of it has narrowed drastically, compared with what we know of peoples in other places and at other times. We are adamant about the domestic *privacy* both of 'the family' and of the reproductive process.[33] But these attitudes are truly modern: as Flandrin has observed, until quite recently the European family 'had many of the characteristics of a public institution, and the relations of kinship served as a model for social and political relations' (1976: 1).[34] While genealogy and the reckoning of descent have evidently lost their social utility, the idea of the *nation*, the outer limits of the relations of reproduction, has notorious persistence and power. At one level it is central to the definition of *ethnicity*, a potent and often vexatious pattern of subdivision within virtually all countries of the modern world. Barth reminds us that we distinguish ethnic groups in the first instance as 'largely biologically self-perpetuating' (1969: 10).

As the word *nation* indicates, it is *birth* which is deemed to establish the fundamental bond between individual people and the modern state, conveying the rights and obligations of citizenship. This is no less true of a state with such a diverse population as the USA. Although so many million aliens have been 'adopted' by rites of 'naturalization', the fact that they remain excluded from the highest political office is a reminder of the fundamental discrimination by birthright.[35] It is a notorious fact in those states in North America and Europe which are the focus of immigration today that *marriage* is an inferior route to citizenship. Officials protecting the 'motherland' have been applying their eyes to bedroom keyholes in an effort to discover whether a marriage is more than a just a legal posture. They warn spouses that if they divorce within three years, privileges of residence or citizenship will be withdrawn. All this is an interesting reversal of the idea that legal marriage protects a couple's rights to sleep together; now it is cohabitation which testifies to legal marriage. All these manipulations indicate the profound significance of the relations of reproduction at the grandest political levels. Our most inclusive political metaphors resort to kinship: 'the Brotherhood of Man' mutually dependent on 'Mother Earth', and perhaps ultimately 'God the Father'

The social organization of reproduction is as important as it ever was; only its meanings have changed. We are simply not accustomed to thinking of reproduction as a function of political parties, taxation systems or the management of economic corporations. Our understanding of the relationships between family microcosm and political macrocosm has been impaired by the vastly increased *scale* of social relations in industrial society, and by a concomitant distension in the social significance of *time*. We have already seen how social organization puts to work the advantages of scale to reduce the material instability of human reproduction. The 'macro' domain of social institutions offers us at least a pretence of stability, continuity and order, in the face of our own wretchedly short individual lives.[36] In the immediate confines of the household we are obliged periodically to acknowledge the realities of instability.[37] By contrast, nations belong in history, and even beyond that in 'time immemorial'. The very word '*State*' is suggestive – the notion that this grand political alliance has somehow overcome the ravages of time. Coercive institutions like the police and the armed forces tell us that 'stable government' matters more than our own brief lives. And yet, despite the best assurances of political authority, history tells us that states themselves develop, decay, segment, confederate, or shatter in revolutionary upheaval.

In political philosophy, the extended family was for long thought of as the prototypical 'state', a little realm presided over by the patriarch. It is interesting to reflect that in European history really large extended households seem to have flourished in the *absence* of effective state control. This was the case with the most famous example of domestic extension and expansion, the *zadruga* of the beleaguered frontier regions of Serbia. Where political protection and mediation were so unreliable, these 'households' sought security in numbers – often as many as a hundred persons (Hammel 1972). Prospects for survival were doubtless greater in these larger fortified settlements than they could ever have been in the compact pattern of domestic development. The latter are viable in our societies to the extent that they are sustained by wider institutions superintended by the modern state.

It is therefore curious that the relationship between 'the family' and the nation state is so often seen as adversarial, with 'the family' very much on the losing side.[38] Others have given it a more sporting chance:

> The war between kinship and authority is alive in legend. In story and fantasy kinship struggles against bureaucratic authority, whether of church or state. It undermines, it challenges, it disturbs . . . When the state fails to protect, people look longingly at the certainty of kinship ... Kinship is resilient and subversive; it is cunning and ruthless. It does not obey the universalistic, meritocratic and bureaucratic rules. (Fox 1983: 7)

If we wish to pursue the truth behind this sort of rhetoric we must recognize that definitions of 'the family' or 'kinship' are not our best starting point, because they are already complex and multifarious social constructions. Here I am urging that we begin at a more fundamental level, and seek to trace the ways in which the relations of reproduction find expression in the mass of social institutions – factories, churches, social classes, political parties and households – which mediate between the ephemeral lives of individual people and the powers of the modern state.[39] The interesting questions are about how the organization of reproduction has shaped the apparatus of the state, and how agents of the state have in turn sought to control the great potency of reproductive processes in the governance of civil society.

## Southern Africa: the political and economic organization
## of reproduction

To illustrate why the organization of reproduction *matters* in our understandings of modern society, I shall outline its importance in interpreting the
moral, political and economic tensions in one of the world's most troubled
regions, Southern Africa. I shall focus on one of the smallest and poorest
countries of the world, Lesotho, which has the unique predicament of being
completely encapsulated within a vastly richer and more powerful state, the
Republic of South Africa.

The early denizens of this mountainous enclave were San hunter-
gatherers, close relatives of the !Kung. They lived in small, mobile units,
very loosely based on reproductive relationships. Over time they were
displaced by immigrant Bantu-speaking farmers, whose family corporations
laid claim to the land. Their lineage heads merged in a structure of
leadership which united the Basotho people politically against their
neighbours. The male elders controlled the productive resources of land and
labour, but they also took care to control their most important *reproductive*
resource – women. In their hoe agriculture women were important as
farmers as well as mothers, and through marriage institutions their
productive and reproductive capacities were moved from one kin group to
another. Men who were politically important usually had more of most
things: fields, cattle, wives and children.

The wealth and political importance of the Basotho a century and a half
ago is in stark contrast to their poverty and dependence today. This was
caused by the establishment of white domination in Southern Africa.
European settlement in the region dates from the seventeenth century, but
it was not until the nineteenth century that racial conflict became acute. The
settlers brought with them the plough, which African farmers readily
adopted. Masters in the production of both seedstock and livestock, the
Basotho travelled widely throughout the region, often cultivating the land of
white settlers, many of whom were desperately poor and inexperienced, in
exchange for a share of the crop. At home, land became more valuable, and
the chiefs who controlled it more powerful. The Lesotho kingdom became
a major exporter of foodgrains and cattle, and a growing political and
economic challenge to white expansion.

By the middle of the nineteenth century there were a quarter of a
million settlers of mainly Dutch ancestry in South Africa. Extending their
colonization north and east, they drove the Basotho out of their most
fertile lands. Seeking to cut their losses the Lesotho king, Moshoeshoe,
made a treaty of protection with the British in 1868. This preserved
Lesotho for the next century as a mountainous enclave within the
expanding South African state. The agricultural revolution which had

been such a mixed blessing to the Basotho was followed by an industrial revolution which consolidated white power in the subcontinent. In 1886 gold was discovered on the Rand, near Johannesburg, and in the next twelve years 100,000 new white immigrants flooded into South Africa. For a while the expanding economy and the demand for food brought renewed prosperity to the Basotho, but soon the white farmers were pressing for stringent land restrictions and trade tariffs against their black competitors.

If the Basotho were no longer needed as farmers, there was an urgent demand for their labour (and the labour of other black southern Africans) on the gold, diamond and coal mines. In 1910 about a tenth of all Basotho men were at work in the mines, and in 1930 the proportion had risen to one quarter. It became South African government policy, eventually known as *apartheid*, to exclude Africans from urban industrial and other 'white' areas for all purposes other than work. The 1913 Land Act restricted black settlement and tenancy, and over the following decades a series of 'pass laws' controlled the movement of black people in all areas outside their 'homeland' reservations. The most significant effect of this was to prevent women and children from settling in the areas where the men worked. Black miners were mostly accommodated in barracks, and were obliged to return home at regular intervals.

Colin Murray tells us in his book *Families Divided*, 'the appropriate question is not "Why are the Basotho still poor?" but "How have the Basotho become poor?"' (1981: 10). From a nation prospering on the export of food Lesotho is now wretchedly dependent on exporting manpower. The country imports most of its food from South Africa, and nearly all households are critically dependent on wage remittances. The South African mines and government agencies 'help' by making sure that most of the money goes straight back home, and is not available for the miners to fritter away. To make matters worse for the Basotho, mine labour has been drawn from increasingly further afield (Malawi, Mozambique, Tanzania), helping to depress the value of wages in 1970 to nearly one half of what it was in the 1930s. With the development of labour-saving machinery, the policy is now to 'give' scarce jobs to South Africa's resident black population rather than to 'foreigners' like the Basotho.

An alternative view of this situation is that the Basotho have been forced for a century to 'give cheap labour' to white South Africans. In 1977 there were 120,000 Basotho miners in South Africa – about a quarter of the black mine labour force. The costs of this can been seen with devastating clarity by anyone visiting Lesotho today. The population has been reduced, in Murray's phrase, to a 'rural proletariat which scratches about on the land' (1981: 19). Agriculture has lost its capital and most of its manpower, and the degeneration of farming practices has caused drastic erosion of the soil (people say that the other main export to South Africa is topsoil). Droughts and crop failure bring a persistent threat of hunger.

Because Basotho men are prohibited from staying in South Africa more than two years, but are obliged to work on the mines for stretches of ten to fourteen months, their home and family life must be organized for them in their absence by the Basotho women. Men now depend on women more than ever, and have a pressing need to try to control them, although for rather different reasons than in the past. The survival of the Basotho now depends intricately on the waged labour of men and the unwaged labour of women – who are now the mainstay of agriculture as well as the people who produce each new generation of miners. But women who cannot, through their husbands or sons, get access to mine earnings are in dire straits. Their problems are compounded by the fact that lung diseases shorten the lives of Basotho men, which helps to explain why in Lesotho impoverished widows form a disproportionate part of the population.

The typical programme of family life in Lesotho goes roughly like this. A young man, for whom no fields are yet available, must seek mine work in South Africa. He sends money to his parental home, but tries to accumulate cash on his own account for his marriage. The importance of marriage traditions are emphasized by the fact that 'bridewealth', ideally including cattle, is still sent to the girl's family. Indeed, tradition has kept up with inflation, and marriage transactions can cost the young man a large part of his earnings. Until they can afford to set up an independent household, the bride must live with and work for *his* parents. When father and sons are remitting wages the household may have a brief period of prosperity. The paterfamilias may take a second or even third wife, but the pressure of the children to marry and move out on their own starts to break up the household. The final phase of this cycle is marked by the elderly widow, clinging to a piece of land which she allows others to cultivate in return for a small share of the crop (a ghostly reminder of the way poor whites were helped a hundred years ago by prosperous Basotho farmers).

Survival depends critically on cooperation among the Basotho themselves, especially among the women who constitute the majority of the resident population at any one time. In their absence, men strive to control women *materially* by keeping a firm grip on access to land and wages, and *ideologically* by insisting on the importance of Sotho traditions: respect for the authority of the lineage elders, of marrying the 'proper' way and of maintaining 'decent' homes. As in other parts of the world, home life in Lesotho is a struggle to balance the reproductive cycle against such economic hazards as weather, crop disease and variable market prices. But life for the Basotho is made a lot tougher by the fact that they have almost no control over the terms of their employment. They have little hope of being able to influence the major force determining how they live today –

the powerful racist state of South Africa. There, the dominant ideology asserts that whites 'made' the industrial economy and the Republic, and that it is their privilege to 'give work' to the black populations around them. Economic prosperity is a white privilege, but this piece of ideology obscures the extend to which the South African economy itself *depends on the reproductive capacity of black women.*[40]

There nothing fanciful about this. The connections are absolutely real – we are simply not accustomed to thinking about them. The mines need Basotho (and other black) youths, and the owners of capital in South Africa insist that this manpower will be bought as cheaply as possible. White South African boys are expensive: to start with, it costs the white community very much more to educate them, and few parents would be happy to see this investment 'wasted' on mine employment. But Basotho mine labour is 'cheap' not because of some quirk of nature or 'free' market forces, but because it was made so, and continues to be made so by notorious political manipulations. The legal framework of apartheid preserves the racial privileges of the whites by prohibiting sexual relationships with blacks, a reproductive key to perpetuating that categoric 'separate development' which allows whites to prosper. Great care has been taken to ensure that mine labour is reproduced in this segregated domain and, better still, outside the borders of South Africa. Basotho boys are not born in South African clinics, they do not attend South African schools, their families are not a charge on South African welfare services, and when they are old and sick they are not hospitalized or buried in South Africa. To die, Basotho men go home to the mountains where they were born. Labour is supplied to South Africa *at immense human cost* to the Basotho people, and most immediately by the unwaged labour of Basotho women.

The reproduction of the South African economy depends on reproducing the impoverished, dependent status of Basotho men, Basotho women, and the whole political and cultural system which *is* Lesotho today. The conventional (white) image of the Basotho dilemma is not that their lives are strung out between two economic and political domains but that they are culturally suspended between a traditional rural past and a modern industrial present. From a black perspective, this contrast between 'tradition' and 'modernity' is dangerous nonsense: the Basotho miners are as 'modern' and as 'traditional' as industrial workers in most other parts of the world. It is the political action of a powerful minority which divides their lives between Johannesburg and Lesotho, and makes their home life look anachronistic. Nor does it make sense to insist that *their economy* is divided between traditional agriculture and modern industry. On the contrary, the interdependence of mining and farming is acutely evident in Lesotho today. The real cleavage in their lives can be found in the organization of *reproduction* rather than production, in the legal ruse of apartheid, and most overtly in the fact that women are at home and men abroad. It is on this division that the economic and political dependence of the Basotho, and the profitability of the South African economy, are constructed.

To repeat: there is nothing 'natural' or 'accidental' about this particular set of arrangements. It is organized and maintained by the regional power of a minority over a majority, which was itself established and is sustained by physical force. The ideological deception surrounding the Basotho predicament goes far beyond the bounds of one racist state. Industrial systems worldwide – even those which like to say they are 'socialist' rather than capitalist – also depend on devious strategies to reproduce a cheap workforce. Even critics tend to shrug and say that this results from irresistible material forces, the pressures of industrialization and the power of supply and demand in the marketplace, which make some people better off and others worse off.

Because social scientists have paid too little attention to understanding the social organization of reproduction in modern industrial economies, we have been unable to reveal the historical lies by which the Basotho and others have been made to suffer: the lie that poverty and backwardness is their fate, that they have no right to the material resources of South Africa and are capable only of mindless physical labour; the lie that Basotho cling to their past 'traditions' because they 'like' them rather than because they have no reasonable alternative; and the subtle lie that makes black men subordinate to whites, and black women subordinate to everyone.

# 4

# The economic organization of reproduction

Human history tells of our collective efforts not simply to secure subsistence, but to improve upon it. Major technical developments in agriculture and industry have obliged us to make radical changes in the organization of our domestic and family relationships. But the influence is not simply one way: economic cause, reproductive consequence. The organization of reproduction on the grand demographic scale, the growth and decline of human populations, has forced us to find new ways of satisfying human needs, making heavy demands on our knowledge, techniques and organizational skills. However, the scale, duration and complexity of these activities makes it very difficult to specify a precise sequence of cause and effect. Ultimately, economic and reproductive processes converge at the intimate level of the household, posing a relentless series of challenges about work and marriage, raising children and capital, sharing resources and dividing them, eating and dying. While it is hard to see the historical effects of these mundane, personal choices and strategies, cumulatively they shape whole societies. What we lack is a plausible theory of how this happens.[1]

The modern social science of Economics has not been very helpful in explaining this interplay, mainly because it has been preoccupied with interpreting the behaviour of modern business firms. On the occasions that they have contemplated reproductive relations, economists have viewed them much as they would any of the other short-term transactions of materially rational individuals in industrial society. Households are construed as small enterprises, and their performance evaluated accordingly. However, in this perspective some of the most important features of reproductive activity remain concealed. Unlike business firms, households and families have the additional and fundamental concern of producing and exchanging *people*, a much more protracted and complicated process than producing and exchanging material goods and services. Treating people analytically as units of consumption or labour reduces the relations of reproduction to simplistic rationales of supply and demand: more food, more babies, and vice versa. What is lost to account is the fact that fundamental decisions and actions are governed by such complex long-term interests as being a provident *father* or a conscientious *son*.[2] Accordingly, important aspects of their economic behaviour can only be dismissed as materially 'irrational'.

While modern social science has driven a wedge between the study of reproduction on the one hand and political and economic processes on the other, everyday usage around the world insists on their close interrelationship. Sometimes this is encapsulated in a single word. Just as a farmer in Lesotho needs the *matla* of oxen, plough, seed and labour to work the land, so a chief needs the *matla* of authority to govern his people, and a husband the *matla* of sexual energy to impregnate his wife. English translations of this useful word seem inadequate: 'strength'? 'potency'? Nevertheless, our own language mixes the metaphors of production and reproduction very thoroughly: pregnant women go 'into labour', men 'spend' their semen; and we talk about a 'family' of industrial companies 'giving birth' to smaller enterprises.[3] In the conventions of modern social science, we are very much more likely to use economic ideas to explain reproduction, than to use reproductive ideas to explain economic institutions and activities.[4] There are dangers in the unilateral, materialist view that reproductive ends are predicated on economic means. If we make the easy assumption that the ultimate purpose of an economy is to reproduce *itself*, we will never consider the extent to which modern institutions like the business firm are ultimately concerned with the reproduction of *people*. The novelty is to insist that *economics itself is part of the social organization of reproduction*. This implies that there are *some* aspects of the elaborate political and economic institutions of our own (and any other) societies which can *only* be explained by understanding the influence of reproductive processes, and which even the most elaborate and sophisticated formal economic analyses will fail to reveal.

In this book I am urging that as social scientists we need to reconstruct our understanding of the relationship between reproductive and economic processes. We can make a start on this enterprise by regarding them as two sides of a single coin. In this chapter I shall begin by viewing the more familiar face of the coin, which assures us that economic constraints and opportunities shape the organization of reproduction. One effect of this is to direct our attention 'downward' to the complexities of individual reproductive behaviour in the household (which happens to be the level of social organization where the discipline of Economics has its semantic roots). An implication of reversing the coin is that we shall be obliged to visualize the

organization of reproduction at the more exalted levels of social organization: in banking and business corporations, in economic classes, and in the
apparatus of the modern state.

## Organizing mating

The anthropologist Claude Meillassoux (1981) has made one of the most
searching explorations of reproductive organization from an economic point
of view. He points out that because fertile women are in short supply, men
have to compete with each other for their services, to control these services
and to 'ration' them out through the institutions we call 'marriage'. The
problem would not arise, he argues, if reproduction could be organized
within the immediate relations of reproduction themselves – that is, among
mothers and sons, or brothers and sisters. But in reality there is little
assurance that there will be enough fertile women in the group of the right
age at the right time to do the job. Men therefore have an interest in gaining
access to women in *other* groups – and in controlling the access of outsiders
to their 'own' women.[5]

The social implications of this are far-reaching. Either men have to go out
and grab suitable women from other families, or they have to organize
peaceable means for redistributing women so that their reproductive powers
are used to the best advantage of all the family corporations in the
community. Meillassoux tells us that 'the physical reproduction of human
beings, the reproduction of the producers and social reproduction at large'
have come to depend on 'the ordered manipulation of the living means of
reproduction, that is: women' (1981: xii). Seizing women implies a state of
perpetual war which may fit the lifestyles of some hunting peoples, but
settled agriculture has depended on the regulation of mating through the
institutions of marriage, whereby 'the progeny of the wife is granted to the
husband's community' (Meillassoux 1981: 33).[6] Accordingly, men make a
social virtue of extending the social organization of reproduction out into the
community. Mostly it is the women who are moved around from one
household to another, but sometimes it is the men who have to quit home
and go to live where the available women are. One of the interesting social
questions which may then arise is whether the children are 'granted to the
husband's community' or are reckoned to belong to the woman's family.

The institutions of marriage tell us much about the necessity and
propriety of orderly reproductive relationships *between* family groups. At
wedding ceremonies the community is witness to the establishment of a
legitimate sexual relationship between husband and wife.[7] By contrast, all
other mating relations *within* households or the immediate family are
commonly regarded as grossly disorderly. This is the taboo of *incest*, the

abomination of sexual relations among close family relations. Because in one form or another this prohibition is well-nigh universal we have come to think of it as profoundly 'unnatural', a view which is strengthened by the knowledge that inbreeding can cause physical defects. However, because incest taboos are so inconsistent they have been a matter of great perplexity for anthropologists. Why, for example, do some societies abominate the marriage of close cousins while others actually prescribe it? These variable attitudes about precisely which relation of reproduction can be incestuous have strengthened the view that such rules are social rather than simply natural in origin. Cultures have much to say about who you *can* marry; incest rules are simply the other side of the coin – who you *cannot* marry. Meillassoux dismisses the genetic and psychological explanations of incest as ideological fuss: because inbreeding is simply unworkable we make a horror show of it. Jack Goody points out that if it is practised regularly incest is 'a policy of isolation' (1969: 70).[8] For this very reason it may be advantageous to families which are rich or powerful, and want to remain so. Repeated close inbreeding is most clearly associated with dynasties of various sorts, notably the Ptolemies of ancient Egypt who produced the famous Cleopatra VI. Such conjugal arrangements mean that the heirs to power and wealth can be kept within very narrow limits: if brothers and sisters produce children, there are no aunts and uncles and cousins to press rival claims to the throne.

Retaining the reproductive powers of women within the household or family in this way is a policy of extreme conservatism which could be described quite fairly as antisocial. More usually, royal families have seen the advantages of using marriage to establish strategic political ties among rich and powerful families, within and between states. Alliances can be renewed, generation after generation, to consolidate the power or wealth of particular groups. Other 'natural' unions, sexual or romantic liaisons which may or may not become full relations of reproduction, are seldom allowed to interfere with conjugal politics. Bastardy was almost routine in the royal houses of Europe.

Marriage everywhere is in a sense at odds with nature. It is a strategic exercise to control the sexual energies of the young and to allow the larger groups to which they belong to construct what they judge to be the most beneficial long-term relationships. Indeed, we should recognize at the outset that they may be prevented from marrying *at all*: hence such institutions of celibacy, perhaps described as a 'marriage' to the Church or to Christ, which take some of the population out of the reproductive arena. In many rural populations, economic and other pressures may oblige a surprisingly large proportion of the population to remain unwed.[9] Leaving mating decisions to the young themselves is a romantic folly peculiar to our industrial societies, and maybe a few others. More generally it is well known that love is blind, and that the young simply lack the experience, foresight and transactional skills to make such vital arrangements, although young lovers are always forcing their families to make respectable marriages out of their impromptu love affairs. Professional marriage brokers have played an important role in many hierarchic societies (notably prerevolutionary China) where families are prepared to pay for information and introductions which will allow their offspring to marry advantageously, or avoid sacrificing wealth and prestige to the wrong union.

If marriage essentially involves men competing for the reproductive services of women it should come as no surprise that the name of the game is to accumulate more wives than the other fellows. With such exceptions as orthodox Islam which allows no more than four, *polygyny* is limited only by a man's wealth and power. Monarchs have had harems of gigantic proportions but the shortage of women means that a majority of men, even in societies which encourage polygyny, have had to make do with one wife. This failure to fulfil the apical norms of domestic development should not be confused with the rule of *monogamy* which *prevents* a man from taking more than one wife at a time. Because this has been the prevalent pattern in European and Asian societies, we tend to regard it as 'normal'. Instead of marvelling at the oddity of polygyny, we should ask ourselves how and why, at some later period in human history, marriage came to be so narrowly restricted.

Because women have little interest in accumulating husbands, or have been prevented by men from doing so, *polyandry* is a great rarity. Different forms of this arrangement, whereby a woman may be married to more than one husband, have been reported in a few very peculiar contexts, for example in certain hierarchic societies in which women can hold high political office.[10] The best-reported cases of polyandry come from the Himalayan region, and are not associated with the privileged position of women. The husbands of a woman are almost invariably brothers who share access to her productive and reproductive services. They also share paternity, regarding themselves jointly as the father of her children. The most plausible explanation says that polyandry is an elaborate tactic to deal with the shortage of agricultural land in a demanding mountainous setting. It is part of a larger apparatus of social institutions which work to hold population growth in check. As a reproductive restraint in these societies, celibacy is no less important than polyandrous marriage. A conspicuously high proportion of people, notably fertile women, remain unmarried and, as in other crowded regions, monasteries take a significant proportion of the population off the marriage market. Polyandry restricts the access of men to fertile women and conserves the ownership of property, a group of fathers passing a farm intact to a group of sons who will in their turn work it and marry as a single household unit. However, cases from Tibet make the point that polyandry is not incompatible with polygyny. If they are sufficiently prosperous, a group of brothers may jointly marry a second or even third wife, still regarding themselves without discrimination as the fathers of their offspring. There are therefore opportunities within this system for accumulating, as well as simply conserving wealth.[11]

To understand the economic and political implications of polygyny, which also manifests itself in many different forms, we must recognize that a wife is a producer and consumer in her own right, as well as a producer of children who are in their turn consumers and producers. In places where, unlike the Himalayas and other crowded farming areas, labour is a scarcer commodity than land, men have good material reasons to compete for access to fertile and able-bodied women. Until recent times Africa has been the continent in which land has been abundant and polygyny very common. In African societies, Lucy Mair has observed, 'polygyny was the privilege of wealth as well as a means to wealth' (1971: 153). Fertile girls were in high demand – no chance that they would be left 'on the shelf' or sent to a nunnery. The marriage market was rigorously controlled by older men as an adjunct of their political and economic power. If, as is usual, the balance of the sexes in the population was roughly even, the only way some men can have more wives is if others have less. One way of achieving this is controlling the ages at which people can get married: if girls are encouraged to marry as soon as possible after puberty, but young men do not marry until they are well into their twenties or thirties, then more older men will have an opportunity to find a second or third wife. This means that at *some* stage in their lives *many* men may enjoy polygyny. The transfer of the productive and reproductive capacities of a woman to her husband's family is usually marked by the payment of often large amounts of goods, cash or services ('bridewealth') to her own family.[12] These can be used to allow one of her own kinsmen to marry in his turn. A young man must wait until he or his family can bear the cost of a marriage transaction. A classic cause of friction in African households is competition between fathers and sons for available bridewealth. An older man may be accused of expanding his own conjugal relations, of robbing a young man of a girl, and of making a 'marriage of lust' rather than sacrificing his personal interests honourably to the cycle of domestic replacement.[13]

Unlike monogamy, polygyny is a tactic of domestic expansion, constrained only by the availability of fertile women. The economic advantage, and responsibility, of it is that it brings labour into the household, both immediately and through reproduction. Seeking to account for the prevalence of polygyny in Africa and monogamy in Europe and Asia, Boserup (1970) has drawn attention not only to the relative scarcity of land (Asia) and of labour (Africa) but also to the technologies which have been developed to bring these two productive resources together. At the heart of this are two very different kinds of agricultural implement, the hoe and the plough. The hoe, ubiquitous in Africa, is well adapted to making full use of women's labour, and has changed remarkably little even in the modern era of commercial farming. The male agricultural implement in Africa is the machete, essential to the slash-and-burn tactics of extensive agriculture. In some places clearing land is about the sum total of men's contribution to farming.

The plough, so characteristic of European and Asian agriculture, has gone through many more technical developments and has come to depend on animal power. It also needs the strength and body weight of a man to drive the blade or share into the ground.[14] Intensive plough agriculture puts a premium on land, equipment, draft power and male labour. It displaces female labour, which may be one reason why European and Asian farmers have shown some preference for sons rather than daughters, and are more ready to hire labour for cash than to marry it. In these societies women's economic roles are more confined to the immediate vicinity of the house, to horticulture and the care of small livestock, to the organization of consumption and to petty trade. It is very striking that, unlike Africa, marriage payments in Asia and Europe generally *accompany* the bride into her husband's household in the form of a *dowry*. Her family provides land and other economic resources, or perhaps a house and furniture which helps to build up what Jack Goody (1976a) calls the 'conjugal fund', essential for the establishment and growth of the household. The greater concern with the reproductive rather than productive role of the single wife is expressed in much greater concern with matters of sexual morality, like virginity and adultery. The acute interest in landed property in these generally crowded areas also means that inheritance and the legitimacy of offspring are matters of great concern. Hierarchies of status and wealth make the choice of a spouse a serious strategic issue. In India today newspaper advertising has replaced some older forms of marriage brokerage as a means of making a match.[15]

In these matters Africa, with its extensive hoe agriculture, offers many striking contrasts. Men have been much less concerned with securing private property in land than with immediate access to labour and the production of descendants who will sustain the family corporation. Studying legal records in Uganda, it came as a minor cultural shock to me to discover that *paternity* suits involved men claiming offspring rather than denying responsibility for them, as was usually the case at that time in Europe.[16] African families may go to extraordinary lengths to ensure that a man has descendants, even arranging for a brother to 'inherit' his widow (the institution of the *levirate*), or to marry another woman and rear children on his behalf ('ghost marriage').[17]

It would be rash to jump to the conclusion that monogamy is more favourable to women than polygyny. Monogamy tends to make a man's rights over his wife more exclusive, whereas polygynous households feel more open, inclusive.[18] The polygynous households I have come to know well bring women into very close dependence on one another within the domestic corporation. Against the husband's externally sanctioned authority they can exert, through the wide range of vital activities which keep the family going, palpable power. The importance of the personality of the senior wife is immediately obvious. For their part, men value good women and often work hard to keep the enterprise together, cajoling, flattering and bribing rather than railing and bullying. The logistics of such a household, its economies of scale and internal division of labour, can give a strong impression of power and efficiency.[19]

In all these considerations we must remember that marriage, like every other aspect of family life, is a process.[20] We have seen, for example, how delaying marriage can reduce mating or allow polygyny. The conjugal relationship and the activities, meanings and strategies associated with it change with the lives of the partners. The various stages of betrothal, wedding, consummation, parturition, menopause, widowhood, and perhaps divorce, may each be marked with ceremonies adjusting individual life courses to the domestic cycle and the life of the community. In our European and Asian heritage, ceremonial interest is quite narrowly focused on the wedding, which is loaded with reproductive symbolism: virginal purity, blood on the wedding night, and so on. African weddings are much less preoccupied with sexual gate-keeping, and the most important transactions may be after the event, endorsing the reproductive and productive progress of the union. Among the Nuer, for example, marrying is a protracted business, punctuated by a sequence of bridewealth payments, and 'It is only when a man's bride has borne him a child and tends his hearth that she becomes, in the Nuer sense, his wife' (Evans-Pritchard 1951: 73). Again, when a woman has passed the menopause her marital roles may change significantly. Divorce is very common in African societies, especially where the marriage is not heavily secured with bridewealth payments. Having brought no dowry into the marriage, the bride does not have the same material stake in the domestic enterprise that the European or Asian wife has. In her middle years, when she has accomplished her reproductive tasks for her husband's family, a woman is most at risk of losing direct access to the productive resources needed for her own continued survival. Her declining physical capacity makes her more dependent on relatives of her own.

Polygyny may be a smart strategy for marshalling labour, but it is not a sensible means of consolidating a narrow interest in property in the longer term. Any arrangement for multiplying heirs divides family capital, which is all very well if land, equipment and other essential productive assets are quite freely available. Polygyny is slowly diminishing in Africa as people move to the towns and as farmland becomes commercially more valuable. I had some interesting discussion of these matters with prosperous Ganda farmers in the 1960s. Although the majority were or had been polygynous, they were alert to the advantages of investing in a smaller number of children and restricting marriage to a single, durable monogamous union of the sort the Christian missions had been advocating in Uganda for so long. These big farmers seemed to feel that such arrangements would be compatible only with fully capitalized agriculture, involving tractors and hired labour. Devoting cash to the education of children would almost certainly take them out of farming into government or industrial employment. Such a change would also remove the satisfaction and esteem of being unequivocally *Ssemaka*, the Ganda paterfamilias.[21]

If the popular media are to be believed, the main characteristic of marriage in our industrial societies is its chronic instability, attributed mainly to the erosion of old-fashioned family ideals. Certainly, the much publicized complexities of divorce, single parenthood and remarriage indicate that reproduction is going through another period of reorganization. The boldest attempt to define the connection between industrialization and domestic structure is that of William J. Goode in his *World Revolution and Family Patterns* (1963). For Goode, if modern marriage is in crisis it is a symptom of its central *importance* to the industrial household. Indeed, he calls his model 'the *conjugal* family', rather than the more familiar 'nuclear family' of sociological jargon. Domestic organization, he concludes, has come to depend very heavily on the married couple, rather than on the authority of parent over child; and in the organization of both production and reproduction, the couple is disengaged from wider family ties. Industrialization has put a premium on mobility: young people commonly find home, work and spouse far away from family networks. They tend not to put down deep roots and aim for fewer children than people in settled agricultural communities. Mating is much more a matter of free choice but, thrust into such close mutual dependence, the conjugal family can easily become an unstable 'emotional vortex'.

With its inward focus on the conjugal pair, Goode's version of what I have called the 'compact' pattern of domestic development has very little to say about the external relations of this basic reproductive group. Bonds with the extended family may indeed have been cut back, but they have been extensively replaced by other institutions.[22] To perceive these more clearly we may have to shift our attention from husband and wife to parent and child, a relationship which is so much at the heart of our educational, savings, public welfare and other institutions.

## Organizing fertility

Why do we go to the very considerable trouble of having children? In every generation there must be some couples who ask themselves this question. The voices of religion or public morality may leave them in little doubt about their social duty to procreate, but sacrificing freedom and relative affluence for the responsibility and economic stress of children is surely a disincentive. The familiar justification that offspring are 'a comfort to us in our old age' seems less warranted now that we can buy long-term security with pensions and investments, and retire congenially to senior citizen communities. There are of course many reasons why people *do* have children, not the least of which are the emotional pleasures of parenthood. These are preceded and probably exceeded by the pleasures of sex, a notorious fact which has reduced the scope for choice in parenting. These animal instincts have been the subject of relatively new fields of enquiry which have extended from population dynamics on the one hand to social genetics on the other. A sublime purpose of our reproductive endeavours may indeed be to 'to get genes into future generations' (Betzig 1988: 9) and to propagate the species, but it is the middle level where our instincts, desires and interests impinge on our social relationships which concerns me here.

Whatever else our genes and our entire species may be up to, most of us are immediately preoccupied with the welfare of ourselves and our immediate dependants. The dynamics of whole populations undoubtedly shapes our personal reproductive decisions, but precisely how and to what effect remains largely mysterious. The emergence of states governing large populations has helped to give reproductive interests a collective voice. Political pressures have encouraged child-rearing at some times and discouraged it at others, setting national concerns about strength in numbers against the material weakness of overpopulation. Ravaged by famine, war and the human costs of rapid development, the Soviet Union used to idealize and reward the 'Mother Hero', bearer of many babies; but we have heard little of this in recent years of economic recession. In America, Hewlett attributes the 'cult of motherhood' to the fact that 'Children were scarce and therefore prized in this long-underpopulated country' (1986: 276); but again we hear much less of this today. In China and other Asian countries rigorous efforts are being made to restrict parenthood to a single child; but in the western European countries, where the birthrate has fallen below the level of replacement, economic incentives are being offered to prospective parents.

In more immediate economic terms, we have already seen how children are variously a short-term liability and a long-term investment, an essential part of the intergenerational transfers which sustain individuals and perpetuate communities. All these pressures oblige us to make choices and to take as much control as we can of the whole business of rearing children, whatever our sexual and genetic urges may be. Throughout history and at every level of society from the individual and the family to the community and the state, people have had preferences about the number of children or their sex, about when they will have children and how much they wish to invest in them, and whether other people's children may be raised as their own. Our techniques for influencing these things have improved enormously in the last few decades, but it would be a grave mistake to imagine that 'family planning' is a modern innovation. Ethnography has shown the acute and active interest people have taken in the two counterpoised problems of the restriction and enhancement of fertility.[23] Angus McLaren draws a lesson for our understanding of our own society:

> Because the conceiving and bearing of children was so important previous generations elaborated a remarkable range of strategies to deal with each stage of the procreative process. It is difficult in fact not to think that we today have a much more impoverished sense of our powers when contemplating parenthood. This is in part because in some ways we have developed a rigid, mechanical view of reproduction. Parents in the past perceived it as mutable – conditioned by diet, exercise, potions and charms. They believed that nature and culture interacted and that their fertility was accordingly their own social creation. (McLaren 1984: 150)

Attempts to stimulate fertility have become a major medical preoccupation in our societies. People in the African and Asian communities in which I have lived have all seemed to show more interest in stimulating conception than preventing it. Aphrodisiacs are copiously available in village market places, and healers of all sorts offer cures for impotence, ranging from a cup of ginseng tea to such diversions as urinating through one's wife's wedding ring.[24] Even artificial insemination is less modern than we may suppose: McLaren reports a successful procedure supervised by the Scottish surgeon John Hunter in 1776 (1984: 13). When all else fails, both men and women may have recourse to surrogate parenthood.[25] The fertile partner may collaborate with someone who is prepared to donate or sell their services, but adoption is by far the most common solution. Virtually every society seems to have some legal process for the transfer of children from one set of parents to another. There are many variations, from short-term fostering to domestic slavery, and such arrangements as the pawning of children to settle debts or raise cash.

It is technically easier to reduce fertility than to increase it. Sterilization

is a drastic measure, and has become generally established as a contraceptive
practice only with medical advances during this century.[26] The entire
childbearing process can be avoided or ended in innumerable ways, and at
any stage. The most obvious is preventing a couple from engaging in sexual
intercourse in the first place. The institutions of courtship and marriage can
be the most effective contraceptive, especially in those European and Asian
societies which take virginity very seriously. Where sex is so tightly licensed,
finding the time and place for non-marital lovemaking can be a major
challenge. The more marriageable the girl, the more likely she is to be
dogged by chaperons. However, it is so often the case that the kinds of
society which police marital sex and make a virtue of abstinence also
encourage prostitution, an institution which is usually based on the
provision of sexual services by people of a lower social class.[27] Commercial
sex has well-known physical hazards, and one of the virtues of marriage as
a social institution is that the partners should *know* each other in the fullest
sense.

Whether married or not, a couple has many means of having sex without
offspring.[28] Perhaps because it is so simple and obvious, withdrawal before
ejaculation (*coitus interruptus*) has evoked great moral wrath, supposedly
pleasing neither the woman nor God. Among the many ways of preventing
insemination, vaginal pessaries and douches seem to have been more
common than male protection, although sheaths made of animal gut and all
manner of other materials have been reported from antiquity to the present
day.[29] Abortion has probably been the most common means of restricting
birth, coming when pregnancy is a fact rather than merely an apprehension.
It is an equivocal act in many societies: the later the abortion the more
closely it may resemble murder. Judgement is determined by theories about
when the foetus or child is deemed to have acquired life and social identity.
These are highly variable, ranging from the instant of conception to several
years after birth. Conceptive and contraceptive techniques are not matters of
personal fancy, they are morally, socially constructed. This is most obviously
true of infanticide – too widely reported to be dismissed as a rarity.[30]
Although it is plainly more expensive in terms of the mother's time and
energy, it may well be less harmful than efforts to induce a miscarriage.
Raymond Firth has described in detail the range of birth-control methods
practised by the people of the Polynesian island of Tikopia earlier this
century. Infanticide might be used when the paternity of the child was in
doubt or when the couple felt they already had 'a family large enough to
consume the products of their land'. Firth concludes:

> When the practice of infanticide by the Tikopia is correlated with their ideas
> of family life on the one hand and their economic situation on the other, it can
> be seen that they adopt a realistic point of view. To them a human life has no

sentimental or absolute value. It is to be considered in relation to its position in terms of a social structure and an economic need; and for them it is preferable to remove unwanted beings immediately from the social scene rather than allow them to endure misery or by their multiplication to be a cause of misery in others. (Firth 1957: 529–30)

The case of Tikopia directs us to a puzzle of considerable importance in understanding human development: whether or not populations expand relentlessly to absorb available resources. This is the controversy established by the late eighteenth-century scholar Robert Malthus. If, as he argued, population always expands faster than food supply, we would expect most people to be in a state of perpetual crisis, at the limits of their resources and threatened with starvation or epidemics associated with dense settlement and poor nutrition. Since this is not generally the case, we must ask what prevents the crisis.

One obvious tactic, of great importance in the proliferation of our species, is migration. In the past, this has been a gradual colonization of one rural area by people from another, whereas in modern times the movement has been a more rapid shift of individuals away from the countryside to urban concentrations. In both cases the immediate mechanism seems to be domestic fission, the quest by younger people for the material resources and opportunities they need to continue the reproductive cycle.[31] Another major tactic in the face of population pressure is to develop the means of production. Malthus's anxiety was that the advantages of any technical developments would be quickly wiped out by vigorous population growth. The effects of industrialization, urban growth and better medicine have indeed resulted in massive population explosions, but latterly these developments have been associated with a remarkably widespread reduction in the rate of population growth. This has been interpreted as a 'demographic transition' from a mainly rural world in which people compensated for infant mortality and short lifespans with high fertility; through a period of industrialization in which rising living standards allowed the population to soar; to a new period in which people saw the material advantages of reducing fertility.[32] Although the recent history of the Third World countries seems repeatedly to confirm this basic pattern, we have to explain oddities like the postwar 'baby boom' in the industrialized countries, a surge in fertility which is now having widespread social and economic consequences.

Attempts to define the relationship between fertility and economic development are complicated by the length of time (many decades, several generations) it takes for cause to become evident in effect; by the large numbers of individual people involved; and by the variety of immediate circumstances and choices which confront them.[33] Our conclusions will be very much determined by how, when and where we pick up the sequence of events. Marx's focus of interest was on the rise of industrial capitalism in Europe, a radical transformation in the social organization of *production* which led him to ridicule Malthus's idea that it was human fertility which ultimately controlled human destiny.[34] Other scholars like Ester Boserup (1981) have looked further back in time and made broader comparisons around the world, and have come to the opposite conclusion that demographic growth can prompt technical innovation in farming or industry, whether by local invention or diffusion from other places.

Whether we are bent on explaining how industrialization has influenced human reproduction, or the converse, our efforts are complicated by the problems of arguing connections between population and resources at the aggregate level on the one hand, and the choices and actions of individual people on the other. Ultimately we must scrutinize the immediate relations of reproduction and production to find answers to such intriguing questions as how and why people adjust their fertility to levels of welfare beyond the reach of generalized poverty and misery. But how are such personal decisions influenced by much broader demographic, economic and political constraints and opportunities?

Empirical study of such motivation is complicated by a remarkably widespread resistance to the idea of thinking materialistically about having children. When I was trying to persuade Ganda farmers to tell me how many children they wanted, they would say piously 'as many as God sends'. Even putting a number on their existing children was considered a temptation to Providence. However, they often expressed their material concerns about fertility in less direct ways: anxieties about school fees, or about pregnancies too closely spaced. So often it seems to be poor people who insist that their children are 'riches', but they plainly do not mean that they are exchangeable for cash. Zelizer remarks that in our societies we think of our offspring as 'priceless', although 'in strict economic terms, children today are worthless to their parents. They are also expensive. The total cost of raising a child – combining both direct maintenance costs and indirect opportunity costs – was estimated in 1980 to average between $100,000 and $140,000' (1985: 3).

This ambivalence certainly reminds us that we have more than just material reasons for wanting children, and that reproductive accounting is not quite like balancing the books of a small firm. The distinction seems to be embodied in rigorous moral codes which insist that people are not simply 'more valuable' than commodities, but that they should be produced and exchanged in a different way. There are many economic ideas which seem distasteful or even silly when applied to people.[35] For example, like most goods, people are *fungible*: they get 'used up' when they lose their fertility and physical strength. But it is essentially social rules which prevent people from being liquidated when they get old, or exchanged freely with other commodities. Nevertheless, we know that throughout history people *have* often been treated as commodities: they have been sold as slaves or as infant adoptees, and in innumerable ways have been controlled and manipulated as 'things'. Conversely, certain *things* may acquire a personality for the people who transact them. Thus we find that in conversation men ascribe a personality *and the female gender* to certain valuable commodities, mainly mechanical objects like ships or cars over which they seek to exercise pleasurable *control*.[36] However, there are very few commodities which, like people, have the capacity to intervene in the transaction of themselves, which is why slaves have rebelled and the labouring classes have revolted. When people lack or lose the capacity to argue their own case they are most at risk of becoming things, whether they are infants on the adoption market, child brides, despised minorities, the mentally deficient or the terminally ill.

These concerns about the limitations of economic explanations should not allow us to lose sight of the fact that material production and exchange are essential to the social organization of reproduction. Producing children is an *important* economic decision in the sense that it involves longer-term considerations than the production of a crop or of most industrial commodities. Having children is rather more like the major undertaking of perennial vine or orchard crops; or (as we saw in the Fulani case) the establishment of a herd; or the construction of a major capital asset like a building or ship (note how businessmen talk of major projects as 'my baby'). However, from the individual's perspective, the reproductive cycle is almost invariably longer than the productive cycle. Whereas a large proportion of important productive decisions are necessarily immediate and short term, reproductive decisions are not. The enterprise of parenting is also more inexorable: as Montgomery and Trussell put it, 'The irreversibility of childbearing' means that 'a household moves through its reproductive span, progressively adding constraints which masquerade as small children' (1986: 259). Because the economic implications of child-rearing extend over so many years, people tend to lose sight of them. The costs of a college education may be unthinkable when the kids are young, and many parents may simply hope that their circumstances will have improved sufficiently when they are faced with the bills fifteen or twenty years hence. But attitudes to long-term business investments are probably very similar.[37]

It is a fact of human reproduction that individuals can only get through their life course by entering into long-term transactions of credit and debt with other people. These relationships both depend on social order and create the fabric of society. Meillassoux (1981) has pointed out that if an individual is to 'balance his books' he must 'pay' in his productive adulthood for his unproductive childhood and old age. If he can do so, he has in an economic sense 'reproduced himself', borrowing from parents and children, and paying them back in different ways at various stages of his life. The books are ultimately balanced by his death and his replacement by one other individual – perhaps his son. His ability to do so will obviously depend on his own efforts, economic and social, in the particular environment in which he finds himself. If, in the give-and-take throughout his life, it is in his capacity to do better than this 'simple reproduction' of himself, we could say that he has helped to 'cover the costs' of an additional person. Meillassoux calls this 'expanded reproduction', a pattern of investment by domestic groups which leads to population growth. This kind of accounting gives us a vivid view of some aspects of the interdependence of production and reproduction. For example, if some outsider (perhaps a landlord) taxes the reproductive group he can take away the margin for 'expanded reproduction'. If he goes further and cuts into what is needed for 'simple reproduction' there can only be one outcome: population decline and premature death (Meillassoux 1981: 54–5).

If we are to think of the value of children in material terms, we must consider very carefully how that value is measured and 'stored' (money? potatoes?) and how it is exchanged (markets? baby bureaux?).[38] Meillassoux has argued that in those societies without money and markets, the value of children can be reckoned only in limited ways – basically by food. If a household produces more food than its members can use, it goes to waste – the extra food is 'valueless'. Likewise, producing fewer children than you have the capacity to feed 'wastes food'. According to Meillassoux, the 'value' of extra food in such societies therefore rests essentially in child-raising, its investment in the production of future producers. But this in turn is restricted by the productive resources available to the household – land and working capital. Too many producers will create food scarcity.

What such societies evidently need to ride out these ups and downs is a system for 'banking' the value of perishable food to cover the consumption demands of children, or for 'borrowing' the future productive value of children, their labour. In our societies we have developed many sophisticated ways of doing this, most of them involving that wonderful medium of exchange *money*. But primitive communities also have means of converting between the short-term value of food and the long-term value of children. Offspring can be moved around from household to household, putting otherwise 'wasted' food or labour to good productive and reproductive use. But we should note that this depends on durable social organization, which offers some assurance among the 'trading' partners that implicit promises will be fulfilled. According to Meillassoux (1981: 58–9), the relations of exchange are more likely to consolidate around the longer-term reproduction of people than the shorter-term production of food. Extensions of the relations of reproduction such as family or lineage are therefore the most usual institutional bases for such transactions. The gist of Meillassoux's argument is that in these pre-industrial communities the social organization of reproduction is of overriding importance. The stark contrast, he says, is with our modern societies, in which the production and exchange of material goods determine the way we organize reproduction. I would agree with Meillassoux only to the extent that a different side of the coin is uppermost in pre- and in post-industrial societies. What we have to explain is the apparent shift of emphasis, the subsumption of reproductive interests by other institutions, not the disappearance of reproduction as a matter of social and economic importance.

Zelizer has noted a remarkable shift during this last century in our evaluation of children:

> In 1896, the parents of a two-year-old child sued the Southern Railroad Company of Georgia for the wrongful death of their son. Despite claims that the boy performed valuable services for his parents – $2 worth per month, 'going upon errands to neighbors ... watching and amusing ... younger child,' – no recovery was allowed, except for minimum burial expenses. The court concluded that the child was 'of such tender years as to be unable to have any earning capacity, and hence the defendant could not be held liable in damages.'' (Zelizer 1985: 138–9).

In stark contrast, in 1990 a five-year-old boy from Phoenix, Arizona, was awarded damages of $28.7 million because as an infant he had contracted AIDS from a blood transfusion. The jury also awarded a million dollars each to his parents 'for the loss of the boy's companionship and the emotional distress of having a child suffering from AIDS'.[39] Zelizer points out that in the nineteenth century child labour had a *price*, but as children were relieved from work – even household chores – their 'sacralization' made their *value* a much more perplexing issue. How should insurance companies compute the 'surrender value' of a materially 'useless' child at death?[40] What was its 'exchange value' on adoption? In both cases the prices now paid reflect sentimental interests which defy conventional economic reckoning. As children became unemployable, computation of their earnings was no longer a sensible guide to their worth (although such valuation persisted in American courts through into the 1950s). But how do you put a cash price on a 'sacred' child? What for example, would be the moral consequences of allowing, as some have argued, the forces of supply and demand to run their course in a straightforward market in child adoptions?[41]

To tackle this vexed question of why the cash price of a child should have soared so dramatically, while children have become increasing 'useless' economically, let us return to the economic accounting of reproduction. Children are a long-term investment, and we should recognize the difference between *present costs* and *deferred benefits*. An important component of the moral obligation of child-rearing is the *trans*generational transfer of costs and benefits: the recognition that a large part of my parents' investment in me cannot be returned to them but can only be credited to my own offspring. This is very evident in our society, where parents seem to invest much more in their children than they get from them in return.[42] In non-industrial communities, parents expect their children to support them in their old age, and to this extent they are more directly 'valuable'. In such societies children in their turn often get their means of livelihood from their parents: land, farms and other capital resources. This is the transgenerational notion of 'patrimony', the idea that we derive our assets from the parental generation and hold them in trust for the next generation. However, we should note that at any stage in these transactions there may be three, even four generations in competition for access to family resources. It is very common for the middle generation to be confronted with a division of loyalties, between 'repaying' parents and 'investing in' children.

## Organizing aging and mortality

The need to assure adequate pensioning services is one of the reasons for 'gerontocratic' tendencies – the concentration of political and economic control in the hands of the elderly. They no doubt like to play on the indebtedness of the younger generation, and to prolong their dependent status by controlling marriage, property etc.[43] The transfer of resources and power between generations can therefore be very painful, whether it is the process of fission within the household, or a change of national regime – the exit of the 'old guard'. Contrary to our folksy images of sweet harmony and unspoken trust in the 'traditional family', arrangements for retirement in rural communities are often extremely tense and rigorously formalized. Gaunt (1983) provides a valuable survey of 'retirement' arrangements in Scandinavia and Europe since medieval times.[44] He notes the widespread tendency for parents to transfer property to an heir in exchange for food and lodging for the rest of their days. There was a keen sense that welfare in old age depended critically on the leverage which could be exerted over property rights sanctioned by custom and law; and on the other side, that retired parents could be an acute burden on an expanding household.[45] Thus, retirement *contracts* between aging parents and children become historically more common, and for periods considerably before infirmity and death struck; pressure of the younger generation to *marry* likewise moved retirement forward.

The major distinction between the industrial societies and their historic predecessors is that the economic relations between generations are not nearly so *direct*, but are mediated by large-scale institutions (like the law of contract). Since medieval times Europeans have been seeking ways of securing their old age independently of family networks, and by the end of the nineteenth century most people depended for support in their old age on savings accounts and pension funds rather than on their own children.[46] In other words, they were buying capital assets which were tied up in special banking institutions, and which were then 'rented' to the next generation. This has meant that people can expect to be provided for in their old age whether or not they have children of their own. All this depends on the next generation's willingness and ability to pay into the system what the parental generation expects. In our societies old age has become a more protracted affair, and to the extent that votes count in our democracies, weight of numbers has added to the power of the senior generation. By the same token, parents and grandparents have become a much bigger charge on the social purse. If, as will soon be the case in Europe and America, the number of old people in the population expecting pensions is significantly greater than the young people who have to pay the bills, the system could well collapse. The question will no longer be 'can we afford children?' but 'can we afford parents?'[47]

The extreme response to this question is *geronticide*, or *senilicide*, the killing of old people. It is a counterpart for infanticide, but appears to be considerably rarer. It has been reported in hunter-gather societies, especially in such harsh environments as the arctic where hand-to-mouth subsistence allows little leeway for the support of disabled people in times of dearth; and in that other harsh environment, industrial society, 'euthanasia' has been debated as a remedy for the high cost of maintaining the aged and infirm. Of course, the worth of older people cannot be judged in crudely material terms. Apart from emotional considerations, older people represent a considerable social investment in wisdom and experience, especially in non-literate agricultural societies. The practical utility of this is evident in dispute settlement, or agricultural decision-making (finely tuned advice based on experience of the weather and environment). These resources are conserved within the *extended* pattern of domestic development.[48] The elderly are reintegrated into other households when their own have reached terminal decline; the institution of 'widow inheritance' , for example, obliges a man to take care of a dead brother's wife. In such societies the unborn, the young, the old, and dead are often seen as being united in a cycle of mortality–immortality. Respected as elders, people are then venerated as ancestors, their graves being important symbols of the continuity of the family corporation. By contrast, the elderly as a social resource tend to be dissipated in the *compact* pattern of domestic development. There has been an increasing tendency in our industrial societies to marginalize old people, detaching them from the broader social exchanges of work, domestic activities and recreation. It is hardly surprising that this has been accompanied by rising suicide rates among the elderly.[49]

## Modernization and the reproductive calculus

The more acutely people are aware of economic constraints, the more likely they are to exert control over reproduction. People in Asian societies tread the fine line between assuring heirs and having more children than they can endow, thereby running the risk of demotion in the social hierarchy as well as material poverty.[50] Concern may extend beyond the number and spacing of children, to gender preferences and their birth order. For example, with plough agriculture in Europe and Asia there is an apparent preference for boys rather than girls.[51] Daughters have to be given dowries, and are 'lost' to parents as a support in old age. In African hoe agriculture men have good productive as well as reproductive reasons to welcome girls, and good political reasons (such as the perpetuation of a lineage) to want boys.[52] In industrial societies, the desire to reduce fertility has become very marked, providing another reason for the popular notion that families are 'disappearing'. In the early stages of industrialization, infant mortality, short lifespans, poor health, the market for child labour, and above all the lack of institutions (schools, paid employment) to secure the investment in children, meant that people cared less about restricting fertility than they do today. It is certainly true that social institutions like pension funds and geriatric clinics have replaced much of the economic utility of children to their parents.[53] But this does not mean we have lost interest in reproduction. If we live in the golden age of the contraceptive it is because in significant ways we care *more* about reproduction than our ancestors did. Anticipating fewer children we have stronger preferences about the timing and spacing of their birth, and perhaps also their gender.[54]

While in the past reproduction was evidently concerned with the quantity of children, in our societies we have acquired an overriding interest in their *quality*. This is taken to mean not simply their physical health and welfare, but the cash investments which they represent. Economists have discussed this in terms of 'human capital', mainly the cost of an education which will increase the future earning capacity of the child.[55] This helps to explain an oddity about family planning in industrial societies: *increasing* wealth is associated with a *reduction* in fertility, whereas in Meillassoux's model of non-industrial, non-market societies, more wealth (food) means more children. In the urban industrial world children do not simply take their place on the family farm, they have to compete as individuals in the labour market. What they have to sell depends largely on what their parents have invested in them, which in turn constrains fertility. For people who are 'upwardly mobile', working hard to make their children more competitive, the advantages are in quality not quantity.[56] In our societies we have depended increasingly on domestic pets to fill the emotional vacuum.[57]

However, high fertility may still be the best strategy for poorer families if there is a demand for unskilled labour in factories and services; or if there are opportunities in the 'informal' or 'black' economy; or if the poor are denied access to other forms of wealth and social welfare. A child who can cover just a little more than its own subsistence costs by selling gum and cigarettes on street corners is a net asset to a poor household. In such circumstances no amount of encouragement from middle-class do-gooders to use contraceptives and cut family size will make economic sense.[58] But faced with absolute poverty, the lack of even these minimal economic opportunities, people will surely cut fertilty.[59] And on the other hand, real affluence will encourage parents to exceed the demographic replacement level of two to three children.[60]

## Time, and the economics of reproduction

Poverty reduces choices to the short term; long-range planning is a privilege of the wealthy and powerful. Throughout this chapter I have stressed the importance of *time* in understanding the relationship between economic and reproductive strategies. Reproductive processes take much more time than most economic processes, and are accordingly less predictable and less easy to change at short notice. As Macfarlane (1978a: 100) puts it, reproductive strategies 'lag' in their response to productive decisions, rather than the other way round (you can usually change farming or trading practices more readily than you can change your children). One implication of this is that major economic events (like a boom or slump) can influence reproductive decisions very quickly, but the effects of those decisions take many decades to play out. By the same token, changes in reproductive patterns happen so slowly that their influence on economic choices is extremely difficult to detect. The fact that they may be more important, in the longer term, than economic processes is therefore disguised. Having a child, for whatever reason, calls for some immediate material responses from a parent; but a baby boom poses challenges for society at large which can redefine major economic institutions and the course of human history.

Referring to European household formation in the sixteenth to eighteenth centuries, R. M. Smith concludes that 'family, demographic, economic, and political systems were linked in a *culturally determined moral economy*' (emphasis in the original). He insists that 'There is no place in this system for a fertility analysis that supposes households of individuals had a determinant and determinable set of preferences for children, which they rationally assessed so as to produce optimal outcomes' (1981: 618–9). Smith no doubt means that in matters of reproduction, ordinary people do not behave like neoclassical economists calculating the production of hats or cars. The 'rationale' of child–raising is set about with complex qualitative issues which are not readily amenable to individual calculation, and instead become lodged in the 'folk wisdom' of culture. However, notions of a 'culturally determined moral economy' may be too mysterious to be analytically useful. The more immediate problem in making economic sense of reproduction is ostensibly much simpler: when they are seeking a balance between production and reproduction, people are juggling interests which are separated by short-term and long-term considerations.

The inadequacy of Economics in coming to grips with these issues is not exactly for want of trying, witness the efforts to make 'human time' accessible to the economics of the marketplace.[61] However, as T. P. Schultz has pointed out, an economics which takes an 'instantaneous' view of transactions is unlikely to make much sense of reproductive reckonings which extend over whole lifetimes: 'Economic models of the determinants of fertility tend to be formulated and tested in static terms.'[62] In modelling fertility decisions, for example, Cain notes a 'Preoccupation with the more immediate costs and benefits of children', rather than such interests as long-term security and insurance in old age. Analyses fix on positive discount rates – 'giving greater weight to near term costs and benefits than to more distant streams' (1985: 146, 145). For example, it is generally presumed that the alternative uses of a mother's labour, (its *current* 'opportunity cost') provide a key index of the value of children.[63] Subsequent efforts have added greatly to the complexity of models without removing this cardinal difficulty in the reckoning of reproductive behavior over time.

To return to the question of how and whether individual people adapt their reproductive behaviour to large-scale demographic pressures: you have to be very privileged and extraordinarily well-informed to base your reproductive decisions on such remote demographic considerations as 'over-' or 'under- population'. Some reckoning of this may be easier on a small Pacific island like Tikopia than in a major industrial nation of several hundred million people. More usually, fertility for ordinary people is a mixture of luck and an assessment of medium-term economic prospects. Having children is an act of faith in the capacity of the economy to provide for the rising generation. But it also assumes that the rising generation will have the capacity to sustain that economy and, by their own efforts and initiatives, make it grow and change.

# 5

# The reproductive organization of the economy

Human reproduction is both a creative and a destabilizing process. It makes people who in turn make up society; but by making them very dependent on others at different stages in their lives reproduction places heavy demands on social organization. In the preceding chapters we have seen how people come to grips with the most basic relations of reproduction, manipulating mating, child-rearing, aging and mortality in accordance with the material opportunities available to them. Now we will turn the coin and examine the economic strategies with which people confront the demands of the reproductive process, and the effect of those strategies on the organization of society at large.

Posed in economic terms, the problem of reproduction is one of changing needs and capacities, whether in the life of one individual, or of a household, or of some wider cooperative grouping. Economic planning, for these people and groups, therefore turns very largely on how to secure tomorrow's needs (child-rearing, welfare in old age) with today's capacities (labour and other resources). Social organization provides 'banking' facilities for these trans-actions, giving us the right to take when we need and the obligation to give when we are able. This is expressed in such complex relations as 'father and son', or 'neighbour', or 'patron and client'. In pre-industrial societies these interdependencies cluster within and around the household, but in the modern industrial world they have been drawn out into a vastly diverse range of social institutions, such as savings banks, stocks and shares, or a good education. Our social interdependence is now teased out into many single strands, linking aspects of us as individuals ('customer', 'pupil') to specialized institutions ('bank', 'school'). The organization of reproduction is no longer tied to the close proximity of household and village, but diffused over vast distances to large organizations – the brokerage firm we telephone to place a new investment, or the government agency which mails us our welfare check.

There are two fundamental institutions which make this wide diffusion of relationships possible in modern society: money and markets. These in turn depend on wider political associations, especially the state. They allow us to move our individual needs and capacities around very rapidly and extensively, putting a price on our energy and the things we produce and allowing us much greater freedom to make exchanges among work, food, land, knowledge and other necessities. They also allow us to buy time: by borrowing we can use tomorrow's money today, and by saving we can keep the cash in our pocket or in a bank until we are ready to choose the particular exchange we want to make.

It is little wonder that we should think of ourselves as living in a world dominated by material interests. This is why some of us look back nostalgically on our pre-industrial past, or out to what is left of the rural world today. There, people seem to be more interested in people than in things. Meillassoux's view of this is that in these non-industrial settings social organization is geared very much more to the relations of reproduction than to the production of material goods, which have value only in so far as they help to reproduce people. By contrast, in industrial societies, the real value of people seems to be their capacity to produce material wealth. Put another way, economic effort seems to be geared to sustaining the enterprise itself rather than sustaining the family or household. There is much truth in this, but we must take care not to drive the wedge too deeply, to split the rural and industrial worlds apart, or to divide the past from the present, or to separate economy from society. The ultimate purpose of an economy is not to sustain itself, but to enable human populations to reproduce. But human life is impractical without economic and political organization – the knowledge and technical means we have developed to extract a living from our environment, and the relationships we have established with each other to make the production and exchange of goods possible.

Modern industrial enterprises do not exhibit the economic variability of the Ganda family farm or the Fulani herd because they are socially so well protected from the disequilibrating effects of the reproductive process. But if the family farm is locked into a more intimate struggle with the reproductive process, factories and business firms also struggle for stability against the ravages of the market, of business cycles, and of governmental caprice. The misunderstanding of reproductive and economic dynamisms makes modern urban nostalgia for timeless rustic bliss as idiotic as peasant images of city streets paved with gold. To make their way through the reproductive cycle the farm family has to keep making changes in the organization of labour, land and movable capital – the factors of production at its disposal. It must also decide how much of its resources it should set aside for investment in future production and as savings for bad times. One advantage for people who depend for a livelihood on specialized jobs in factories, offices and workshops is that they are spared the task of managing *all* these diverse factors of production. In that respect at least, life in our 'complex' modern society is 'simpler'.

## Organizing labour and capital

Labour is the factor of production most obviously linked to the reproductive process. Mating and child-rearing adds to it, aging and dying subtracts from it. In expanding its personnel the household simultaneously accumulates needs and the basic means of satisfying them – a workforce. But generating labour without regard to capital and the other means of production can be hazardous. Some strategies of domestic development are more conservative about this than others. As we have seen, the *extended* pattern aims for security in numbers, but not by encouraging expansion so much as by constraining fission.

Pasternak (1972), for example, reports that Taiwanese farmers build up larger households as an insurance against the notorious uncertainties of rice farming. Very often the only remedy for storm damage, disease or the collapse of prices is to apply heavy doses of labour to the farm. A prudent farmer will keep this on hand by delaying fission and retaining the services of sons and daughters. In the less stable *compact* pattern, with its more rapid rate of fission, the household must either exercise reproductive restraint or else send its offspring out to match their labour with whatever capital the world can provide.

Le Play was much impressed by the extent to which in the *stem* pattern of development, households pursue their own precise adjustment of people to material resources. A central concern of the Irish countrymen of County Clare, as described by Arensberg and Kimball (1968), was to avoid the build-up of consumers, by allowing only a single marriage on the family farm each generation. One son lived and worked with his parents in the long-term expectation of marrying and taking over the farm. If they could not marry out, his siblings either had to remain spinsters and bachelors or move out and make shift for themselves, often by emigrating. This points to the dependence of the stem pattern on external arrangements. Berkner's reconstruction of an eighteenth-century Austrian community reveals how, in struggling to prevent long-term consumer surpluses, the stem household also had to deal with short-term labour deficits. Young adults were recruited from neighbouring households 'as a labour substitute for children'. As servants or wage-earning lodgers they applied their capacities to the needs in one stage of the domestic cycle, while helping to relieve pressure in their own parental households (1972: 413).[1]

Berkner notes that there was nothing casual or relaxed about these transactions. Servants were bound strictly to serve out a full agricultural year, and could not be dismissed at short notice. Both sides were acutely aware of the value of the labour and its compensation. It is considerably easier to think quantitatively about labour – numbers of people, manhours and so on – than to assess its *quality*. This can be of as much concern to humble peasants as to managers of modern hi-tech enterprises. Parkinson's famous 'law', that work expands to fit the time available, draws attention to variable *effort*, a quality of labour which is extremely difficult to measure, but which has a profound effect on productivity.[2] An even more complex quality is *skill*, a mixture of aptitudes, learning and experience which, like the physical and mental capacities entailed in effort, must be developed in individuals over time. For economists this is 'human capital', a long-term investment made through upbringing, schooling, apprenticeships work experience, etc.[3] Parents usually have a better idea of, and muɹe control over, the quality of labour which they themselves have raised, than the abilities of a hired stranger. The skilful employer (whether as parent or chief executive) extracts as much as he can from his workforce, but employees have much leeway for adjusting the quality of their work to what they reckon their rewards are worth. Where a cash wage is not involved, this can be very subtle. For example, a son who knows he will inherit a particular field may work it more carefully than a servant or a tenant who knows he will quit in a couple of years. On the other hand, a son can campaign for the right to marry and set up on his own by dragging his feet and lowering the quality of his work.[4]

Compared with the peasant household, the modern factory or business firm makes fairly constant demands on its labour force year by year, calculating and negotiating flat hourly wages or piecework. Pay is geared to profits and the demands of shareholders, and to the capacities of individual workers rather than their *needs*. As we saw in the Ganda case (chapter 3) the pressures of reproduction have a very direct effect on the peasant farming enterprise. This was the central concern of the agricultural economist A. V. Chayanov, who explained how the cycle of changing needs determined how the Russian peasant household put itself to work.[5] The demand for and supply of labour, and the rewards it can expect, are variable and for most of the time are out of phase with each other. Chayanov applied his model to agricultural survey data to show why, at one stage in its development, members of the peasant household needed to work harder to make ends meet. But by the same token his model explained why household members did not need to work equally hard all the time. When the dependency ratio drops so that there are more hands to mouths, subsistence can be secured with less effort.[6]

Putting it another way, where the economic unit and the reproductive unit coincide, the effects of reproductive dynamism can be seen in the varying *intensity* with whch the group uses the resources at its disposal. Thus, Lee (1979: 67–71) tells us that variable dependency ratios are expressed in the importance of *effort* in understanding the viability of the !Kung camp. Adjustments are also made in techniques and output: the choice of a more or less labour-intensive crop, or the use of a machine in preference to manual labour. Older people in declining households often revert to hoes and vegetable gardening, lacking the strength and other resources to plough grain fields. Obviously, all of this affects the division of work within the household according to sex and age. In this regard we should note that however burdened by domestic routine they may be, women's work patterns are no less variable than those of men.

The assumption that households in the non-industrial world are economically self-contained is a major obstacle in understanding how reproduction and production are organized in wider social networks and institutions. For all its interest, Chayanov's model of the Russian family farm is deficient in this regard. Picturing each household as an isolated unit, he largely ignored the long-term social relationships between households within a community which allow the 'banking' of available labour and skills and their transfer from one unit to another. This leads to a very partial picture of domestic dynamism: Chayanov's rudimentary model focuses on the *expansion* of the household, adding a child every three years and assuming that extra land is available to support the necessary increases in production. His account stops short of the stages of fission and decline in which, as we have seen, the relationships *between* households become vitally important. Thus, critics have complained that he has little to say about the processes of marriage and inheritance which provide many households with the necessary resources for growth.

The point is that durable social networks are essential in dealing with the disruptive effects of the reproductive process in *any* community, rural or urban. This is particularly evident in densely settled parts of the world where there are keen pressures to keep all land at the highest pitch of productivity and override the ups and downs of the domestic cycle. In the long term, inheritance rules may prevent an elderly couple from hanging on to their land when they can no longer sustain reasonable yields. Similarly, in the short term there are concerns about the 'wastage' of available labour: at busy periods like planting or harvesting, communal work groups take advantage of small variations in ripening times to move all available labour rapidly around the fields of each villager in turn. One implication of these various forms of cooperation is that economic management is not always in the hands of individual household heads. Decisions about sowing or harvesting, for example, are often made by senior men of several households who plan the movement of communal labour from field to field. Their control over the *timing* of agricultural operations is often backed up by ritual authority – divining ritually the day on which the earth may be broken, organizing first-fruit ceremonies, etc. Agricultural economists who, like Chayanov, confine their reckoning to the domestic unit may therefore fail to understand these outward extensions of the family farm. Outside observers are mystified how accounts of cooperative transactions are kept. How do people balance differences in yield or labour contributions, and prevent 'free-riders' from taking advantage of the system? Answers are complicated by the fact that 'accounting' is done through the medium of social institutions: credit and debt get translated and absorbed into other rights and obligations, like 'kinship' or 'chiefship' or 'citizenship'.[7]

In chapter 3, I explained how the social organization of domestic groups allows people to trade the incapacity of infancy and old age against the productive period of their adult lives. But this is not like buying and selling fruit in the market. The closest relations of reproduction involve *transgenerational* exchanges, and the long-term accounting of who owes what to whom implies a sort of contract-in-perpetuity among family members. This draws attention to the 'timefulness' of economic resources. Capital, especially 'fixed' resources like land or buildings, tends to 'move' – to change hands and value – more slowly than labour. Dealings in capital therefore depend much more on durable relationships which provide a basis for trust over long periods. In most societies, the relations of reproduction provide the medium for these transactions: family ties are a vehicle for moving access to productive property from one generation to another. For the quick quid pro quo of balanced short- or medium-term exchanges (help in felling a tree or building a house) people more usually have to reach outside the reproductive nucleus and the household, into the wider community.

Anthropologists have accordingly noted that while access to capital such as land is commonly managed in family groups, people may actually go out of their way to exchange labour with someone who is not a relative.[8] In the absence of family corporations in our societies we also pin much of our faith on political and legal institutions which guarantee our title deeds. It is notable that banks, important custodians of capital in our modern societies, go out of their way to convey an impression of permanence and solidity, incorporating a lot of marble and cast-iron into their architecture. Labour bureaux look very different.

Certainly, managers of all enterprises, factories or family farms use social relationships to secure a dependable supply of labour. We have seen how marriage can be used to tie up labour, keeping fathers obligated to sons or sons-in-law, or by transacting the services of women from one family to another. Industrialists use other kinds of commitment, ranging from pensions and tied housing to the oppressive use of class power. However, labour can be more difficult to control than capital because work, unlike land or factories, can be traded on a day-by-day or month-by-month basis. Indeed, individuals seem to prefer short-term working arrangements with those with whom they have no lifetime responsibility, perhaps because they allow for much more rapid accounting and efficient bargaining. Kinship can add unwelcome moral clutter to a brief working relationship, which is probably why brothers commonly avoid working for each other.[9]

For economists, 'capital' is essentially 'the produced means of production'. This reminds us that to have value, capital must be developed, used, owned and in general be drawn into the social relations of production. Livestock and seed are variable forms of capital of great importance in farming communities, but it is important to recognise that productive land is also 'produced' and is highly variable over space and time. Although often described as 'fixed capital' it acquires, maintains and improves its value strictly according to the use people make of it. It follows that, although capital may 'move' more slowly than labour, it can be run down, improved, wasted, fragmented, accumulated and exchanged for other productive resources.

Because the management of capital is dynamic it plays a vital part in the social organization of reproduction. Its availability may explicitly determine the establishment of new households, and thus the rate at which reproduction in the community proceeds. When she marries, the Ganda wife expects to be given her own *lusuku,* a plantain garden over which she has exclusive control and with which she makes her contribution to basic household subsistence. Without it, the marriage is neither viable nor respectable. Where property is held in family corporations a new household usually acquires its share of 'patrimony' on the authority of the elders. The village chief in Lesotho controls the allocation of land, and custom declares that each household is entitled to three fields. In crowded areas couples are obliged to wait until the decline of another household makes land available. Until then the Sotho wife knows she will have to live with and work for her husband's family.

The transfer of resources from one generation to the next is usually backed up by weighty social and legal institutions, especially where extended family groups no longer manage the ownership and transfer of productive property. Jack Goody has pointed out that this involves a variety of strategies which may be broadly related to different productive and reproductive systems. It is important to note that *devolution* of property (what we generally think of as 'inheritance') can occur before the death of the holder (*inter vivos*) as well as after it (*post mortem*). Although in the compact pattern of development people hang on to most of their property until they die, fission and the marriage of children usually involve some *inter vivos* transfer of assets from the parental generation. Devolution in the European 'stem' pattern is concentrated into this stage, with settlements being made both on the single heir who marries and takes over the farm, and on the other children who are 'dispossessed'.[10] Boserup (1970) and Goody (1969, 1973) have pointed out that in the societies of Europe and Asia dependent on plough agriculture, *dowry* has been the characteristic way of devolving property *inter vivos* to women. Marriage assembles the productive resources which allow reproduction to proceed: with her dowry a woman brings assets of land, cash, or perhaps a house to add to the 'conjugal fund'.[11] Men, however, are more likely to receive their main share of property on the death of their parents. Thus, although it is devolved at different stages in the reproductive process, property is passed to both sons and daughters (Goody calls this *'diverging devolution'*). Where fragmentation of capital could be economically disastrous, it usually *'converges'* on a single heir according to a selective rule like primogeniture or ultimogeniture (first- and last-born). In African pastoral societies property often devolves *laterally* on a man's death to each of his junior brothers in succession, before dropping a generation to each of their sons in turn. This is closely related to the business of managing viable herds in larger lineage groups.

One further point to note about the ownership and devolution of property is that some of it is distinctively female, and some of it male. Thus mothers often endow daughters with clothes, cooking utensils, gardening implements and other objects which males do not normally use.[12] Female property can amount to extraordinary accumulations of wealth, much of it 'stored' in the form of female ornaments.[13] In many parts of West Africa women buy, store and exchange hundreds of metal bowls. These are often used as a kind of currency which is ingeniously kept out of male hands. Much basic trade in West Africa is done by women, who sometimes use these utensils to back up deals with each other, in preference to banknotes whose value has proved much less solid.[14]

The bonds of kinship can be mobilized to assemble capital for individuals who need it at particular times. This is a means of scratching bridewealth or dowry together, cattle or cash being drawn out of one family network and diffused into another. Negotiations are intense and precise, although the extremely complicated transactions do not work like a 'market' as we would understand it, because who you are in the family hierarchy determines what you are entitled to, and when. In the extended pattern of domestic development, the conservation of material and human resources calls for managerial skill, especially in matters of domestic fission – control of marriage, inheritance, etc. However, short-term accounting among individuals is probably less necessary and less burdensome. A three-generation household holds the old 'pensioners' and young prospective heirs together as a unit without the need to allocate specific resources to support each.[15] By contrast, the compact pattern of development implies that the household and its resources are reapportioned as each generation matures. In this pattern people usually get involved in a frenetic race to build up, largely by their own efforts, the capital they need to bolster themselves and their households against the harsher effects of reproductive instability. This is the 'self-exploitation' to which Chayanov's model of the expanding Russian peasant household drew attention. With prompt fission, young people are liberated, and may relish the challenge of independence. But it is they, above all, who need – *and demand* – the assistance of organizations beyond the range of family ties.

If the compact pattern in our industrial societies has come to depend on the social paraphernalia of banks and mortgages, in the rural world it still depends on collaboration within a much closer neighbourhood. Writing elsewhere about *The Dynamics of Productive Relationships*, I focused on the way in which rural households enter into *share contracts* with each other, so that people who lack one kind of resource (such as land) can make a deal with people who lack a complementary resource (such as labour).[16] 'Sharecropping' as we know it in European and American history is often seen as a vicious arrangement in which people who monopolize land get rich by letting small parcels out to people who have no land. In this arrangement they do not pay a fixed rent each year in cash or produce, they pay a predetermined *share* (a half, or maybe two-thirds) of their crop to their landlord. Arrangements are complicated by the fact that landowners often share in the working of the land, providing tools, or fertilizer, or even labour. However, share contracts do not always favour the owner of the land. For example in Africa, labour is often the scarcer resource, and the person who brings it into the contract may have the upper hand. To be labourless is as debilitating as to be landless; this is certainly the case in Lesotho, where many sharecrop contracts involve elderly widows who have a piece of land but no means of working it. They typically make contracts with younger people who organize the plowing and weeding, and the harvesting of the crop. These younger Basotho usually have movable capital because they work on the mines in South Africa and have cash to buy oxen, ploughs etc. What they lack is fields, and they must wait until the older generation is ready to part with them. Meantime, rights to a field may be the poor widow's best hope of survival.

In rural communities where no individual or small group has monopolized land or labour, share contracts can therefore be a means of achieving the best 'mix' of productive factors. Surplus labour in one household can be applied to surplus land (or seed, or equipment) in another. Choosing from maybe a hundred or more neighbours in the wider community, people can match their resources, making short- and medium-term adjustments to the pressures of the domestic cycle. This way they are less dependent on close relatives, and do not necessarily have to wait until they inherit land, or have saved the cash to buy oxen or ploughs. One of the most interesting aspects of these contracts is that they can involve complete strangers, unrelated neighbours, or close kin, and that it can be difficult to trace any categoric difference in the arrangements. Sometimes a man will make a much tougher contract with his own son than he would with a stranger, perhaps because he knows he can not take his son to court if he defaults on the contract (Heady and Kehrberg 1952).

In this context, share agreements form a very flexible social and economic system for evening out the temporary inequalities which arise from the reproductive process. Because they mediate between the changing needs and capacities of households as they go through the reproductive cycle, the contracts themselves are dynamic, their terms adjusting to favour one party or the other as the years pass. Although providing much leeway for negotiation, the arrangements depend on a set of well-established, institutionalized expectations about what the contract should specify. Each major version of the contract usually has a name, and a whole population is bound to accept its basic terms by civil or customary law.

Sometimes sharecropping is intricately involved with other social processes, notably the accumulation and devolution of productive assets. In Malaysia, for example, a father may make a sharecrop agreement with his own son, thereby keeping control of his land and continuing to get the benefit of his son's labour by claiming a share of the crop. Meanwhile the son gets a bit of independence, and may be able to marry. Year by year the father will take a smaller share of the crop, until eventually he gets nothing. At this point the land is effectively his son's – he has acquired it by working it, and by a process of property devolution *inter vivos*.[17] In a similar way, American historians have described the 'agricultural ladder' in which young people without resources begin their domestic careers by working as hired hands, renting a piece of land, saving enough to buy some, and eventually becoming prosperous farmers in their middle age. What is often ignored, though, is the other side of the process: the way in which these prosperous farmers in turn hire in labour, lease out land they can no longer work, and eventually sell or bequeath their property to the next generation.

Hunter-gatherers like the !Kung are little concerned with matters of inheritance because they do not claim the factors of production as private property in the first place. In our industrial societies, however, getting control of as much property as early in the domestic cycle as possible is the key to survival, if not success. For most of us, property is no longer vested in family corporations, which means on the one hand that we have more strategic freedom to dispose of it as we wish (keeping our children guessing about their inheritance), and on the other, that we must depend for its protection on other social institutions, the most important of which is the state. Not only does the state apparatus provide the documents which say who we are and what we are entitled to, it is (shades of the extended family) the residual heir of our property, and the residual custodian of our children.

The state also produces and controls another kind of document, *money*, which enables us to acquire, mix and dispose of the factors of production very much more easily than through these other institutions like inheritance, or sharecropping, or communal labour. Thanks to money and the markets in which it operates, we can now turn land into wages, or a building into school fees, in a matter of hours. This has become not just a convenience but a necessity, given the acute cyclical pressures of the compact pattern of domestic development in industrial society.

## Organizing consumption and investment

For any economic unit – persons, households, firms – the most basic strategic challenge is striking a balance between what is consumed today and what must be saved and invested to secure future needs.[18] We would all like to control the future, but such things as variations in weather or market fluctuations interfere with our most careful calculations. The reproductive process adds a further set of variables, a pattern of changing needs and capacities which are continually altering the reckoning of consumption and investment. Trying to get a grip on a future which will always remain uncertain requires a great deal of imagination, energy, cooperation and good organization. It also takes a lot of faith and self-confidence, as the managers of big industrial firms and small family farms both know very well.

It is often said that economists have concentrated on explaining production and exchange, to the neglect of consumption.[19] If we (men) have lost sight of the fact that organizing consumption is *work*, it may be because it is usually *women's* work. An important issue in modern feminism is that housework is not accounted or rewarded, or even considered to matter, in the same way as male activities in production and exchange. Preparing food and other items for 'consumption' like clothes and shelter is intimately connected with the *work* of reproduction, which is so profoundly woman-centred. Around the world, close symbolic connections are made between eating and sexual intercourse and the 'work' which both entail.[20] Olivia Harris (1981: 149) remarks that so much of women's work is *body* work, another reason why it features little in 'proper' materialist discussions. Those who are not involved in the serious work of consumption may not appreciate that it is as responsive to reproductive dynamism as any other aspect of domestic organization: the nature and cost of clothing are highly variable over the life-cycle (Wynn 1970); pap, beefburgers and vintage port are likely to have distinct chronological positions on the family menu.

It is ironic that although we live in what we like to call 'consumer societies' we have evidently lost much of the sense of value which people through the ages have attached to food and its preparation.[21] Apple pie is now made in superabundance by national baking corporations not by Mom. In a place like Lesotho food is scarce and absorbs a much larger proportion of a household's resources. Processed food (including beer) even serves as a form of capital and currency, being saved and invested back into agricultural production as payments for labour. Indeed, the idea of 'earning your keep', of working very explicitly for food and accommodation, has been a basis of domestic service and apprenticeship in our societies well into this century.

In rural societies in which cash is not widely used, people translate food into labour, labour into capital, and capital into social relationships in more direct but no less complicated ways than we do. Rather than being simply 'worth' so-many dollars, cows in Africa may embody the privileges of an elder and, through marriage, are 'worth' the fertility and energy of a wife. A cow is also 'worth' something more than itself, at some future date, if it is kept healthy and breeds. *Capital, chattel, cattle*: in our language, the words all derive from the same root, indicating complex interrelationships among property, people and consumable investments. Without cash as the common denominator, the nature of transactions can be very difficult to decipher and evaluate. People in communities seek security by bringing material goods and social relationships much more closely together than we do in our shops and markets and banks.

Setting aside capital to create future production involves practical tasks such as saving seed or raising breeding stock, or pricing manufactured goods so that there will be enough profit to pay for repairs and replacement of machinery. But in rural households where the organization of human reproduction is part and parcel of the economic enterprise, the meaning of these managerial decisions is very complicated. It is little wonder that the economic theories and methods devised to explain how business firms reckon profits in industrial societies make little sense of important aspects of the family farm. Why, above all, is it often so much *less* productive than anyone with a little business sense would expect it to be? This has been one of the most vexatious challenges to rural development planners in the Third World. If these farmers are not chasing profits, what motivations *do* they have? What sort of calculations are they making about what to consume, save and invest? Some scholars have suggested that peasants lack the imagination or knowledge to raise their goals and thus their productivity; others have argued that the jealousy of neighbours in small communities prevents the ambitious from expanding production and getting rich.[22]

Research has piled up evidence that none of this is necessarily true. Earlier assumptions that peasants were too stupid or fatalistic to make *any* calculations have given way to a recognition that it is our Economics which is too simple-minded to interpret the complexity of their organization. The idea of efficiency which enables us to talk about 'capacity' is an invention of modern Economics, and small farmers can hardly be blamed for not knowing what this objective measure of their 'capacity' is. Chayanov made this point in discussing the Russian peasants: they were not measuring their efforts according to some generalized market value, they were responding to their own changing needs with the variable capacity available to them. Chayanov pointed out that the motor of the peasant economy is the reproductive cycle, but modern Economics has taken little interest in reckoning the costs and benefits of this.

Where farmers are not measuring their land, labour and capital according to prices set in regional markets, their 'economizing' is based on more local and immediate reckonings of changing needs and capacities. Ordinary communities offer an array of households at different stages of the domestic cycle, some 'rich' and in their prime, some struggling to get established, and some 'poor' elderly couples making do with their dwindling capacities. The prosperous established household which is a goal for newly-weds stretching their economic imagination and their capacities, is a nostalgic memory for the elderly couple. It is important to understand that the idea of a general *average* economic performance or of a 'normal' or 'ideal' pattern of productive efficiency, which plays such an important part in economists' analyses, is meaningless in this sort of reckoning. Peasant farmers do not look for inspiration to some abstract norm or average of productivity, drawn like a loading line across their granaries, fields or dinner-tables. As their needs and capacities change, they have the much more realistic example of people who have already 'made it' ahead of them in the cycle of domestic development.[23] These are the 'rich folks' (perhaps their own parents) to be imitated and envied. The great consolation is that soon enough this senior generation will be declining and dying, giving others a chance to take their place.

## Organizing surplus and savings

Our involvement in the reproductive process makes our judgements about wealth and welfare dynamic and relative, rather than stable and absolute. Especially on the family farm, the value of labour, food or land is dictated most immediately by the domestic cycle, not by markets. However, the same basic truth applies in our own societies, hence the old home-maker's complaint: 'Just when you've managed to make ends meet, somebody comes along and moves the ends.' Most of us do not expect to be able to sustain the same basic levels of income and expenditure throughout our lives. Households prosper or feel the pinch in different ways as domestic development proceeds. Newly-weds have to plan for the future, expending extra energy and sacrificing consumption for investment. Established households have the productive power to choose whether they will invest more or consume less. Variable need and capacity mean that accumulating *and decumulating* is the rhythm of our economic lives: in the stage of decline households eat their investments. This basic rhythm must appear very dreary to the young and acquisitive. It is hardly comforting to know that as the domestic cycle progresses people lose what they have gained, and that for all the striving, the world stays very largely the same.

It must also look dreary to economists, who have been more concerned with the aggregate sameness of rural economies than with the reproductive turbulence which underlies it. Taught to attach particular importance to the notion of profit, they find it difficult to imagine why people seem content with 'satisficing' when they could use their extra capacity in the easy periods to get rich. This has become an important aspect of the longstanding debates about the meaning and historical significance of *surplus*. What a 'surplus' is and what you can do with it depends on the kind of social and economic system you live in. In most contexts, prudent people try to produce as much as they think they need immediately, *plus* something as a safety margin, *plus* something (for example, seed) to give some assurance that the next cycle of production can proceed. It is production beyond these very basic requirements which interests us here. Lee (1979: 455–6) points out that accumulating 'surplus' would be pointless to the !Kung, because they need little capital and have no interest in lugging extra consumables around with them. If they do produce more than they need (a big kill) it makes sense to share it out as widely as possible, a sort of social banking arrangement which allows them to benefit in turn from other people's gains. With flexibility in the relations of production comes a fluidity in the relations of exchange which Lee calls 'a form of primitive communism' (p. 460).

For active agriculturalists, eating to the point of obesity is thoroughly counterproductive. Saving for future consumption is also limited by the storability of goods; peasant granaries are notoriously vulnerable to raids by human as well as animal and insect pests. In any case, accumulating productive resources like land or cattle makes more sense in meeting the longer-term demands of domestic growth. Again, perishable goods can be 'banked' in social relationships, perhaps by translating feasts into prestige.[24] More notoriously, outsiders who can apply brute force (brigands, feudal lords) can prey on peasants; but the trick is never to extract surplus to the point at which their *reproduction* is no longer viable. Economists like Chayanov would conclude charitably that surplus capacity in rural societies is not being 'wasted', but is being used to 'buy' extra leisure: people work less. But virtually all of these evaluations depend on a phenomenon which has not penetrated very deeply into small-scale rural communities: the market. Trading in markets gives people a sense of the relative value of their labour, food or land which is distinct from that determined by their own needs and capacities. In a word, it puts a *price* on their assets and produce. Defined and mobilized by the market, the idea of a surplus is extended far beyond the limits of consumption. Indeed, a symptom of market involvement is a shift in many social definitions towards the organization of production and exchange. In The Gambia, for example, it has been noted that the basic household group is now less frequently identified as the people who gather round the cooking pot (*sinkiro*), than as the work group (*dabada*). This shift in attention away from the women's sphere of influence parallels the greater involvement of men in producing crops for international markets.

Reproductive pressure is perhaps the most important dimension of the intriguing social phenomenon of *greed*. It is important to understand that acquisitiveness, the urge to accumulate, was not created by the marketplace: it was already a fundamental force in the processes of domestic establishment and growth, the quest for security in the face of reproductive instability.[25] By putting a price on surplus capacity, market institutions release people from the limitations of 'banking' within networks of kinship and community, and provide opportunities to turn latent surplus into more widely transactable currencies (cash and gold), and back into wealth of a more familiar kind (land, cattle). By the same process the market is as likely to be a medium of dispossession as of accumulation. Some people can turn their own productive of efforts and assets into liquid assets which they can then use to buy out the productive resources of other people.

Economists and others may like to think of markets in the abstract as 'free' and responsive to individual will but, as social institutions, access to them is never entirely open, nor are they ever entirely evenhanded. People lacking influence as well as skill can easily be fleeced. This is partly because markets do not develop in isolation from other institutions – banks, lawcourts, civil governments – which set the terms about who may trade what with whom, and under what conditions.[26] There is thus a political presence in all market transactions which puts some (landlords, factory owners) at an advantage over others. Markets have been the means by which ordinary people are made to pay for those same institutional frameworks into which they are being drawn, and to which they become subordinate: aristocracies and armies, courts and police. The trouble is, as James Scott (1976) has pointed out, such outsiders, cushioned by their own accumulated wealth, tend to be insensitive to variable harvests and the ups and downs of the domestic cycle. The *fixed* demands they make for rent or taxes may be met quite easily by a household in its prosperous phase, but may cause great hardship in the stages of establishment and decline. In such circumstances people have little incentive to step up production beyond what they need to survive – hence the accusations of 'laziness'.

Market institutions inject new meanings into the organization of production. Goods become commodities: they acquire value not from the personalities who produce and use them but through those larger, impersonal political-economic institutions.[27] A great virtue of an efficient market is that resources such as land and labour can likewise be traded *speedily* for one another: if you have the money you no longer have to wait for a workforce to grow up within your own household, or for a parent to bequeath you a plot of land.[28] Money, markets and trade have in turn led to the development of specialized banking institutions, the prime function of which is to mediate these transactions through time and space. Selling credit from savings held on behalf of depositors calls for a high degree of credibility and trust, which is one reason why banking has been so closely associated with the emergence of states and civil governments. Banking has also depended on large-scale systems of communication based on literacy and numeracy. Legal contracts have allowed the extension of personal trust to dealings between strangers, and bookkeeping, with all its paraphernalia of invoices, bills and balances, is still the basis of modern accounting.[29] Currencies, contracts and accounting have all come to depend on the political control afforded by government, and this in turn has allowed banking houses to expand from tight family nuclei to business partnerships and eventually to the large corporate bureaucracies of today.

Because the histories of banking have been much more concerned with the provision of credit for trade than with the personal interests of ordinary depositors, the importance of banks in the economic organization of reproduction has remained obscured. The earliest banks, in classical Greece and Rome and later in medieval Europe, were associated with the storing of surplus wealth in the form of valuables, and later cash, for safe-keeping. For the Greeks, temples were the most secure places, but in Christendom the churches were preoccupied in accumulating their own wealth, and were hostile to usury.[30] The jewellers and goldsmiths who manufactured most of the storable wealth also had the facilities for keeping it secure, and they and other merchants with larger houses provided deposit services for a fee. However, especially when they were holding 'liquid' deposits of cash rather than candlesticks, they were able to put the stored capital to work in their own or other merchants' enterprises, earning interest for themselves and their depositors. This interest was often paid as an annuity, an early form of pensioning.[31]

The history of modern banking is usually traced to the medieval city-states of Italy and to the provision of credit for long-distance trade.[32] Fairs were the clearing houses where money-changers set up their benches (*'banci'*) and took fees for converting the numerous currencies. Soon they too were accumulating deposits and financing trade on their own account. These concentrations of capital were very enticing to princes and governments, always in need of funding for public enterprises, especially wars against other states. As early as 1171 Venice was issuing four per cent government bonds to raise an army to protect its trading interests in the Byzantine empire.[33] Although sometimes the public was compelled to buy these issues, government bonds have always proved attractive to private family investors, mainly because of the *long-term* security they offer. If the state cannot guarantee payment thirty years hence, who other than God can? For their part, governments have found the slow maturation and easier rates of interest preferable to commercial loans.

Citizens, especially merchants with reduced ties to farming and extended families, resorted to banks not only to fund business ventures but to buy security for themselves and members of their households.[34] This component of private long-term savings has remained fundamental to the operation and stability of banking corporations. If merchant banking is associated with rapid, speculative investment at high rates of return, the business of the 'main street' banks dealing with personal deposits and loans is closely geared to the reproductive cycle – saving for weddings, homes, retirement – which has the virtue of providing a more stable, long-term source of banking capital. These protracted interests and motives are not well understood by those whose time horizons are limited to the rapid transactions of the marketplace. On the strength of a survey of incomes and savings in Oxford, England, in 1952–3, Lydall offers the following 'impressionistic picture' of savings patterns over the domestic cycle:

> Young men and women, before marriage, do not normally earn very large incomes. They spend what they earn very freely, with little thought for the future. Immediately before and after marriage, however, they begin to set aside what surplus they can for building up a home. In the next twenty years or so they are usually preoccupied with supporting their children, and their savings are not, on balance, very great. After middle age, the number of dependents declines more rapidly than income, expenditure on durables also falls away, and people begin to put aside larger sums for their old age. After retirement they usually draw down their capital in order to supplement their shrunken incomes. (Lydall 1955: 150)

Modern banks are at least tacitly aware of these patterns in their customer relations. For example, they seek to purchase a lifetime of profitable business by seducing impoverished college students with credit cards and other perquisites. The future they are purchasing will include a pattern of long-term loans, for education and – of soaring importance in recent decades – mortgages for house purchase. Contemplating strategic responses to the 'family life cycle squeeze', Gove et al. (1973) suggest reducing needs (i.e. children), reorganizing the household budget, or seeking to 'improve the temporal fit of income and "needs"' by anticipating a later squeeze and making savings. They conclude, 'The uses of savings and debt as devices to ease the life cycle squeeze undoubtedly are conditioned by factors in the wider economy' (p. 187). I am reversing this perspective here, arguing that the need for savings and loans arising from the reproductive process 'conditions' institutions in the wider economy. To understand how this happens we have to step outside the narrow confines of the marketplace and see the development of economic and political institutions in the long term.

At times the merging of reproductive and political interests through the medium of a bank has been very explicit. An example is the Monte delle Doti (literally the 'dowry mountain') which was set up by the Italian city-state of Florence in the fifteenth-century to help pay for its war with Milan. Fathers were invited to make a cash deposit in respect of their daughters for a term of up to fifteen years; the principal plus generous interest was paid to the son-in-law upon the consummation of the marriage – not paid to the girl or her father.[35] By the 1450s the fund was worth four million florins, and was providing dowries for relatively humble Florentine shopkeepers and artisans as well as the wealthier merchants. At this stage it was clear that the Monte was driven by the enthusiasm of investors rather that the need for capital. Donald Brown observes that the Monte delle Doti 'went beyond material interests in the usual sense to link the very reproductive interests of Florentines with their city' (1988: 269). Despite periodic solvency crises and church opposition, enthusiasm for the fund continued unabated well into the sixteenth century.

Since the earliest times, another important source of banked capital has been deposits held in trust for minors, or for the payment of annuities to widows. By the end of the seventeenth century the Orphans' Fund had become the most important source of credit for the development of the city of London. Constituted as a bank by Act of Parliament in 1694 its reputation was second only to the Bank of England, formed in the same year.[36] National banks, which usually reserved the right to issue money, grew up in association with national debts, combining the private and public interests of welfare and warfare. The Bank of England was set up to raise cash for the French wars, and in just ten days sold its first subscription of 1.2 million pounds to middle-class investors. The European and North American banks were essential to the capital investment of the industrial revolution.[37] Between 1750 and 1815 the number of private joint-stock banks in England more than doubled to well in excess of 700.[38] The next round of bank building came in the nineteenth century, when the lower-middle and working classes were seeking to secure the reproductive process in the hostile urban-industrial environment.[39]

The reinvention of banks today in countries of the Third World reveals the same converging interests of trade, personal savings and state intervention. The 'rotating credit' club is a universal example: people get together and contribute small sums which are disbursed by rota, lottery, or according to need. Very common among newcomers to towns and cities, these banks provide security for sickness and death in the first instance, and a means of raising small amounts of capital for investment. They often accumulate an array of supplementary functions, from recreation to dispute settlement and political representation. As they have grown they have become bureaucratized, acquired offices and salaried officials, and have been subjected to increasing government regulation. A few have made the transition to major banking corporations.[40]

Money, markets and banks have made many aspects of reproductive organization more efficient – for some, if not for all. Along with the web of political institutions of which they are a part, they provide means for combating the insecurities of the reproductive cycle. Each individual can convert surplus capacity into currency, which can be banked to fund periods of deficit. Labour – one's own or other peoples' – can be traded for cash, converted into capital, and saved to meet such longer-term demands of the reproductive cycle as marriages or security in old age. Moreover, wealth can be used not simply to produce more people, but to *produce more wealth*, more capital. We can see this in the development of the family farm into a *firm*, an economic organization which may have capital shareholders who are not relatives, and has such legal protection as limited liability. The enterprise is no longer at the mercy of the reproductive cycle; through broader institutional guarantees it can even sustain a life of its own. But what the firm does *not* do is produce new producers; for that it still depends essentially on individual households. The cost of greater personal economic independence is our greatly increased dependence on a much wider set of social institutions. By protecting our wealth they help us to overcome the insecurities of the domestic cycle. But it never *removes* these insecurities: they are always there to provoke both our greed and our need for cooperation, and thus to provide a vital momentum for human progress.

The name we usually give to this particular kind of progress is *capitalism*. A key virtue of market institutions is that productive wealth accumulated by individuals in one generation can be banked and passed on to those in the next, placing them at an advantage over other people. This wealth must then be guarded, hence political arrangements which work to protect private rights to *property* – land, buildings, machinery, etc. The competitive accumulation of wealth results, over time, in distinct classes of people. The more privileged must work to sustain their position not only through the apparatus of the state but by setting up boundaries of speech and dress, manners and morals. These social institutions are a vital part of their own mode of reproduction – most obviously expressed in a fussiness about who should marry whom. Part of this game of cultural politics is to dictate the morality of reproduction and production to other, less privileged people: preaching the value of 'knowing your place', or of 'an honest day's labour for a fair wage', is an important part of keeping a ruling class in business from generation to generation. Inevitably, those who can only sell their labour want more control over capital resources – a desire we usually call 'upward mobility'.

A problem of major historical significance is that, however much they succeed in accumulating and controlling wealth in the form of capital, no dominant class can fully control the supply of that other vital factor of production, labour. This is essentially because human labour must be *re*produced, and this takes place not in the factories and offices of the bourgeoisie but in millions of working-class households, and most directly through the unwaged labour of women. Keeping a tight grip on the reproduction of labour is thus a major political challenge for the capital-owning classes – as we have seen in the case of Lesotho. But the pretence of a minority to control the production of people is a marvellous piece of ideological grandiloquence.

# 6

# Generation, gender, and social class

In seeking to explain how the organization of reproduction is a historical force, I am challenging the assumption that it has little relevance in the explanation of social change, or that it has somehow lost its importance with the modernization of the world. This intellectual confusion underlies longstanding debates about the differences between our agrarian past and our industrial present, and between the intimacy of family relationships and the alienation of social classes. Today it continues to obstruct our understanding of such pressing contemporary issues as the political significance of gender, and of the 'generation gap'.

The misunderstanding is endemic in social science, and has become a symptom of the mutual incomprehension of the ideological Left and Right. For example, it loomed large in the political debates leading up to the Russian revolution of 1917. On the one hand there were the Narodniks ('Populists') who favoured more gradual reforms based on the interests and capacities of ordinary people, and on the other the Bolsheviks, who were for the revolutionary transformation, violent if necessary, of Russia into an industrial socialist state. Between the two there raged a debate about the nature of the Russian peasantry, and how they might be persuaded to change in a way which would make the expansion of industry possible. The contesting points of view are now associated with the populist economist A. V. Chayanov (see chapter 5) on the one hand, and the revolutionary Marxist leader V. I. Lenin on the other. The focal issue was how to explain the economic *differentiation* of the peasantry. Was it, as Chayanov argued, mainly an expression of the ups and downs of the reproductive cycle, today's 'wealthy' households becoming tomorrow's 'poor' households? Or, as Lenin believed, was the difference between wealthy and poor more permanent, evidence of the expansion of capitalist relations of production and the resolution of the rural population into distinct classes of landowners and labourers? It was very much a question of interpretation, because the two authors were arguing from essentially the same Russian survey data. The explanation each favoured affected the kinds of change they would recommend: a relatively homogeneous population could be worked upon by administrative persuasion (Chayanov), but a privileged class would probably have to be dislodged by violent revolutionary action (Lenin).

The debate continues apropos of the modernization of the 'Third World' today.[1] If anything, convictions about 'cyclical' differentiation, pre–capitalist society and reform on the one hand versus 'historical' differentiation, capitalism and revolution on the other, have hardened.[2] These dogmas make it doubly difficult to strike a sensible compromise, to the effect that a particular peasantry is neither necessarily 'classless' in the longer term, nor polarizing relentlessly along capitalist lines.[3] Two different kinds of explanation are at odds here: the one arguing from the organization of *reproduction* to explain social *continuity*, and the other fixing on the organization of *production* to define social *transformation*. What is lost in this dialectic is the influence of *reproduction* on social *transformation*.[4] Thus, neither Chayanov nor Lenin was interested in whether patterns of domestic development *helped to create capitalism* in the Russian countryside.

Inattention to the organization of reproduction has driven a wedge between our understanding of what goes on in households and what goes on in society at large. We can neither come to terms with how domestic processes bear upon those grand interactions of social classes which (according to the Left) make history; nor can we trace how the mass of individual interactions which (according to the Right) constitute society, are modulated by such fundamental categoric differences as age and sex. In tackling issues of *gender* and *generation* both Left and Right have had recourse to those material explanations which have held sway in modern social science generally – the relations of production and exchange. The failure to treat gender and generation as fundamentally reproductive categories has resulted in a notable tendency to confuse them with economic *class*, and for explanations of the relationships among all three sorts of category to break down. Again, alternative questions are suppressed: To what extend are social classes themselves defined by *re*productive processes?[5] Precisely what kind of influence does the organization of reproduction exert on the structures of modern industrial society?

From a materialist perspective, the subordination of younger people and of women in general to adult men bears a strong resemblance to the distinction, so important historically, between a labouring proletariat and the owners of capital. Women *are* labourers and also *produce* labourers, but both of these capacities have been controlled, along with other material resources, by men. This piece of patriarchal mischief has been traced to the organization of agrarian households. There, as we have seen, economic and reproductive processes are fused; and it is there, consequently, that a resolutely materialist approach becomes confused. While turning its back on the wider social domains of reproductive organization, it stops far short of an understanding of the reproductive nucleus around which households themselves are formed.

## Generation and political economy

In an effort to put these private and public domains of reproduction back together I shall begin with an examination of generation, an aspect of reproductive organization which has been somewhat neglected recently in favour of the exploration of gender. As I noted in chapter 2, the fact that human reproduction is differentially timed means that there are no natural and universal boundaries between one generation and another. If they do not 'really' exist, why then do we bother with the notion of generation at all? Apparently there is a need for people in most societies, including our own, to *construct* the idea out of the general hubbub of reproductive relationships, as a way of summarizing important distinctions among people of different age and experience within the wider reaches of community and society. What are these differences, and why are they important?

In non-industrial societies generational categories are often more explicit than in ours. This is made very evident in names, terms of address and greetings, for example in the extension of the family idiom of 'mother' and 'father' out to all senior people in the community.[6] Some societies seem to go to inordinate lengths to synchronize generations, arranging periodic ceremonies to shift a whole age group up from junior to more senior status. Examining one particular case in which the political-economic organization of generation has been carried to extraordinary lengths may help us to come to grips with the relationship between reproduction and the meanings of both class and history.

The Karimojong are migrant pastoralists who inhabit some 4,000 square miles of flat, dry plain in north-central Uganda. In the 1950s, when they were studied by Neville Dyson-Hudson (1966), they numbered around 60,000, and although they were thinly dispersed they had a strong sense of independent political identity. This depended much less than other pastoral peoples on the idiom of kinship, and they reckoned relationships by descent only to a depth of about three generations. For their coherence as a people and for the organization of numerous important activities they depended instead on a system of *age and generation sets*, into which the whole male population was grouped. In such societies, men themselves explain that age sets 'ensure that men of similar age and/or generation move through life in time together' (Baxter and Almagor 1978: 13). But why? What is the virtue of synchronizing lives in this way?

As figure 6.1 illustrates, boys were recruited as a batch every five years into a specific *age set* with its own name and identity. Five age sets in turn constituted a single *generation set* which consisted of men in an age range of twenty five to thirty years. At any one time Karimojong society was thus divided into a senior and a junior generation set. They distinguished each other as Red and Yellow, one set wearing copper (red) and the other brass (yellow) ornaments. Karimojong history was measured by the alternation of Red and Yellow generation sets through junior to senior status. In a grand ceremony every twenty-five to thirty years, which drew together Karimojong from all quarters, Red would relinquish its senior status to Yellow, and a *new* Red set of juniors would be opened.

A complete historic cycle of generation sets was reckoned to consist of two pairs, Red–Yellow–Red–Yellow, extending through a period of 100–120 years. The system thus expressed continuity over time for the Karimojong, as well as political unity over space. It also emphasized the opposition between adjacent (father–son, Yellow–Red) generations, and the bond between alternate generations (grandfather–grandchild, Red–Red or Yellow–Yellow). Karimojong would say of the rising generation: 'they re-enter the place of their grandfathers' and 'they will take the ornaments of their grandfathers.' But Dyson–Hudson makes it clear that the system was not some wonderful natural mechanism. Its coordination across so large a population and geographical area depended on conscious reckoning and adjustment (1966: 158, 204).

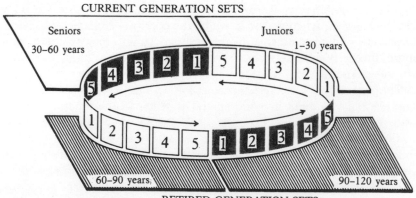

**Figure 6.1**  Age and generation set organization of the Karimojong (an interpretation of the model in Neville Dyson–Hudson, *Karimojong Politics*, Clarendon Press, Oxford, p. 157)

*Asapan*, the inauguration every five years of a new *age* set and the initiation of a batch of boys, was a major event throughout all Karimoja. It was prompted by the relentless process of reproduction, but in turn exerted an important influence on the scheduling of domestic development. Once initiated, a boy became adult and could marry, but according to a rigid sense of priorities, a youth could only be initiated into the *generation* set *below that of his father*. Children in one household joined *age* sets in approximate birth order, but full brothers usually joined the same age set, regardless of their age. The fact that an ox had to be sacrificed for each ceremony added a significant material cost to the advancement to adulthood.

While Red–Red or Yellow–Yellow relations were emotionally warm, Red–Yellow relations bore the brunt of much economic and political tension. As Dyson–Hudson puts it, 'The adult male population is divided into two classes: those in authority and those in obedience, the leaders and the led. Each of these classes is seen as related to a defunct class which they were inaugurated to replace.' This, he says, is 'a restatement of the father–son relationship in a public idiom. Not only are adjacent generation-sets considered related as fathers and sons, they usually are fathers and sons... As individual fathers, their authority is final in the context of domestic affairs: as members of the senior generation-set, their authority is final in society at large.' The elders were thus 'a class sanctioned to wield authority and exact obedience, in public matters', something of great political value to this scattered population (Dyson–Hudson 1966: 162, 170–1). Individually, elders could direct the labour of juniors within the domestic domain, and collectively they commanded them as an 'army' in defence and in cattle raids on neighbouring peoples. The Red and Yellow ornaments would immediately inform Karimojong who met on a chance encounter about their basic relationship to each other. No need here to work out genealogical connections, or compare addresses. Red–Yellow carried a fundamental implication of inequality, and so, too, to a lesser extent, did the more 'brotherly' relationship between adjacent *age* sets. These differences were not just a matter of ornaments, they were expressed in access to productive and reproductive resources: the 'wealth' which goes with being a paterfamilias, and the 'poverty' which is the lot of a dependent son. In this case the power and prestige we would associate with a dominant class was conferred on the entire cohort of older men.

There are striking parallels between Karimojong age organization and social class relations in our industrial societies. The typical progression of males through the domestic cycle is very like a transition from 'proletarian' to 'capitalist'. A boy begins with little or no property, and his labour is at the disposal of his parent. The paterfamilias controls the means of production, the land and other resources needed to make a living. The institutions of community and society reinforce his privileges: he is the legal patron of other family members, and his rights and duties are backed up by religious codes. As we have seen, this authority extends beyond the economic realm to management of the reproductive process itself, and the business of deciding who may marry when.

Why do younger Karimojong put up with their subservience to the elders? (Why do sons everywhere put up with their subservience to their fathers?) Why do they not rebel and seize power and wealth? In a sense they do, as time moves on and the pressure to turn over the generation sets increases. The phase of domestic fission is therefore very evocative of class conflict, raising as it does questions about access to productive resources. The elder generation is concerned to hang on to its authority and privileges, but passing time, the aging and death of the elders, whittles down their numbers and their claims to authority. They certainly do their best to hang on as long as possible; one ideological tactic at their disposal is their power to collectively curse juniors who have displeased them. But pressure builds up inexorably among the lower ranks for a succession ritual – which only the elders can sanction. The aging juniors resent their economic and political subordination to the old brigade, and are likely to be particularly hostile to their 'poaching' brides from an age cohort which the juniors consider to be rightfully theirs. If promotion to elderhood may be thought of as a kind of upward class mobility, the Karimojong are remarkable in that they synchronize this process ritually across the entire population. The Red–Yellow opposition could be thought of as an uneasy intergenerational truce. The competing interests are the familiar ones of domestic fission, but here they are given a concerted voice. In most societies the generations do not have this sort of solidarity, and the youngsters have to struggle on a more individual basis to make their way in society. In Karimojong social organization, the intergenerational tensions which are a dynamic force in all societies become a coherent central motif in their *historical* understanding of themselves.

Our own thinking may not be so very different. But in our societies each generation, each overlapping cohort of subjective viewpoints, is left to form its own collective vision of society and experience of history. It draws on certain generally available, chronological cues to categorize itself as a generation: the Depression, Vietnam, etc. There is a moral dimension: each generation likes to claim that it has virtue on its side, and has had to face more serious economic and political challenges. This can go beyond a way of speaking to a way of acting. If we doubt the political force of generational conflict we should recall the world-wide revolutionary fervour of the junior 'underclass' in the years 1968–72, and the 1989 revolt against the gerontocracy in China.[7] These movements are so impressive because they translate the squabbles between parents and children into a much wider arena than the household, pitching one generation as a mass against the other. Husbands can feel much the same categorical alienation when their wives resort to the rhetoric of feminism.

Periodically, a generation makes itself evident by force of numbers: by dying in a war, or by deferring marriage in a period of economic slump. These effects are amplified by the demographic scale of industrial societies. As Reuben Hill puts it, 'Each cohort encounters at marriage a unique set of historical constraints and incentives which influence the timing of its crucial life decisions' (1970: 322). How, we may ask, did households at different stages of development respond to the Great Depression of 1932–3? It seems likely that those in decline suffered most heavily, while those in the early stages of expansion were better placed to take advantage of Roosevelt's New Deal programmes.[8] The point is that people neither make history nor respond to historical events as an undifferentiated mass. The reproductive cycle produces categorically distinct interests across a whole population, and how each generation responds will depend on its particular life experiences as well as its sheer size. As the proportion of old people increases in our industrial countries we can be sure that they will do their bast to hang on to their wealth and voting power to secure their welfare.[9]

Although competition between generations may not be as concerted as it is among the Karimojong, the 'motor' of the reproductive process is massive in its effects. Most influential are the acquisitive pressures on the younger generation, which give society much of its historical momentum. Juniors must accumulate, must displace their seniors, and must in their turn ultimately relinquish control, divest, decumulate. But resources are not passed on mechanically and without a struggle. They must also be *created*: new lands must be colonized, livestock bred and *technical innovations* made. This progressive force is continually pitted against the constraints of environment and the limitations of technology. But all around us we see evidence of the extent to which youthful ingenuity has prevailed. This rhythm of progress is thwarted only by the countervailing rhythm of aging and death.

Consider the possibility of a whole society which consisted exclusively of a younger generation: that, surely, would be extremely dynamic and progressive. Perhaps surprisingly, quite a few such societies exist. Almost invariably they have one central purpose: the pursuit of rapid economic development. An example is the Malaysian government's enormous land development programme.[10] Between 1957 and 1980 more than a hundred thousand households from poor rural areas were resettled on two hundred rubber and oil palm plantations cleared from the jungle. The many applicants were screened on the basis of 'need' (family poverty) and 'suitability' (efficient, able-bodied labourers). Whole communities were thus created consisting of younger married couples with several children, additionally motivated by the fact that they had little or no land at home to support them. This active and acquisitive labour force helped to guarantee the remarkable economic success of the Malaysian land development schemes for several decades. The abnormality of these communities was evident in many ways, for example in the chronic overloading of the local schools. The Bukit Besar scheme, which I visited in 1972, had ten simultaneous first grade classes spread out over morning and afternoon sessions.

By the 1980s, however, the schools were emptying and the children were taking their educational advantages to the expanding towns and cities. After reaping the short-term benefits of this 'unnaturally' skewed population, the Malaysian government is now confronting the long term costs: both the settlement scheme populations and the tree crops they have been tending are aging simultaneously.[11] Dwindling crop yields are exacerbated by the declining physical capacity of the settlers themselves, and additional labour (much of it drawn from neighbouring Indonesia) has to be hired to do the work. Billions of dollars of investment in more than two hundred schemes is now under threat, and the government is understandably vexed to see its ardent young proletarians turn into aged, underproductive capitalists. Recently it has even felt obliged to renege on original contracts to hand the land over to the settlers. The dream of profitable, self-sustaining smallholder communities has evaporated, and the settlement schemes remain government-managed estates.[12]

Evidently, the Malaysian planners either did not understand or chose to ignore the significance of the reproductive process in the making and breaking of their land development schemes. Experience tells us repeatedly that the success of economic projects is not guaranteed solely by the efficiency of productive arrangements. Either optimism, shortsightedness or plain ignorance blinds us to the fact that the generational cycle involves decumulation as well as accumulation. Folk wisdom may know better – 'riches to rags in three generations' goes the old saying.[13] Individuals move out of one social class and into another, but the *consolidation* of a dominant class undoubtedly depends on its capacity to resist this sort of mobility. For a minority to retain control of capital it has to keep outsiders at bay, and prevent its own offspring from dropping out. This is hard work, involving the sort of economic, political and *cultural* tactics we shall consider in the next two chapters. Reproduction poses the most serious threat to the maintenance of class power. But if reproductive processes are excluded from a definition of class, then class itself is doubly deficient as an analogy for understanding the inequalities of generation and gender, and their impact on modern society.

However conspicuous they may be, political and economic definitions of generation and gender are always secondary *social constructions* of the fundamental reproductive distinctions. This is why trying to explain inequalities of gender and generation from a political-economic point of view has proved so frustrating. For a start, the two sorts of categorization (class on the one hand, and generation and gender on the other) are not mutually exclusive. Thus, Dyson–Hudson is at pains to point out that Karimojong generation sets do not equalize wealth: there are still richer and poorer elders, more and less advantaged youths. In a broad survey of age-set organization in Eastern Africa, Baxter and Almagor make the point that the sets do not corporately own or control productive property: that remains vested in households and patrilineal descent groups. Consequently, 'When the interests of domestic and familial loyalties diverge from those of set loyalties, set loyalties are likely to be the ones which give.' Indeed, as domestic issues claim more of their attention, older men may 'ooze away' from involvement in their age set (1978: 22, 13).

In a zealous effort to apply Marxian explanations to pre-industrial societies, the French anthropologist P. P. Rey (1979) has used the model of class conflict in industrial societies to explain the relations between 'exploiters and exploited' in societies like the Karimojong. Juniors keep their own company in a kind of working-class solidarity in the face of the economic and political domination of the elders.[14] In reaction to Rey's argument, but still from a materialist perspective, Meillassoux points out that people distinguished as a generation within a community cannot constitute a class, because the one is defined by the passage of time and the other by access to material resources.[15] Elders can only be elders by virtue of having been juniors; but people do not have to be proletarians before they can become capitalists (1981: 80). Classes, Meillassoux implies, are fixed, but people are not: 'Age, even understood in its social sense, is only a transitional moment in the life of an individual.' However, classes are only 'fixed' because we choose to think of them so. A central interest in maintaining class status is to resist downward mobility within and between the generations – in other words, to counteract the turbulence of the reproductive process.

## Gender and political economy

Similar problems have arisen with political-economic explanations of gender. The central dilemma for feminists thus becomes one of loyalties: to a 'class' of women, or an economic class which is comprised of both sexes. Classes are historical developments, but women's subordination seems timeless.[16] Playing men at their own materialist game, likening women to a revolutionary proletariat, may actually obscure the issues, for example by reducing explanations of women's subordination to arguments about the nature and value of their labour, and whether or not it should be 'waged'.[17]

It seems that feminists are gradually returning to the view that an explanation of women's subordination must be sought in the organization of *re*production. Rossi declares firmly, 'Gender differentiation is not simply a function of socialization, capitalist production, or patriarchy. It is grounded in a sex dimorphism that serves the fundamental purpose of reproducing the species' (1985: 161).[18] However real and potent class distinctions may be, they are also historically more recent than reproductive categories of gender and generation, and are thus in some sense more superficial. Generation and gender are categories which divide households, social classes and whole societies. Social classes, on the other hand, divide whole societies *but do not divide households*.[19] Class conflict widens the gap between households; it does not necessarily close the generation or gender gap *within* families. Nor does class differentiation eradicate distinctions of gender and generation, it *superimposes* itself on them. Thus, Mackintosh argues that women's subordination is 'mediated' by the household in a way which gives women inferior status in the labour market. This implies a reversal of the more familiar pattern of cause and effect: 'in the long run inequality in the wage sphere can only be overcome – and indeed could be relatively easily overturned – were the relations of reproduction, and the form of the household which they create, first to be transformed' (1984: 14).

If the reproductive process is very clearly central to the definition of generations, its significance in the definition of gender is less obvious. In earlier chapters we have seen how the central role of women in reproduction exposes them to male control in transactions within and between households, and how the subordination of women is expressed in the organization of domestic activities. However, households are not static, and neither are gender definitions. Within the cycle of domestic development the rights, obligations and social identity of a woman change. At the risk of overgeneralization, in the period from puberty to marriage she is quintessentially feminine: most sexually desirable and most rigorously subordinated. Child–rearing gives her authority over a rising generation, and requalifies her conjugal relationships. It is striking that after the menopause, as their authority is further enhanced with age, women acquire '*more male*' (rather than 'more female') attributes: owning property, speaking up in public debates, and perhaps being entitled to smoke a pipe or wear pants.[20] We might therefore say that generation qualifies gender.[21] There is some parallel 'feminization' of male roles and identities, but the reproductive cycle is very unlikely to bring women those privileges which give male elders the appearance of a dominant class. The whole confraternity sees to that; as Meillassoux puts it, the junior males work as 'clients' of elders in a joint exploitation of the productive and reproductive capacities of women (1981: 80).[22] In Dyson–Hudson's account Karimojong women 'have no part in politics' (1966: 210), and accordingly no relationship to the age or generation sets other than by vague association through brothers or husbands.[23] Baxter and Almagor (1978: 11) explain that in these systems the status of women is defined essentially within the domestic frame.

It seems that Karimojong women, like their sisters elsewhere, are doubly restricted by the social organization of reproduction. For men, the reproductive process makes one generation subordinate to another within each household; but for women, it takes subordination one step further, dividing each generation. This double bind has remained with women during the historic development of the third form of subordination, social class, an economic and political categorization which transcends the distinctions of gender and generation consolidated within the agrarian household. Until recent years, and then essentially by virtue of changes in the social organization of reproduction, upward class mobility for women independently of men in our societies was as unthinkable as the idea that they might have a place in society outside the home. From the materialist perspective, while *all women* are labourers and have the capacity to reproduce labour, control of capital has passed to *some men*. The predicament of proletarian men now begins to look a lot more like the dependent, labour-generating status of women. 'In all stratified societies,' says Obbo, 'men too are the victims of progress or development, but the women often see themselves as "victims of victims"' (1985: 212). Indeed, it has been argued that economic development in most countries of the 'Third World' has not liberated women from the domestic domain, but has actually reduced whatever political influence and economic independence they might have had in the past.[24]

Beneria and Roldan (1987) have explored this intersection of gender and class categories in the predicament of home-based industrial workers in Mexico City. From an avowedly materialist perspective they describe how the system of capitalist production takes advantage of the gendered divisions of labour within poor households to secure an unskilled, unstable, insecure, under–rewarded, semi-legal, and predominantly female workforce. Seeking out the cheapest segments of the labour market, industrial subcontracting capitalizes on the domestic isolation of women which virtually eliminates any form of collective bargaining, and on their readiness to reduce their dependence on men by getting some control over their own income.[25] The analysis is unusually sensitive to the reproductive careers of women: 'one must go back to the various milestones in a woman's life history, each one of which, by being defined within a particular context of class, gender, and family relations, progressively shapes the future class insertion' (pp. 101–2). Marriage is the pivot, the only real opportunity a woman has for altering her cardinal class identity.

But, in the final analysis, Beneria and Roldan remain, like the homeworkers they describe, immobilized at 'the crossroads of class and gender'.

They extrapolate the predicament of women from relations of production and exchange, allowing reproduction to slip away in a series of economic metaphors (the 'reproduction' of labour, capital, etc.). Even their basic definition of the household as 'a locus or social sphere made up of a number of individuals who share a common place to live and a budget' (pp. 111–12) evades reference to the reproductive process. The inevitable conclusion is that homework 'is a form of capitalist production at the household level that represents a disguised form of subproletarianization'. As a class-within-a-class, women are left with minute opportunities to 'renegotiate gender relations within the household' (p. 165). At Beneria and Roldan's crossroads, class relations are given highway priority, and questions about the social origins of gender categories are halted. In the final analysis we are left with little sense of why it is *women* who so overwhelmingly constitute this 'subproletariat'.

To return briefly to the case of Lesotho, described in chapter 3. Industrial capital and its owners in South Africa depended on the supply of black labour and have found in the apartheid system an effective means of controlling that supply. The labour force is male, but is produced as always by women, who are forcefully segregated from the mines – the regions and processes of material production. South African industry controls the productive capacities of Basotho men by controlling the reproductive capacities of Basotho women. Rigorous efforts to explain the predicament of the Basotho in terms of the material definitions of social class produce a series of partial truths. Insisting that Basotho men 'exploit' these women by putting them to work in the fields is about as informative as saying that the old widow who hires labour to work her fields is a 'capitalist', or that the young men who send wages home to support their parents are *Lesotho's* 'proletariat'. Such piecemeal definitions of 'class' chop the peoples of southern Africa up into a confusing array of categories whose oppositions to each other are economically, politically and historically very much less significant than their opposition to the white owners of capital. Indeed, the idea that the black population is at odds with itself has always served the purposes of white domination.

It is not the organization of the economy which explains the system of exploitation in southern Africa, so much as the political organization of *reproduction*. The creed of apartheid – a political system whose basic tenet is that whites shall not engage in reproductive acts with peoples of subordinate, labour-supplying races – makes this obvious. And yet, apartheid is consistently seen as racial subordination, not the subordination of women by men. The long-term success of the South African enterprise depends on the fact that it is not rooted in something so modern, so obvious, as class relations, but in a categoric distinction of much greater antiquity. What makes the ideology of gender such a powerful instrument is that ultimately it is shared by white and black populations alike. It is an inequality which has been, in a fundamental sense, beyond question. Working in Lesotho, I had a feeling that black men were in some roundabout way complicit with whites in the mechanisms of black subordination. Basotho men would tell me how important their wives were, but how necessary it was for a husband to be in control of his household and its affairs within the community. How else could a man be sure that he had a home to return to?

All this suggests that the power to transform South Africa rests less with men and their political-economic capacities, than with women and their reproductive capacities. This, of course, suggests an almost unimaginable political upheaval – something little short of a global feminist revolution. The possibilities for that may be slightly greater today, but it is more likely that, as so often in the past, the predicament of Basotho women will be mitigated piecemeal through political reform of the relationships among men. However there is a danger that in lamenting the economic and political subordination of women we continue to overlook the social significance of their reproductive *powers*, and thus the history of their influence on society.

To understand the subordination of women we should perhaps begin by liberating women from *our thinking about* family and household,[26] and recognize that, through their central concern with reproduction, they, at least as much as men, have always been instrumental in the construction and transformation of social institutions. They may have lacked a strategy to put this power to work in their own interests, but as social scientists we too have lacked the means of understanding their potentialities.

# 7

# Reproduction and the rise of industrial capitalism

Theories of the historical development of 'the family' have provided a weak and misleading surrogate for speculation about the social organization of reproduction. Modern social science has a simple story to tell: In agrarian societies (past and present) social, economic and political relationships have been sustained primarily within 'extended families', thought of both as ramifying networks and as large household groups. 'As society became more dense, more complex and more organized, there developed a series of semi-public bodies, town authorities, parish overseers of the poor, schools, banks, etc., which took over many of the functions previously performed by the kin and by the family' (Stone 1975: 21). Continued proliferation of these institutions, it is assumed, threatens to put the family out of business altogether.

Recently, new historical evidence has challenged this account. On the strength of detailed research in western European parishes, the social historian Peter Laslett could declare that 'There is no sign of the large, extended co-residential family group of the traditional peasant world giving way to the small, nuclear, conjugal household of modern industrial society' (Laslett 1969: 200). In England, so much at the heart of the industrial revolution, the encapsulated 'nuclear family' could not have been created by the economic transformation of society, because it was already widely in evidence long before that transformation began. It is now clear that what I have called the compact pattern of domestic development has been prevalent throughout the population since the fourteenth century and probably before.[1]

The discovery that industrialization was not responsible for the compact or nuclear family has encouraged historians to turn conventional theory around and take up the cudgels on behalf of the family as an active force in history. Family structure, some of them have argued, is not a casualty of economic change, but has played a significant role in shaping industrial society. 'The long-recognized effect of the economy on the family has too often obscured the converse – that the family may have important consequences for the economic system,' declares Furstenberg. 'To understand the complicated relationship between the economy and the family, we cannot simply view the family as the dependent variable in the relationship' (1966: 327).[2] Here, I propose that 'the family' is not the appropriate agent in assessing cause and effect, because 'families' are themselves complex and diverse products of change. Nor do we have any reason to conclude that just because it existed before the industrial revolution, the compact or 'nuclear' family *caused* anything. Instead, we must look *within* the family for the more fundamental processes which account for its multifarious forms – and for the structure of many other social institutions besides.

To explain the significance of reproduction in the making of history is an unfamiliar and unconventional exercise, and a task of monstrous proportions. What follows can only be regarded as a piece of intellectual effrontery, a selection of indications rather than a proof. My central purpose is to find a context for the social organization of reproduction in explaining the events leading up to and ensuing from that great historic trauma we call the industrial revolution. Accordingly, I am mainly concerned with what has happened in western Europe over the last eight centuries, and the consequence of these developments for the world at large.

## Family dynamics and social growth

I shall begin by picking up a few strands of the story in England a thousand years ago. The mass of the agrarian population lived as serfs or villeins in small households, economically and socially dependent on feudal lords, manors and the great estates. As elsewhere in Europe, the lord could exercise very detailed control over the family development of his dependents: allowing or preventing fission, setting the terms for retirement, and perhaps even enjoying the rights of the first night with the newly-wed bride.[3] The church was no less influential in family affairs. It had been expanding its wealth and power since the third century AD by intruding its moral force deeply into processes of reproduction and production in all classes:

> For the Church to grow and survive it had to accumulate property, which meant acquiring control over the way it was passed from one generation to the next. Since the distribution of property between generations is related to patterns of marriage and the legitimisation of children, the Church had to gain

authority over these so that it could influence the strategies of heirship.'
(J. Goody 1983: 221)

The monasteries endowed themselves with vast estates by stepping between
heirs and their inheritance, exchanging care of body and soul in sickness and
death for land. They turned over much of their property to the capital-
extensive rearing of sheep, pioneering the cloth production on which
industrialization was subsequently based. Not content with making a virtue
out of celibacy, the church narrowed the choice of spouse by expanding the
definition of incest, and meddled in all matters from wet-nursing to care of
the elderly.[4] The apparent aim was to reduce the strength of 'real' family
corporations in favour of the spiritual family of the church. Throughout
western Europe ordinary people were obliged to make somewhat furtive
'customary' marriages, often when they were very young. This reinforced
the pattern of small, externally dependent households, the conjugal pair
struggling to raise progeny for an unsympathetic but underpopulated world.[5]

In the middle of the fourteenth century, plague swept Europe, reducing
the population of England from about four to two and a half millions. The
sudden shortage of labour gave some power to the working poor, who finally
shook themselves free of their feudal bonds. For them this was a mixed
blessing, because as the lords gave way to private landowners the common
people's access to capital resources was further reduced. Moreover, a new
class was in the making, with trade as its power base. It was recruited in large
measure from the smaller landed families, who depended on laws of
impartible, primogenital inheritance to hold together their estates and their
privileges. According to Trevelyan, 'the younger sons, after being brought
up as children of the manor-house, were sent out into the world to seek their
fortunes. This had the effect of increasing the adventurous and roving spirit
of the new English nation' (1945: 145). Throughout Europe, these younger
sons were at the forefront of the mercantile revolution. Explicitly separated
from their 'extended families' they were obliged with some urgency to
construct new economic and reproductive relationships. They established
compact households in the towns, and built up new forms of capital in their
trading enterprises.[6] An important minority invested their education in the
expanding professions (law, the army) and in the administrative apparatus of
the state.

'The history of the change from mediaeval to modern England might well
be written in the form of a social history of the English cloth trade'
(Trevelyan 1945: 279). With feudal patronage a thing of the past, the
merchant class did much to fill the gap. Small towns sprang up all over the
country, inhabited by the merchants who 'put out' the manufacture of
woollen goods to the poor farm-labouring households. Increasingly, the
merchants sought material and spiritual security not in family ties or in the

church, but in town-based institutions of their own making – conspicuously the guilds. Initially, these 'formed a sort of artificial family, whose members were bound by the bond not of kinship but of an oath, while the gild-feast, held once a month in the common hall, replaced the family gatherings of kinsfolk' (Gibbins 1912: 92). In their heyday around the fourteenth century, the guilds provided the new middle class with banking and insurance services, regulated wages and profits, and set the foundations for civic government.

This class of self-made men did much to extend the influence of money and markets. According to Trevelyan, their new wealth 'overthrew status and custom in favour of cash nexus and the fluidity of labour, it brought to the newly emancipated villein great opportunities and great risks, and to the capitalist farmer and landlord temptations to grow rich quickly at the expense of others' (1945: 283). In town and country the quest for capital led to the erosion of old rights and privileges, most notably access to common land for grazing, fuel and other vital purposes. The law encouraged these 'enclosures' and, especially in areas depopulated by the plague, vast tracts were turned over to the production of wool. These appropriations benefited not only the wealthy landowners but also a rising class of small 'yeoman' farmers. But the mass of rural people found that their subsistence depended increasingly on cash wages, rather than on patronage, communal exchanges or payments in produce.

Throughout England from the fourteenth to the seventeenth century, the social organization of reproduction in all classes remained based in the compact household. There is little or no evidence of the extended pattern, and the stem family seems rare.[7] Laslett identifies a well-established 'structural principle' in north–west Europe which 'requires each newly married couple to set up on their own, to live by themselves and not with the families of either set of parents – to take charge of their own domestic enterprise' (1983: 531). The conjugal bond was central, a companionate ideal of marriage contracted freely by the couple themselves. 'The one hard and fast rule', says Macfarlane, 'was that the young couple should be able to form an independent unit at marriage' (1986: 321).[8] A household rarely outlasted the death of its head.[9]

In previous chapters I have explored the material implications of the compact pattern, noting how acute economic pressures give rise to the pronounced cycle of accumulation/decumulation, early fission as each new generation matures, and external dependence. Furstenberg reckons that 'some of these very tensions in the family may have facilitated the process of industrialization' (1966: 327). Let us now consider how these pressures, in so many thousands of households, came to influence the course of English economic history.

In recent years social historians have taken up the challenge of reconstructing from documentary traces the lives of households and whole communities in Europe *through time*. This involves extremely laborious tracking of individual lives through parish records of births, marriages and deaths, and the scrutiny of tax and land registers etc. The results have been very illuminating, revealing not only the smallness of households but their dynamism, and the variety of strategies for dealing with reproductive pressures.[10] Hans Medick has compared the cyclical ups and downs of English rural households with the nineteenth-century Russian farm families described by Chayanov. However, unlike his Russian peasants or the Ganda farmers described in chapter 3, economic expansion and contraction in English rural households was severely inhibited by alienation from the land and the loss of communal rights. Capital deficiency made households very conservative about the production of labourers and consumers. As Levine puts it: 'In the relatively stagnant preindustrial, semicommercial economy in which the household was the primary unit of production and consumption, controls over nuptiality and, to a somewhat lesser extent, over fertility were of vital importance in keeping population size roughly in line with resources' (D. Levine 1977: 45). The key tactic was to delay marriage, thereby slowing down the rate of domestic fission and replacement.[11]

The compact domestic pattern was sustained not simply because households were good at coping with internal pressures but because their need for external support was being met in various ways. Containing on average fewer than five persons[12] the typical household, says the historian R. M. Smith, 'appears to have been highly vulnerable to "life-crises"' which prompted a good deal of collaboration with wider family and neighbours: 'certain hardships such as the death of a spouse, unemployment, sickness, or senility would have made it difficult for households to have been self-sufficient' (1981: 606). Personnel changed continually, with non-relatives drafted in to achieve a degree of economic stability.[13] The wider ties of kinship undoubtedly sustained households in lean times, but families no longer controlled access to essential capital resources. With the expansion of money and markets, people increasingly sought security outside family networks, for example by contributing to community welfare funds. These were the basis of the parish poor relief system, which in turn provided the foundations of the modern welfare state.[14]

Dependent on their own resources of labour, the overwhelmingly rural households were readily drawn into manufacturing for the cloth trade. In the seventeenth century,

> industry was still organized largely on a loose domestic basis, work being commissioned by middle men... Many industrial workers would have a cottage and a bit of land, perhaps as much as six acres: the spinning wheels

and looms on which, for example, Yorkshire kerseys, Lancashire fustians, and Norfolk worsted were manufactured would be found in the operatives' own homes, while yeomen with small holdings would also engage in industry as a part-time occupation. (Ashley 1952: 13)

Among the farreaching implications of this 'proto-industrial' organization of production was what we might call the 'involution' of domestic labour. The new 'cottage industry' depended squarely on woman power, but men were drawn out of the fields and into the domestic domain. Along with the children, they were set to spinning and weaving and the many other tasks of cloth production.[15]

The sheer importance of these relations of production for the emerging *national* economy was reflected in a public revaluation of 'the family' in the sixteenth century. By this time the word had become synonymous with small *household*.[16] The Reformation (from 1517 onwards) entrenched in the Protestant mind the moral vision of a compact, socially responsible household. Instead of celibacy and ecclesiastical interference in property and fertility, companionate Christian marriage and the natural development of the population were idealized.

In Protestant territories monasteries and nunneries were dissolved and their physical structures and endowments given over in most instances to public charitable and educational uses. Marriage laws became simpler, clearer, and more enforceable, and were applied less arbitrarily. A new freedom and privacy came into the lives of the honorably married who had no sins to hide, while for the sexually unprincipled and wayward, correction was now nearer at hand from the new, vigilant marriage courts. If governmental monitoring of moral and domestic life increased through the agency of conscientious marriage courts, so too did the security of marriage, its new publicity and communal oversight now its best defense. (Ozment 1983: 49)

'Most significantly,' says Ozment, 'home and family were no longer objects of widespread ridicule.' Paternal authority was affirmed, but so too was the conjugal bond, and the interdependence of man and wife in the domestic domain. Parenting was shared to a high degree but wilful indulgence of children was resisted.[17] Historians have debated the extent to which *patriarchy* was an invention of this period.[18] If so, it was probably mostly ideological bombast: with little capital to control, parents 'possessed no sanctions against adolescent children who wanted to leave the house and found a new nuclear family unit' (Medick 1976: 303). Men no doubt had to 'talk tough' to preserve the productive and reproductive integrity of their households.

According to Ozment, 'Parenthood was a conditional trust, not an absolute right, and the home was a model of benevolent and just rule for the "state" to emulate.' Reformation morality proposed a new moral bond between the private domain of the household and the public domain of the state: 'Privacy and social extension were not perceived as contradictory. . . To the people of Reformation Europe no specter was more fearsome than a society in which the desires of individuals eclipsed their sense of social duty. The prevention of just that possibility became the common duty of every Christian parent, teacher, and magistrate' (Ozment 1983: 177). This new *political* image of the family has many ideological overtones. While the middle class extended their influence over state, monarchy and civil society, it was to be expected that they should make a virtue of the responsibility of *all* households to civic institutions; and while they continued to prosper from work put out to the predominantly rural mass, it was reasonable that they should advise that *all* families should take responsibility for their own productive and reproductive affairs. These messages were reinforced in parishes throughout the land by a new middle-class professional – the *family* clergyman.[19]

If ideology now emphasized the moral stability of the household, and fostered the notion of the family as the foundation of society and polity, the reality of reproductive instability was heightened by the expansion of manufacturing and trade, the growth of towns and cities and the division of society into more distinct social classes. Survival in Elizabethan London depended on adaptability and ingenuity, which in turn created the social fabric of the city. The immanence of death meant a continual regrouping of household personnel – adoption, fostering, remarriage. 'Without the buttresses of household organization, wider kinship networks, neighbourly sociability, and the more formal company structures, this inherently fragile grouping of parents and children was inadequate for the satisfaction of physical and emotional needs' (Brodsky 1986: 140). The intense pressure to *accumulate* in the early phases of the compact pattern of domestic development, which had driven the merchant classes, now became an increasingly urgent force for the mass of the population. Hard work and good fortune took some rural craftsmen into the ranks of broker and merchant, or enabled them to employ ten or twenty people in what might be called 'proto-factories'. But craft work offered little scope for saving, and the hand-to-mouth existence of the majority diminished their capacity to provide for sickness and old age, with the result that chronic poverty became evident throughout the land. Likewise, the decreasing ability to endow children with productive resources encouraged earlier domestic fission, which exacerbated poverty. From the mid-sixteenth century the government was obliged to respond with a series of Poor Laws which provided some halfhearted institutional support (workhouses, parish relief) but which basically contrived to drive the population to greater productive efforts.

## The reproductive organization of the industrial revolution

By the eighteenth century the pressures within the rural household must have been acute. To an extent unknown before or since, the productive and reproductive organization for an expanding national society was confined within these four cottage walls. In effect, the internal dynamism and external dependence of these households was a major asset to the expanding national economy. A more self-contained, extended pattern of domestic development would not have released the same productive and reproductive energies which now invigorated the national economy.[20] But at the same time, the compact family structure was generating economic and political liabilities which, *en masse*, would soon have momentous historical effects.

From the perspective of rural households the most urgent problem was that while material security and access to wealth depended on their own labour power, producing labour was becoming too costly. Reproductive restraint was no solution while wages and piece rates remained low and variable. Indeed, the proto-industrial households were already producing more children than their strictly agricultural counterparts, which could only increase the cyclical stress.[21] People lacked the power of communications and organization to press collectively for improvements in the returns to labour. And so it was that from within those proto-industrial households there emerged the *labour-saving* machines which would transform the world.

Sometime in the mid-1760s James Hargreaves, an illiterate weaver, invented the spinning jenny. In 1779, at the age of twenty-one, Samuel Crompton, the son of a small farmer in Lancashire, devised a more efficient spinning frame or 'mule'. The competitive advantage of such machines was immediately obvious, and while many rural people sought to adopt the innovations, others responded to this further devaluation of their labour with sabotage. Very few of the famous inventors were left unscathed, the discontent reaching a climax in the Luddite riots of 1812–18. They were also at the mercy of the merchant class, to whom they often lost the fierce struggle to register rights and patents. In retrospect it is remarkable that, as common people themselves, any of them managed to appropriate their own inventions. Hargreaves benefited little from the rapid proliferation of his spinning jenny at home and abroad, and only a belated act of conscience, a public subscription, saved Crompton from dying in poverty.

For all their ingenuity, these labour-saving innovations did not in themselves make the industrial revolution. Without a complementary set of capital-enhancing developments emanating from the merchant and professional classes, it is unlikely that the efforts of Hargreaves, Crompton and the others would have had such great effect. The revolution evolved from the 'functional interrelationship between family economy and merchant capital' which was as old as 'proto-industrialization' itself; more precisely, it arose from the political and economic tension 'between household production based on the family economy on the one hand, and the capitalist organization of trade, putting-out and marketing of products on the other' (Medick 1976: 296). Initially, the rustic geniuses used the familiar materials of wood and iron to make their looms and frames, and the farmyard power of cattle and horses to drive them and transport the product. Steam and electric power, steel and the complex mining and smelting processes which it entailed, and the communications systems which made the technical revolution economically feasible, all emanated from the capitalist class - or, more specifically, from the professional engineers who worked for them.

One of these was James Watt (1736–1890) the son of a merchant and town councillor who became a mathematical instrument maker for Glasgow university. A prolific inventor, he is noted for harnessing steam and for the metrics of power.[22] After a lucrative career as a merchant in New York, John McAdam (1756–1836) returned to his native Britain and, while working as a surveyor for the Bristol Turnpike Trust, invented the road-making system for which he is famous. By then he was in his sixties. Richard Arkwright is an interesting case of a man whose life extended across the class divide. The youngest of thirteen children raised in a poor Lancashire household, he joined forces with such craftsmen as John Kay and Jedidiah Strutt to produce a number of spinning, weaving and knitting inventions. Surviving sabotage and patent theft he accumulated enough wealth to invest in one of the first steam-powered cotton mills, and was eventually rewarded with a knighthood.

During the 'industrial revolution proper' (usually reckoned as the six decades from 1760 to 1820, the reign of George III) the social relations of *production* were reorganized drastically. Dramatic increases in the scale of operations took industrial work out of the household and subjected people to new terms of employment, hierarchies of supervision and the intricate regulation of work in the factory system. We can date from this period the misleading notion that 'work left the family': in reality, industrial employment left all the other productive and reproductive tasks behind in the household – unobserved, underrated, unpaid, but still the most essential social business. Certainly, the family went 'out to work': initially, mechanization increased the demand for the quantity of labour rather than quality (operating the machines called for less skill than producing cloth manually) and accordingly men, women and, notoriously, children were employed. Between a third and a half of the cotton mill labour force in England in the 1830s was aged under twenty-one.[23] Households congregated in the expanding towns and cities, profoundly dependent on wages and often a great deal more wretched than they had been in the era of cottage industries.

It is important to note that industry could expand so rapidly because labouring households *had already* stepped up the supply of labour.[24] Nevertheless, households responded to industrialization with new reproductive strategies: fertility increased, not because infant mortality was significantly reduced but because young people married and left home sooner.[25] All these strategies increased the pressures within the compact pattern of domestic development, and the quest for relief outside the household. Especially when they moved to the towns, family members grouped and regrouped – sometimes seeking protection in numbers, more usually seeking advantage in compactness and mobility. As Hareven graphically puts it, 'Households functioned like accordions, expanding and contracting in accordance with changing family needs and external conditions' (1978: 65). But 'the extended family' now had a different connotation: it had become 'a private institution to redistribute the poverty of the nuclear family by way of the kinship system. The extended family of the peasant, on the other hand, served as an instrument for the conservation of property and the caring of the older members of the family' (Medick 1976: 295).

## The rise of the English working class

During the six decades of the industrial revolution the population of England nearly doubled, from 7.5 to 14 millions. The demand for food triggered parallel technical developments in farming, and mechanization in the countryside in turn drove more agricultural labourers off the land and into the towns. Very slowly the impoverished proletarian mass, more by weight of numbers than by concerted action, became a political force.[26] Their misery became an embarrassment to their rulers, and gradually the institutions which were designed to extract their labour – the factories, workhouses, lawcourts, police – were augmented by public organizations more overtly concerned with their welfare.

The precedent for this sort of institution-building had been set by the entrepreneurial middle class. They built the industrial towns and presided over the new social order which went with them. But most important, they constructed the apparatus of the modern nation state. Between the seventeenth and nineteenth centuries the bourgeoisie undermined the landed aristocracy. After the English Civil War (1642–6) they consolidated their power in parliament, retaining the monarch as a convenient political figurehead.[27] Although they maintained their exclusive associations (freemasonry dates from the eighteenth century), *their* institutions – the banks, schools and universities, inns of court, even the trading corporations themselves – increasingly became *public* institutions. These were the means by which the middle class secured their economic and reproductive interests; and central to these interests was the subordination to them of the working class which generated their wealth.

Like the church in the medieval period, the bourgeoisie dictated the values which sustained that other institution upon which (so they said) the state was founded – the Family.[28] Although they extolled its universal importance to 'the nation', there was a fundamental difference between those families which were organized around the benefits of accumulated capital and those which were struggling to reproduce labour. Those who had the wealth and the power of association to cope, handsomely, with the effects of reproductive instability could make a virtue of the compact household. The working class could not and generally did not; compact, hungry, economically dependent households were cheap for the capitalist, and very expensive for the worker. In the streets, pubs and music halls middle-class pieties about family and marriage were turned upside down and ridiculed. By the middle of the nineteenth century expanding markets and technical innovation still provided working people with opportunities to accumulate the wealth on which, much more than family ties, the quest for security now depended. Never before had so many had the opportunity to get so rich. But a great mass became trapped in the miserable routine of poverty. Poor households had to sell labour, and the only way they had a chance to accumulate savings was to sell more of it. Its price was low not so much because the market was glutted, but because the households which supplied labor were also obliged to bear most of the costs of reproducing it.

While the compact pattern of domestic development, with its cyclical pressure to accumulate, was an instrument of national economic and political growth, its dependence on external support laid it open to the predatory control. As Rowntree discovered (see chapter 3), expanding capitalism was an unsympathetic patron: it did not discriminate according to variable need and capacity in extracting labour from poor households. Impersonal relations with bosses offered no relief when family crises met the brick wall of flat and inflexible wage rates. E. P. Thompson tells us that the period 1790–1840 brought the working people of England 'intensified exploitation, greater insecurity, and increasing human misery. By 1840 most people were "better off" than their forerunners had been fifty years before, but they had suffered and continued to suffer this slight improvement as a catastrophic experience' (1968: 231). Forged by the industrial revolution, the working classes throughout Europe began to exert massive pressure on the structure of European societies. Explosive class war in England was widely anticipated, but instead the revolutionary energy was released in a mass of social reforms, extending well into the twentieth century. Middle-class philanthropists played their part, but as working people found a more concerted political voice they were able to transfer much of the burden of organizing reproduction to their employers and to the public institutions of the new nation states.

We should not underestimate the degree of control which the factory owners, merchants and the whole middle-class consortium had come to exert over the domestic lives of working people. They designed and built the houses inhabited by their workers. They set 'family wages' at the lowest level of adequacy to ensure that *all* household members would work and would continue to reproduce more workers.[29] They controlled the rhythms of daily life with the factory siren and the clock, replacing the cycle of farming seasons with daily shift work. The bourgeoisie provided the magistrates, the 'beaks' who intervened in marital and parental disputes and who largely invented the domestic legal codes for the cities. They paid for the clergy, who preached the doctrines of a frugal, docile and dependent family life, and buried the dead in the new municipal cemeteries. The bourgeoisie paved and lit the city streets, and paid the police who paced to and fro between the dwellings of rich and poor.

The merchant companies also built and staffed schools for their own progeny, and saw to it that the state built and staffed separate schools for the masses. For, as industrialization progressed, the demand for more *skilled* labour increased. One reason for this was economic expansion overseas, the quest for raw materials and new markets. While the people of these farflung territories became unskilled labourers for the European empires, further technical developments had increased demand for the *quality* of labour at home. And so, by the end of the nineteenth century, reproductive strategies shifted once again.

A notable expression of this was the revaluation of children and of the role of the mother as a domestic child-rearer. According to Minge-Kalman,

In the middle of the nineteenth century the development of the need for educating wage-laborers created a previously-unknown institution of 'child-hood' which soon extended children's dependency into adolescence. The cost to the family soon became considerably greater than the foregone labor of children who no longer worked for the family. Since the beginning of the concern with education, children have subtly but rapidly developed into a labor-intensive, capital intensive product of the family in industrial society. (Minge-Kalman 1978: 466)

Once again, the new trends were fixed in legislation. In Britain the Factory Act of 1833 forbade the employment of children under nine and insisted on at least two hours of schooling daily for children under thirteen. Elementary education became compulsory in 1880 and 'free' (that is, state-funded) in 1891. Doubtless this helped to discipline a rising generation for the factory regime as well as for the duties of citizenship.[30] It is also clear that to compete in the labour market households were obliged to invest more in 'human capital'. Children were therefore sent back into the domestic domain for longer periods of dependence on their parents, and obliged to achieve at least functional literacy and numeracy (the famed '3Rs'). Education defined the expanding professions, and soon the upwardly mobile were competing with the middle classes in the production of fewer, higher quality children (investment being in favour of boys well into the twentieth century).

There was still security in numbers for the large segment of the working class which continued to produce unskilled labour. It is also clear that they continued to depend on wider ties of kinship ('the extended family') and neighbourhood. Village-like solidarities persisted in the industrial cities well into the twentieth century.[31] However, it is no less clear that from the late eighteenth century the working class were inventing institutions of their own, with the prime function of helping them to bear the heavy costs of reproduction. The most famous initiatives were the co-operative societies, which began as resistance to employers' efforts to control consumption. The Toad Lane Co-operative in Rochdale began as a means of providing the impoverished mill workers with food and basic necessities outside the company store. Only later, under the inspiration of Robert Owen and others, did the movement begin to compete in the relations and processes of industrial production.

In the nineteenth and early twentieth centuries, the working class reinvented, on their own account, the banking institutions of the bourgeoisie. Their development has a striking sameness: early informal, voluntaristic origins in rotating credit and mutual assurance funds; and then massive growth leading to bureaucratization and regulation by the state. In England towards the end of the eighteenth century there was a proliferation of trade and craft friendly societies, collecting funds to subsidize working people in marriage, childbearing, sickness, old age and death.[32] Problems in managing the huge sums of money they generated prompted parliamentary enquiry and a mass of legislation. The formalization of life insurance schemes also created a new profession of actuaries and a science of Vital Statistics, the measuring of people's lives so that their economic and political effects could better be understood – and manipulated.[33]

Many of the working-class savings banks, originating around the turn of the nineteenth century, were set up under the guidance of middle-class philanthropists, believers in the virtues of frugal self-help and upward mobility, who helped underwrite their liabilities. Initially these were 'institutions of the character of banks, but on a modest scale, in which the poor could deposit the smallest sums they could from time to time spare, certain of being able to draw them forth when they pleased, with accumulated interest' (Chambers and Chambers 1875: 513). The importance of *women* investors in these organizations is notable. One of the very first modern savings banks, established by Priscilla Wakefield at Tottenham in London in 1799, 'received contributions from women and children, who were promised pensions when they reached the age of sixty, weekly payments in case of sickness, and other inducements towards saving' (McCulloch and Stirling 1936: 6). Later in the nineteenth century, as many as 40 per cent of the annuities provided through the Post Office and other savings banks were bought by the numerous women domestic servants of the period (p. 71ff.). In addition, there were around two thousand 'penny banks' throughout England in 1875, instilling frugal virtues in the young. Once again, the extent of public investment in these banks prompted the state to intervene and regulate funds and interest rates through the Bank of England.

As the industrial population, drawn from scattered rural areas and speaking many different dialects, acquired a degree of political cohesion, they were able to exert more direct pressure on the organization of production. After much struggle, trade unions were legalized in Britain in 1871, and throughout this period populist and socialist political parties sprang up in rivalry to the middle-class Whig–Tory orthodoxies.[34] Of no less significance were the non-conformist churches in which working-class people sought liberation from the moral dictates of the established clergy. Through the power of the secret ballot (1872) and especially universal suffrage (which brought British women into the electorate for the first time in 1918), governments were obliged to embrace the new policies of '*social welfare*', a catch-all notion with the physical health and material security of families and households at its heart. During the first few decades of the twentieth century 'the welfare state' in the European countries took a managerial interest in every phase of the reproductive cycle, from birth and infant care to schooling, employment, pensioning and burial. The development of local government brought such amenities as baths and libraries, clinics and crematoria to the common people. This public intervention in the standard of living has been expressed in the marked upward shift in life expectancy for the population as a whole since the late nineteenth century. A non-contributory old-age pension scheme was established in Britain in 1909. In 1911 the National Insurance Act incorporated the existing friendly societies and trade unions schemes into a system to insure all working people against sickness.[35] These policies meant increasing the burden of taxation on the middle classes, and did not pass unchallenged.[36]

## The organization of reproduction in modern society

The reproductive explosion in the first phase of the industrial revolution was in a real sense the making of the New World. Frustrated by the declining demand for unskilled labour, poor people were encouraged to take their poverty, and their productive and reproductive energies, to the Americas. There we can speculate on the effect of a large number of immigrants from a single European country gathering in a single American factory within a short space of time. Not only were they likely to import a distinctive set of family ideals, they were most probably all young people at a roughly similar stage of domestic growth. As Tamara Hareven (1982) has shown, these cohorts exerted a profound influence on the organization of industrial enterprises.

In eighteenth- and nineteenth-century America there was much variation in household organization. Not only were immigrants bringing with them different domestic styles, they were making their own hectic adaptations to the new and unpredictable world: expanding, contracting and relocating as need and opportunity arose.[37] However, by the middle of the twentieth century, observers were remarking enthusiastically on the striking uniformity of the Great American Family. Domestic development had a sameness across ethnic groups, regions and social classes which suggested that the new society was pouring families into the same basic mould. 'In the United States, as in other industrial societies, the ideal family consists of a legally constituted husband–wife team, their young, dependent children, living in a household of their own, provided for by the husband's earnings as a main breadwinner, and emotionally united by the wife's exclusive concentration on the home' (Keller 1980: 69). Only those who eschewed the modern world – such communities as the Amish and Hutterites on the rural periphery – could hope to retain an extended pattern of domestic development. In magazines and radio situation comedies people could relish the details of one broadly familiar way of domestic life. In their zeal to conform, people studied manuals on sex and child-rearing, and young ladies were instructed in the new discipline of 'domestic science'. After the Second World War, construction firms like Levitt were so confident in their understanding of the apical norm that they could put whole tracts of identical houses on the market; superficial cosmetic modifications (colours, facades) let people believe that they were a little different from their neighbours.

It is plain that this 'homogenization' of American households had a great deal to do with their common exposure to the forces of industrial capitalism. Italian, Irish, Armenian, Hispanic and African families were clustered into the same urban industrial landscape, dependent on the same employers and public services, producing and using the same commodities. The regimes of factory, firm and government, which were fundamentally the same in Manchester New Hampshire and Manchester England, penetrated individual lives in intimate detail, putting a uniform schedule on the ages at which people entered and left school, went to work, could expect to marry, and were obliged to retire. Hareven has remarked that an effect of the proliferation of industrial institutions has been to routinize domestic cycle transitions: 'Families are now able to go through a life course much less subject to sudden change than that experienced by the majority of the population in the nineteenth century' (1978: 61).[38]

This conformity does not imply that households had become passive or inert, plastic material compacted into the industrial mould and distributed, like mass-produced widgets, over the urban landscape. Their sameness is an expression of their cumulative success in making social institutions more responsive to their variable needs and capacities. Hareven points out that 'The increase in uniformity in family time has coincided with a growing diversity both in career and opportunity choices and in familial and non-familial arrangements' (1978: 67). It was the expanding scope of modern social organization which permitted, for a few decades at least, a more stable and thus more uniform pattern of domestic development. However, by the 1950s the effects of earlier changes in reproductive organization were becoming evident. Most conspicuous was the decline in fertility over the preceding hundred years. During the nineteenth century in America the birthrate dropped from around eight live births per mother to about three.[39] Between 1890 and 1952, the proportion of women who had been married but who were still childless past the childbearing age rose from 8 per cent to 19 per cent.[40] An inevitable result of this is that the average size of households declined, encouraging observers to imagine that 'the family' was under threat of extinction.[41]

Over a century, the pattern of domestic development had become more emphatically compact. Comparing the 1890s with the 1950s in America, Glick concluded 'that the intangible values associated with membership in larger families tended to be replaced during the first half of the twentieth century by a different set of values that favoured the prospect of surrounding a smaller number of children with a better environment from the economic and civic viewpoints' (1957: 66). A painful symptom of this was the trauma of fission. Zuckerman has explained how twentieth-century American parents have put themselves 'hugely and hopefully in the hands of child-care counselors', finding a charter for modern family life in Dr Spock's reassuring *Baby and Child Care*. Arguing for *guilt-free* early fission in the compact family, the book 'disdains dependence on parents and urges instead an independence defined as an efficacious reliance on peers' (Zuckerman 1975: 206–7). Although publicly normalized, American households had become decidedly more exclusive in their composition: from the later part of the nineteenth century, 'Families shared their household space with other kin only as a last resort' (Hareven 1978: 65). After the First World War it was no longer normal for households to include lodgers or relatives beyond the range of the nuclear family.[42] As a result, the long-time trend has been toward smaller households, as indicated by the decline in the median size of household from 5.4 in 1790 to 4.5 in 1890, 3.3 in 1940, and 3.1 in 1950.[43]

These changes have prompted many false conclusions about the fate of 'the family': diminished in numbers, it has supposedly lost the communitarian 'self-sufficiency' nostalgically associated with life on 'Grandma's farm';[44] an introverted relic of its former self, its alienation from society is now almost complete. 'Why', Edward Shorter asks at the beginning of his inquiry into *The Making of the Modern Family*, 'did the family decide to cut the ties that held it within the surrounding social order?' (1975: 4). The short answer is that it did not: for all but the poorest, the reduction in household size was a symptom of the extension of reproductive organzation out beyond the compass of 'the family'. Shorter's lament that 'No outside institutions at all intrude upon the intimacy of the couple, and men and women come together and wrench apart as freight cars do in a switching yard' (p. 8) is incredible if we consider the extent to which the conjugal relationship has been circumscribed legally, fiscally and in other ways. The more salient questions are about what modern 'family' relations have done to society.

One effect of changes in reproductive organization has been the *proliferation* of households at a time when it is generally assumed that modern society is putting them out of business. In proportion to the population there are many more of them than ever before. This is because, after the middle of the last century, more people were getting married and establishing their own households, and were doing so slightly younger; and because so many more households had come to consist of single persons.[45] We have already noted the strategic advantages of this compact pattern of domestic development: the small, mobile units were well adapted to the shift from a predominantly agricultural to an industrial way of life. Less obvious are the pressures which this dynamic mass of households has been exerting on the formation of industrial society. With a large proportion of each generation dispersing to new localities in search of employment, the demand for social institutions beyond the range of the family was intensified. Thus, the modern American family has been seen as a 'dynamic system' creating 'pressure lines' – the need for income, credit, etc. – which *en masse* imprint themselves on social institutions (Gove et al. 1973).[46]

Pressure to shift the costs of reproduction out from the compact household into the wider social domain can been seen in a second conspicuous trend in American vital statistics since the middle of the nineteenth century: greatly increased longevity. Between 1900 and 1980 the proportion of people over sixty-five in the population tripled to 12 per cent. Men can now expect to live into their early seventies, women eight years longer.[47] A product of social pressure for better management of public health, as well as the development of medical techniques, the social effects of this have been profound. A woman born in 1951 could reckon on having fifty-two years of life ahead of her after bearing her last child, and the 'empty nest' phase after the departure of her last child could extend for several decades. The prospects for grandparenthood have been greatly increased. It is reckoned that in 1750 the average woman would die *twelve years before* the birth of her last grandchild, whereas in 1970 she would live *twenty-five years after* the birth of her last grandchild. With life expectancy extending into the nineties in the twenty-first century, great-grandparenthood will become a normal experience for most women.[48] At the same time, this increases the proportion of people living alone, with its deleterious effects.[49] It also increases the proportion of people who live outside of households in the conventional sense: in hospitals and other 'institutions'.[50]

People have responded to this extension of the lifespan by inventing new social institutions rather than by extending domestic organization. Households remain locked into the compact pattern, but now elderly couples are confronted with a greatly extended period of domestic decline. An increasing proportion of them eventually move into retirement communities or sheltered housing, and only a minority go to live with adult children.[51] The impact of this reproductive pattern on contemporary social structure has been profound and extensive. A potent example is pensioning: individuals save and invest in institutions outside the family in order to achieve 'independence' in old age. This is turn generates a very large proportion of the capital managed by banking and investment corporations. Much of American and European business is in fact structured and sustained by this relatively new distension of the reproductive cycle.[52]

After the 1960s, public confidence in the Norman Rockwell image of the stolid, generic American family seems to have yielded to anxieties about its moral and material disintegration. It was not 'the family' itself so much as 'society' which was blamed for this. Viewed from the political right, 'the family' is still our social bedrock, threatened most by declining public morals and a society bent on robbing it of its proper functions: child-care, feeding, clothing and sheltering, the complete containment of sexual activity, etc.[53] The implication is that families are no longer doing enough for society. Yet, in the opinion of the political left, the household is still expected to do too much:

> Its ability to produce and reproduce itself in a coherent and orderly fashion, and above all to survive without preying on subordinate forms of social organisation, have rendered it subject to every form of exploitation... But crushed, oppressed, divided, counted, taxed, recruited, the *domestic community* totters but still resists, for *domestic relations of production* have not disappeared completely. (Meillassoux 1981: 87)

Minge-Kalman is likewise indignant about the burdens families still bear:

It has been the family that pays most of the cost of reproducing the educated laborers necessary to industrial production. . . The family has not ceased to be a productive group, but its function has been transformed from a producer of food to primarily a reproducer of laborers for the highly educated labour market of Western industrial societies. (1978: 455)

However, there are dangers in becoming fixated by some vague understanding of the 'the family' or household as a beleaguered social agent, locked in battle with social structure.[54] It is difficult to make sense of the contest in such a simple form: the people who make up families are, after all, the same people who make up society at large. The opposition is politically more complicated, and concerns *some* people who are concerned to make *some others* pay the costs of reproduction by shaping and manipulating social institutions. The issue, in other words, is complicated by distinctions of social class.

Moreover, let us remind ourselves that households are internally differentiated: they too are shaped in various ways by reproductive and productive processes. We therefore have to regard Meillassoux's assurance that the household can 'survive without preying on subordinate forms of social organisation' with scepticism. Gender relations in particular remain concealed behind these masks of the unitary 'family' or 'household'.[55] Industrial production is indeed still heavily subsidized by households, but most specifically by the under-rewarded labour of women. Since the middle of the nineteenth century the closer spacing of fewer children was partly offset by the extension of dependent childhood into the late teens. The idealization of motherhood, so conspicuous in America for the first half of this century, was another way of policing the domestic domain: the place of women should not be anywhere other than in the home.

## From baby boom to baby bust

The transformation of this ideology, and of much else in the society around us today, may be traced to a brief but very 'fundamental shift in the organization of reproduction. Shortly after the Second World War, in the industrial countries, and most conspicuously in the US, there was a surge in fertility which reached a peak around 1956. Many explanations for this 'baby boom' have been offered, ranging from the release of reproductive energy by the returning servicemen, and the emancipating effect of women's employment during the war ('Rosie the Riveter'), to mass optimism about postwar economic prospects.[56] As this wave has moved through history it has caused expansion and contraction in educational facilities, changes in commodity markets (music, clothes, foodstuffs), cannon fodder for Vietnam, shifting electoral strategies, and pressure on jobs and housing.[57]

One of the most dramatic effects became evident in the 1960s when the demands placed on household resources by the boom babies drove women out to work.[58] In 1940, one woman in eight was out to work; in 1955, one in five; and in 1976 one in two.[59] Men remain very ambivalent about this 'invasion' of 'their' labour market, resisting the new competition for jobs but obviously benefiting from the augmentation of household income. There has been some female movement into middle-class 'male' occupations (in 1983 a quarter of the Harvard Business School graduates were women) but the labour force and the labour market remain profoundly divided along gender lines. In the early 1980s women still earned only two-thirds of what men got.[60] Denise and William Bielby (1988) have shown the entrenched resistance to hiring women in many occupations, although the fact that women work harder for the money suggests that economically rational employers (men, of course) ought to prefer them to men. Despite the overall drop in male employment and a tendency to retire earlier, men have not made a compensatory move into housework, which means that 'most employed wives are holding down two jobs' (England and Farkas 1986: 99).[61] One response has been the rapid development of domestic technology, the washing machines, vacuum cleaners and easy-care fabrics. These cut down the drudgery if not necessarily the volume of 'women's work', but also increase domestic consumer demand and thus the need for more earnings.

It has been argued that these changes encouraged many women to reevaluate the opportunity costs of their labour: first of their *own* labour, and latterly of the labour of *reproducing* labour.[62] The 'women's liberation' movement of the 1960s was quick to observe the difference between unpaid work in the home and paid work outside it. The high opportunity cost of reproduction certainly helps to account for the 'bust' which followed the baby boom in the 1960s and 1970s.[63] In this period there was a revolution in the development and use of female-controlled contraception, notably the pill and intra-uterine devices. Further reduction in infant mortality has cut the time spent in pregnancy, although mothers may still be hampered by the extended years of maternal responsibility. This has provided an impetus for the extension of child-care arrangements outside the household, in factories and offices. Babysitting cartels extend their tendrils into suburbia: parents who may not even know each other use carefully controlled plastic currency to buy and sell time.

Changes in conjugal roles have added to these pressures for public institutions which subsidize reproduction. Marital instability is signalled by the much-quoted statistic that half of all American marriages will end in divorce. This may have made some people more cautious about entering into wedlock, although, intriguingly, divorce has not deterred the majority from remarrying. There are many signs that the terms of marriage are being renegotiated. Its continuing popularity seems to turn more on its romantic and sexual than its reproductive and economic aspects. Because children greatly complicate the process of divorce, some parents may be discouraged from marrying, and some married couples from having children. Certainly there has been a parallel increase in both cohabitation and children born out of wedlock.[64] The mood of caution is expressed in the increasing preference for pre-nuptial contracts, specifying in varying detail individual conduct in the marriage. In effect, they are largely *post*-nuptial agreements, to the extent that they anticipate such things as the disposition of property and access to children in the event of a divorce. The virtues and vices of these arrangements are debated in agony columns, pulpits and parlours, critics pointing out that this is yet another extension of legal authority into intimate personal relationships. A significant objection is the impracticality of inscribing in tablets of stone a relationship which is necessarily dynamic. Some lawyers accordingly advise periodic renegotiation – which can only be good for business.

To the extent that they now have more economic power within marriage, women can with greater assurance quit.[65] An unwelcome cost of this new authority may be the upsurge in conjugal and parental violence in our societies, as males succumb to frustration and uncertainty about domestic authority and conjugal roles. A steadily increasing proportion of households have been pared down to the care group of mother and children (a very small minority of 'single-parent families' are based on the father).[66] Once again, the vexed issues of access to and custody of children dramatize the increasing dependence on the mediation of civil institutions. The continued importance to society of the domestic domain can be seen in the keenly restitutive approach which state agencies take to the premature disintegration of households. They promote, for example, the legal fiction of a single household after a couple divorces, moving children back and forth between the custody of their parents, and appointing officials (social workers, child psychologists) to help sustain the ghostly semblance of unity. It is the children who inhabit this curious 'meta-household', which for them is a reality consisting of two bedrooms and two sets of toys, access to two budgets, and complicated extended families of 'step-kin' and 'half-kin'.

'Parenting' has certainly been reorganized, occupying less of the life course and being less anchored in the institutions of marriage; but, says Alice Rossi, despite its complexities there is little sign of it 'falling out of fashion, at least among women' (1985: 166–7). Conjugal breakdown thrusts the single parent into closer dependence on public institutions. While still bearing the cardinal responsibility for children, women have been exerting political pressure for substitutes for the security which was previously sought in marriage. The more radical claims have extended beyond child-care services which would enable women to go out to work, to direct demands for domestic wages. Child-rearing is, in effect, a labour-intensive social service. Its costs have been met in some small measure by social welfare payments and reverse taxation – parental allowances paid in the form of deductions and rebates.[67]

Debates about these matters are rife today. Women's declining enthusiasm for reproductive labour in the 1960s and 1970s has been followed by a 'baby craving' which has led to last-minute races against the menopause, as well as to dubious adoptions and to outright theft of children from Third World countries. The clash of pro-Life and pro-Choice in abortion turns largely on the issue of whether women should be *socially obliged* to sustain a pregnancy. This reminds us that what is private and what is public in the organization of reproduction has never been resolved, and is likely to remain as contentious in the future as it always has been in the past.[68] The household is, as ever, the little realm in which women and children are 'protected', the proper container for those sexual activities which remain at the heart of the reproductive process.[69]

There are certainly signs of a conservative backlash about women's place being in the home. In recent years the fastest growing employment category in the US has been temporary office help, a system which offers the (female) worker 'flexibility' in exchange for very little in the way of security, health-care provision, pensioning and other perquisites – usually on the tacit assumption that these are covered through a husband. Rather than women revolutionizing the economy, the economy may simply be adapting to them as it has in the past. One of the last acts of the Reagan administration was to revoke restrictions on the 'putting out' of work to self-employed people in their homes. The stated virtue of this is that it allows women to be 'decent' mothers and wives, while availing themselves of the market for labour.

## Family and state in the late industrial world

Zaretsky has concluded that; 'Far from the state "invading" or "replacing" the family, a certain kind of alienated public life and a certain kind of alienated private life have expanded together' (1982: 218). Here I have argued that to comprehend this interrelationship we must consider how family and state are linked through the social organization of reproduction. While the economic and political structure of society has changed drastically, the European households in which industrial processes were born have changed remarkably little: 'The system of mate selection, the marital relationship, and parent–child relations in the pre-industrial family all show striking similarities to those in the family of today' (Furstenberg 1966: 337).

The constant factor has been the compact pattern of domestic development, with its characteristic internal dynamism and stimulus to the growth of external institutions. During the twentieth century, households have had considerable success in transferring responsibility for the organization of reproduction out into the public realm presided over by the modern state. This is not just a favour granted by magnanimous governments, it is a service demanded and achieved by ordinary people in civil society. Now, as individuals, we are likely to be born, educated, employed and to die outside the household, in institutions which have developed since the eighteenth century.

In Sweden there is bewilderment that the elaboration of welfare policies designed to support and sustain 'the family' has had something like the opposite effect: fertility has reached an extremely low ebb, households are smaller and dissolve more rapidly, marriage seems to be falling out of favour and single-parent households abound.[70] Anxiety about the demise of 'the family' as we have conventionally understood it has distracted attention from something much more interesting: the *reorganization of reproduction* in the emerging *post*-industrial age. The pioneering experience of Sweden is in striking contrast with those new nations in Africa and Asia which have produced relatively few public reproductive institutions, and in which household units have often increased rather than shed their economic and political functions.[71]

These developments underlie the most fundamental division of political opinion in the world today: whether welfare in its most comprehensive sense is the responsibility of governments or of private individuals. All states have institutions which organize reproduction on the grand scale. The difference between the socialist states and the liberal democracies is the extent to which we pay for these institutions as private individuals or collectively, as joint owners of the economy. These are indeed very different political-economic principles, with farreaching consequences, but they tend to overshadow the inherent *sameness* of the great mass of organizations on which citizens of the USA or the USSR have depended. If we have little difficulty recognizing a school or hospital in each country, or even a factory or bank, it is because we share the same basic challenges of reproduction and, with industrialism, have tended to organize solutions in fundamentally similar ways.

Nor has the distribution of benefits in the social organization of reproduction been very equitable. In the next chapter we shall see how some groups have succeeded in manipulating reproductive subsidies and services very much to their own advantage.

# 8

# Wages, salaries and the political economy of reproduction

This chapter seeks to illustrate how institutions in our own societies which we may think of as 'purely economic' or 'purely political' are also defined by reproductive interests. Without due attention to this, even the most detailed political-economic explanation will be incomplete. I shall examine one pair of social institutions which are close to the heart of economic and political relations in modern industrial societies: *wages* and *salaries*. I shall argue that they represent different strategies for funding the process of reproduction, and that this essential difference between the two systems of reward has remained obscured *because* they are instruments of class power and tactics for class survival. If social scientists have failed to recognize this, it may be a measure of their ideological complicity, doubtless unconscious, with the interests of the salaried class.

We have no reason to believe that the struggle against reproductive instability in modern industrial society is any less intense than it was in the epoch of the family farm. The difference is that much of the burden of that struggle has been lifted from the immediate relations of reproduction in the household and transferred to a much wider range of social institutions. However, these institutions are not neutral or evenhanded in their support of the reproductive process. As in the past, reproductive security is pursued in the economic domain by control over the means of production, and the accumulation of wealth remains the most effective weapon in the battle against reproductive instability. The institutions of industrial society, including the state and the apparatus of government, have developed around this competition for wealth. But the most obvious inequities are embodied in distinctions of social class. To be firmly established as a member of a class which derives its power from its privileged access to capital is still the best way of dealing with the material stress of reproduction.[1]

However, maintaining control over capital and reproductive privilege is hard political work. Although wealth may come easily to some, consolidating an upper-class position is a much longer undertaking. To join the group and benefit from its protection, to make the transition from 'upstart' or 'nouveau riche', one has to acquire many credentials, ranging from housing and hobbies to talk and table manners. Above all, one has to have demonstrated the capacity to reproduce *within* the privileged class: to endow offspring with competitive advantages and to consolidate gains from one generation to the next. Reproductive strategies are therefore of acute concern. Like any other enduring community, a ruling class gains real coherence from webs of reproductive relationships woven by strategic marriages. Class, it is often said, is a matter of 'breeding'. Reproductive strategies *protect* class privilege; and class privileges protect the reproductive process.

This elite 'groupiness' is usually most intense near the centres of power. By contrast, the mass of working people can cohere only by finding a broad, categoric identity, some shared symbols to which they can attach themselves. This is the 'class consciousness' perceived by Marx. Their reproductive strategies are much more concerned with survival in the short term than the entrenchment of power in the long term. 'Family ties' therefore have a very different significance, entailing a good deal of competitive give and take. Especially those who lack access to wider social institutions (health plans, pension funds, etc.) must depend, as in the past, on ramifications of reproductive relations or on contingent ties of neighbourhood and friendship. Dependence on family ties – the relationships of reproduction – is a *physical* survival strategy for the working class, and a *social* survival strategy for those who dominate them.

Class power brings control over social institutions, most importantly the apparatus of government, in which class power is in turn consolidated. Over time, privileged groups turn existing institutions to their own advantage (the church, lawcourts) or *invent* social institutions which reinforce their privileges (clubs, political parties). In this work, people in power make alliances, most obviously with upwardly mobile groups in the 'middle class' who would dearly like to join them. By controlling the distribution of profits and the allocation of rewards *over time*, the owners of capital favour a particular group of functionaries which we can best identify as the *professionals*. These are the managers of business, and those who have achieved respect by the provision of essential services (classically in the church, the army, medicine and law). Today their greatest concentration is within the administrative apparatus of the state. The *salary* is a device which ensures that they are funded in a manner which (in varying degrees) allows them to bear comfortably the costs of reproduction. By contrast, the conservation of profits in capitalism requires that the working class should be obliged to cover as much of the costs of its own reproduction as the exercise of class power will allow. In this, the *wage* is an ideal device for perpetuating dependency.

## Reproduction and the social structure of rewards

Although in popular usage and in social theory we seem to imply that there are clear-cut differences between 'wage' and 'salary', the distinction remains extraordinarily vague. We have a broad expectation that salaries will be larger than wages. The liberal economist would probably interpret this simply as the result of 'free' bargaining in the market for labour: those with greater skills and capacities command a higher price. But this still leaves a great deal to be explained. It is not just the price of labour but distinct social categories of employee which are distinguished by the two terms. The implication of class privilege is inescapable: *wage* denotes the value of skilled or unskilled manual (proletarian) labour, *salary* its professional (middle-class) counterpart. Most importantly, this is a socially institutionalized distinction which defines transactions in the labour market – it is not the labour market itself which creates the discinction: a labourer does not bargain for a salary, he bargains for a wage. Although he, too, may feel the distinction to be a vague one, the labourer has tacitly accepted a definition of rewards which serves to keep him – and his dependents – in their place.

Wages and salaries differ not so much in *what* is paid, as *how* it is paid. The most important distinction is in the way rewards are organized over time: although some wage-earners may take home more at the end of the week than some salaried employees, it is much more advantageous *in the long term* to have a salary than a wage. A wage is, as it were, nearly instantaneous, almost timeless: it is measured by the piece, the task, or the hour. Wage rates in aggregate may be raised or lowered by short-term changes in factor markets; otherwse, individuals raise their earnings by moving between differentially rated jobs, depending on the skills they acquire and whether they are prepared to move around.[2] John Rex (1961: 142) has pointed out that a pronounced distinction between the middle-class bureaucrat and the proletarian is that the former sells his labour by the *lifetime*, not by the hour, day or week. An expression of this is the durable contract, the idea of 'tenure' and security of employment. Notice of termination, for example, is characteristically much longer for the salaried than for the waged employee. A salary typically includes many long-term financial interests, notably contributions to mortgages, health and education programmes, pensions and life insurance.[3]

One of the most distinctive features of the *salary* is that it is incremental over the employee's lifetime. It usually increases most steeply during the period in family development of most acute demand, the 'homemaking' phase when children are young.[4] The most common pattern is an age-related ladder of pay increases, often punctuated by promotion thresholds (which are used as a sanction against poor performance rather than a means of screening out competitors). This pattern and its attendant privileges are most likely to be guaranteed by formal organizations – industrial firms, government departments, universities, etc. Self-employed professionals are significantly more vulnerable to loss in earnings as they get older, which may well be explained by their greater exposure to 'market forces'.[5]

Figure 8.1 considers these temporal distinctions between wage and salary in the light of an illuminating survey by Harold F. Clark of *Life Earnings* among various occupations in the US during the 1920s. During their careers, the average income of professionals, notably doctors, engineers and architects, rose steeply to about ten times the annual earnings of an unskilled labourer. For more humble professionals like college professors, the curve flattened out quite soon, even more so for semi-clerical occupations like librarianship.[6] At the level of the unskilled labourer, in much closer proximity to the threshold of poverty, the pattern of life earnings was virtually flat. Clark found that his evidence 'fails to show that higher wages

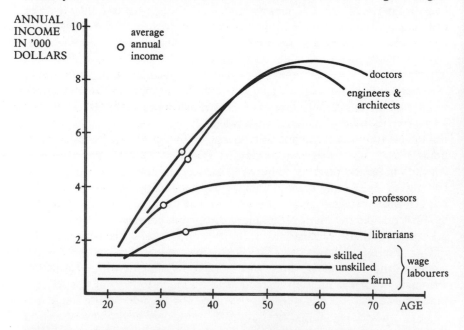

**Figure 8.1** Wage and salary structures compared: annual income by selected occupations in the US, 1920–1929 (*Source*: Based on data in Harold F. Clark, *Life Earnings. In Selected Occupations in the United States*, Harper, New York, 1937)

accompany long periods of service. Instead . . . in unskilled and semi-skilled labour the pay is determined by the kind of work done and not by the length of service' (1937: 138). We can picture Rowntree's cycle of working-class poverty (see chapter 3) compressed against this unyielding ceiling of the wage rate: around the age of thirty-five, when the worker's domestic needs are greatest, his wage affords no relief, while his salaried counterpart enjoys a steady upward swing in earnings until his mid-fifties. Subsequent studies confirm that the lower-paid occupations have notably 'early ceilings' (Oppenheimer 1974: 240) and start to drop sooner than salaries, largely because of the declining value of physical labour. As figure 8.1 indicates, the working life of wage labourers (with the exception of the poorest, the farm workers) ended earlier than the professionals. At retirement the latter enjoy pensions and other deferred benefits, while wage-earners are confronted with Rowntree's second major trough of material need.

The different structures of lifetime earnings are further illustrated in figure 8.2, drawing on Lydall's 1953 survey of life earnings in Britain. This compares 'salaried and self-employed workers' ('managers, professional, technical, clerical and sales employees') with skilled and unskilled manual workers (Lydall 1955: 141–2). Again, it reveals the steep upward curve of the professional's salary and the relatively flat earnings pattern of the unskilled worker. The significance of these earnings patterns can be seen by comparing them with Wynn's illustration of the changing prosperity of a 'family of modest means'. The steep upward curve of the professional salary would alleviate the marked squeeze which the 'modest' family experiences in the period of child-rearing. The sustained high level of professional earnings when offspring are no longer dependent allows the accumulation of pensioning and endowment funds, which offsets the tendency towards poverty in the stages of domestic decline.

The lack of such privileges places acute demands on working-class income strategy. Much of the compensating action must be taken *within* 'the family' or household. Survival depends on tightening belts, begging and borrowing, and forcing people other than the main (male) breadwinner out into the lower reaches of the labor market. In principle, this is very evocative of the 'self-exploitation' of family labour which A. V. Chayanov diagnosed in his celebrated studies of the Russian peasantry (see chapter 5). In the industrial world, formal piecework or overtime systems and opportunities for informal earnings allow some scope for the *intensification* of labour.[7] However the principal means of raising household income remains the transfer of women's (and often children's) labour out into the wage-earning category.[8] I say 'wage-earning' advisedly, for women generally, even those with highly paid jobs, are much less likely to be rewarded according to the salary paradigm.[9] Recent studies have revealed the extent of female labour force participation, and the notable class differences. Figure 8.3 indicates the

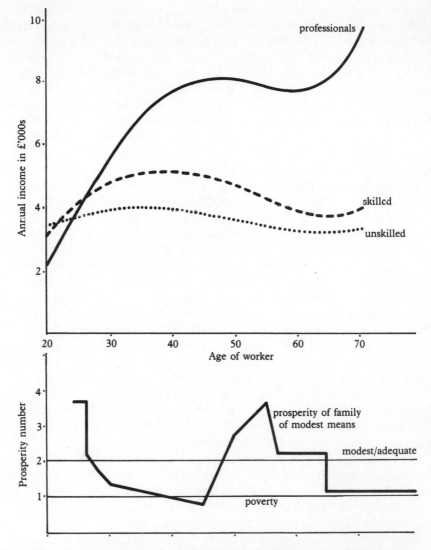

**Figure 8.2**  Wage and salary structures, after Lydall; with 'prosperity numbers in the life-cycle of a family of modest means', after Wynn (*Sources*: Harold Lydall, 'The life cycle in income, saving, and asset ownership', *Econometrica* 23(2), 1955, pp. 141–2; Margaret Wynn, *Family Policy*, Michael Joseph Ltd, London, 1970, and see also figure 3.2 above)

proportion of wives who are 'out to work' in different income categories in 1967, and reveals that women in low income households are much more likely to work during the high-stress period of child–rearing, and less likely

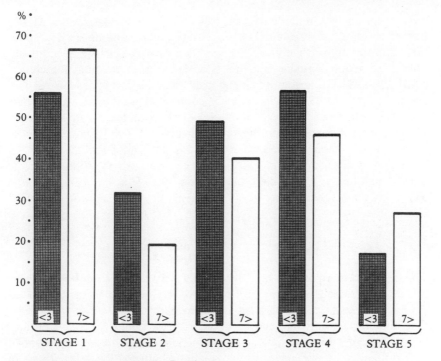

The family cycle stages specified by Duval are:

1  Couple with no children under 18 years old; wife aged between 16 and 34;
2  Couple with two children under 6 years old;
3  Couple with children aged between 6 and 17;
4  Couple with no children under 18 years old; wife aged between 35 and 54;
5  Couple with no children under 18 years old; wife aged 55 or more.

Shaded bars: annual income of husband *less than $3,000*.
Unshaded bars: annual income of husband *more than $7,000*.

**Figure 8.3**  Proportion of wives 'out to work' in five stages of the cycle of domestic development, by annual income of *husband* (*Source*: Evelyn Millis Duvall, *Family Development* (4th edn), J. B. Lippincott, Philadelphia, 1971, p. 494, based on US Department of Labour data, 1967)

to work after middle age.[10] At both these stages the more affluent women are likely to be supported by the salary structure of their husbands.[11] On the other hand, the *costs* of having to work outside the household during periods of peak need in the reproductive cycle bear very heavily on working-class women – most conspicuously when there is no other breadwinner in the household.[12]

Middle-class professionals can afford to make a virtue of their 'self-reliance', their capacity to fund their own welfare 'privately' rather than depending on government handouts (tax breaks, which characteristically favour high-income households, are not thought of as 'handouts'). Hence Becker's curious observation: 'The reduced importance of the family implies that members of middle-class and upper-class families gain the freedom and privacy of action available only to poor families in traditional societies' (1981: 243). What this disguises is the heavy middle-class dependence upon, and privileged access to a vast range of supporting institutions, from banks and private hospitals to professional associations and the state apparatus. Working-class dependence on the state is structured both by poverty and by class position – their relation to the means of production. Provision of child-care is vital to working-class mothers who *have* to work, and little more than a luxury for middle-class mothers who *choose* to work (and often feel guilty about 'abandoning' their children).

## The salary: privileges and apologies

The middle-class riposte to these arguments is that the costs of reproduction in the professional world are very high, mainly because access to salaried employment requires a long-term investment in education. Little wonder that middle-class parents have an acute interest in the social institutions which organize this high-quality reproduction. Economists have found it very difficult to devise adequate explanations both for the inflated cost of access to professional employment, and for its high levels of reward. The most plausible explanation has been couched in terms of *'human capital'*, the notion that by ability, education and experience people build up knowledge and skills which increase in value as they get older.[13] 'One prediction of human capital theory is that the greater the amount workers invest in themselves, the more rapidly their wage profiles will rise and the later the profiles will peak' (J. P. Smith 1977: 220). Note the capitalist premise: we are not talking about rewards for a certain quantity of *work* done, but for the quality of an *investment* made. Precisely what does this investment consist of? Where it is stored? How and when can it be cashed in for a larger pay-check? The main problem with which this approach must contend is that these values do not derive simply from 'free' transactions in labour markets. Senior doctors are paid more than four times the salary of junior doctors, but does this mean that we are four times more inclined to seek the services of a senior doctor when we are sick? The chances are we might have greater confidence in the skills of one who was trained recently. Alternatively, do we care so little about whether our plumber is in his teens or his fifties that we reckon their work is worth the same wage?

The answer seems inescapable: salary rates and structures are being protected from market forces by *social institutions*. Things are arranged so that some important individuals do not have to sell their labour for what people are prepared to pay on any particular day. The question which remains is why some particular resources of 'human capital' need and get special institutional means for their accumulation (schools, universities), transfer (qualifications and certifications) and storage (professional status), while other sorts apparently do not. Institutions are not simply helping to protect 'real' values when markets cannot cope, they are actually dictating those values. At this point 'institutional economics' runs out of ideas.[14] Why some people's values carry more weight than others is a matter of how much power they wield within society.

Because the social organization of rewards transcends economists' conventions of individual rationality and unfettered markets, the *measurement* of human capital and efforts to *prescribe techniques* for structuring salaries have both proved very perplexing.[15] The essence of such a privileged system of rewards, say Lupton and Bowey, is its dependence on implicit social *rules*, such as 'the young ought to defer to the old' or 'the young ought to be asked to contribute their energies and skills that their youth endows them with' (1983: 14). Reproductive organization extends the logic of a salary far beyond the compass of short- or medium-term bargaining for skills and labour. It guarantees that the professional will be lifted *at the right time* above the stresses of the reproductive process. '1960 census data on earnings patterns by age indicate that in only relatively high-level professional, managerial and sales occupations do average earnings peak at the same time family needs are peaking' (Oppenheimer 1974: 227). The young professional does not gain immediate compensation for the drain on parental resources, indeed the initial steps on the incremental ladder are often lower paid than wage rates for the same age cohort (an infamous temptation for middle-class youth). But soon a steeply rising pattern of increments and promotions carries the employee away from the first of Rowntree's poverty 'troughs', when pregnancy and young children stretch the dependency ratios uncomfortably. Thereafter, increments continue a more gradual rise, to finance the education of offspring and to build up a pension fund for the final phase of threatened poverty in old age.

The salary permits intergenerational transfers of professional status in ways which a wage does not. Admission to, and upward mobility within the salaried category is jealously guarded by the professional class – conspicuously by creating formal associations which protect their interests, and erecting barriers of paper qualification. Historically, medicine and law set the standards, and now people are made to plod through examinations before they can sell houses or insurance – on the pretext of protecting the public from inefficient service. The relevance of subjects studied can be very obscure: an Oxford or Cambridge degree in Classics was for long considered the best qualification for admission to the British diplomatic service. 'A good education' expressed in paper qualifications subsumes a broad range of other social aptitudes and graces. Their complexity and subtlety means that suitability for professional employment is still ultimately a matter for personal appraisal in job interviews (Lupton and Bowey 1983: 96). On the other hand, recruitment to wage labour is characteristically impersonal and more factually concerned with physical aptitudes and skills.

The salary may be seen as part of a mutually reinforcing fabric of economic institutions. For example, its temporal structure bears directly on the middle-class acquisition of (mainly domestic) property. Not only do the higher rates of reward allow greater opportunities to invest, salary structures readily accommodate mortgaging arrangements. Wage-earners have remained trapped in the insecurity and higher long-term cost of rentals. It is striking that financial institutions will accept a professional *career*, with its promise of security and increments, as *collateral*, for a home loan.[16]

The value of the time which the worker sells by the hour or by the piece bears little relation to the value of the products which the owner of the enterprise sells. The difference is profit, which provides the return to capital and pays the managers and other professionals. Maintaining the gap is hard work for the minority which enjoys the higher rewards. Powerful ideas about wealth and about the organization of production and reproduction are key assets in the struggle to minimize intrusion into their ranks. So long as disputes about earnings are kept within the conventional definitions of wage and salary, the labourer can be underpaid for the value of his work. Thus, in a country like Britain, collective bargaining has been preoccupied not with the long-term structure of rewards, but with the rate per hour or piece, the duration of the working day or week, the scheduling and rates for 'overtime', or the differentials between one job rating and another.[17]

Salary negotiations, on the other hand, are much concerned with the pattern of increments, promotion ladders, the deferred gratification of a pension, and family-oriented perquisites such as health-care and mortgage provision. Such things are seen as an example of middle class providence, rather than an intricately constructed, class-based scheme to ride out the stresses and insecurities of the reproductive process. Salaries are not set by something so crude and immediate as the market; professionals seldom bargain for better rewards by withdrawing their labour – going on strike. A salary, with all its advantages, has come to be regarded as an *entitlement* of the middle class; and as Amartya Sen (1981) has explained, entitlement is defined by society, not by 'free' markets. Middle-class investment in the education of their offspring (giving them a meal ticket which they can cash in later in their lives) is not simply a matter of faith in future demand for that kind of labour; it depends on the power to assert who is *entitled* to cash in a particular qualification for salaried employment. On the other hand, entitlement to the insecurity of a *wage* helps to keep workers on their toes – producing the wealth which the middle classes draw as salaries, as well as reproducing the cheap labour on which industrialization has depended. Through the political means at their disposal, the middle classes have had to work quite hard to keep working-class discontent in check. One expensive way of doing this is to extend the privileges of a salary. In certain new, high-technology industries there has been a tendency to 'salarize' earnings, giving workers longer-term contracts with incremental rewards and family-related perquisites, and the enticement of upward social mobility.[18]

## Salaries in the late industrial world

These brief comments leave unexplored many questions about the historical origins of the wage–salary distinction. For example, I would speculate that in the pre-industrial period of mercantilism a hierarchy of age-related promotions (apprentice, journeyman, master) distributed profits in an incremental pattern which may be a prototype of the salary. Regional variations are also of great interest. Japanese industry is well known for its extensive use of the salary principle. In marked contrast to the organisation of factory labour in Britain, Japanese firms like Hitachi have bought 'not a skill but a lifetime's work' (Dore 1973: 111):

> British manual workers reach their peak earnings in their twenties. Thereafter there is little change in their earnings level until (for those who are not made foremen) they decline somewhat in their fifties and rather more in their sixties. Japanese workers' earnings rise throughout their working life at a rate which does not vary greatly, though the gradient steepens somewhat in the late thirties and levels off after 45. At the end of their working life they are likely to earn two and a half times their beginning wage. The pattern for British university graduates is similar to that of Japanese manual workers. (p. 110)

The fusion of reproductive and productive interests in the Japanese system is remarkably explicit: 'A man's family are peripheral members of the company family'; whereas 'the British system sharply separates the man's role as employee from his role as husband and father, and the firm disclaims responsibility for, or jurisdiction over, the latter' (Dore 1973: 209, 210). Japanese workers receive specific allowances for each family member, and special funds contribute not only to education but to the cost of weddings and other rites of passage. Dore remarks wryly that in Britain family allowances are paid 'only to members of the middle class such as university professors who are not particularly noted for starving themselves to feed a family' (p. 103).

The Japanese system derives from family-based rationing strategies after the Second World War, and was supported by both employers and trades unions. While some have associated it with the economic 'miracle' in that country, others have objected that it is 'paternalistic', co-opting workers into the firm-family rather than confronting them with their predicament as an alienated class. At any rate, the wage principle has been regaining ground steadily in recent years. The incremental system of rewards was always sustained by government bureaucracies and larger corporations rather than by smaller businesses, which could be proportionately less confident about their capacity to secure the future of their employees.[19] As in the other advanced capitalist economies, the segmentation of labour markets into the more and the less skilled has been polarizing income patterns. In Europe and the US, the contraction of the privileged middle class has been reinforcing the distinctions between wage earners and the salariat.[20] At one stage, Japanese industry intimated the possibility of a more humane system of rewards, responsive to the welfare of the many rather than simply the privileges of the few. Today it seems that latter-day industrialism, however else it may have changed, is no more enthusiastic about alleviating reproductive stress in its dependent workforce than it was a century ago, when Rowntree investigated the dynamics of proletarian poverty.

# 9

# Moral crises and utopian experiments

'The little utopia of the family', declared the architect-philosopher Lewis Mumford more than half a century ago, 'is the enemy – indeed the principal enemy – of the beloved community. This fact is notorious' (1923: 49–50). The family: that nexus of human passions, that tight arena of birth, procreation and death which seems perpetually to undermine our quest for social stability; the joy and the agony of human flesh, as against the dreams of immortality built into the monuments of antiquity and the architecture of our own attempts at civilization.

The last two centuries have made us increasingly conscious of what seems to be a widening gap between the intimate world of the household and the mass of institutions on which we all, as individuals, now depend. We have come to think of this as a set of uneasy oppositions between 'the individual', 'the family' and 'society', a contest over rights, duties and loyalties. Society is threatened by the decline in parental control, but society snatches teenagers from the homes where they belong. The fate of 'the family' evokes a powerful mixture of emotions: primeval feelings of loyalty and frustration, and of regretful pleasure when one more of its functions is liberated by society. In this kind of reckoning, family members stand exposed as individuals to the threats and opportunities of a bewildering array of new institutions, and must struggle to make up their own minds about the costs and benefits. Rather than having status ascribed to them by birth, and decisions minimized by family routines, they must work in vastly wider arenas to construct their own social identity.

## The family – right and left

There are some serious differences of opinion about whether families make society, or vice versa. Politicians on the right, who tend to judge things from the point of view of individual freedom, keep telling us that the 'family' is the foundation of national society (often implying that if parents kept better control of their kids, public order would be easier to maintain). On the other hand these same conservatives, who resent the intrusion of the public domain into the private, complain most loudly about the declining role of 'the family'. It has been robbed of form and function by the prodigious expansion of society and of state power. Compressed into a fragile nucleus, it can no longer work as a moral force in our lives.[1] Religious fundamentalists in America are most vigorous in their condemnation of the erosion of family rights and duties, castigating the double-income-no-kid couples, working mothers, public day-care for children, and above all any kind of tinkering with the reproductive process. This last is construed as a strictly conjugal sexual relationship, which belongs unequivocally in the private domestic domain, behind the bedroom door, under the bedclothes, and preferably in complete darkness. Through a combination of free choice and divine will, mature adults thus furtively create the raw material of American society. Suggesting that it might be otherwise is very explicitly equated with communism and 'the forces of darkness'.

For their part, politicians on the left are inclined to argue that without firm government and extensive welfare policies families cannot survive and prosper. Socialists are certainly much more sympathetic to institutions beyond 'the family', hardliners tending to view the latter with suspicion as a vestige of an old, redundant and corrupt moral order. For them the question is whether 'the family' *should* have a future. In the nineteenth century, the expansion of capitalism was nurtured by family institutions, but with the arrival of the communist utopia the predatory bourgeoisie itself would be dissolved, taking its familistic ideology with it. In the *Communist Manifesto*, Marx and Engels demand:

> Do you charge us with wanting to stop the exploitation of children by their parents? To this crime we plead guilty . . .
> The bourgeois claptrap about the family and education, about the hallowed co-relation of parent and child, becomes all the more disgusting, the more, by the action of Modern Industry, all family ties among the proletarians are torn asunder, and their children transformed into simple articles of commerce and instruments of labor. (Marx and Engels 1967: 100–1)

In tune with this philosophy, socialist states have been assiduous in extending reproductive organization outside the household. In the USSR efforts were concentrated on child-care services which would release more women for the labour force. However, in spite of early intentions to dissolve it, the virtues of 'the Soviet family' were soon being reasserted. A popular Soviet 'Book for Parents' first published in 1937 declared: 'The family is a natural collective body and, like everything natural, healthy, and normal, it can only blossom forth in social society. . . The family becomes the natural primary cell of society. . . In delegating to you [parents] a certain measure of societal authority the Soviet State demands from you the correct upbringing of its future citizens.'[2]

The problem with all these arguments is that they take a very static, idealized view of family life, assuming that households are the uniform modules out of which stable societies are made. Our own experience tells us how different households can be – each is a small eccentric society in its own right. ('Every household', says a Ghanaian proverb, 'has its own special way of cooking a chicken'.) We might be happy to think of a nation composed of thousands of reduplications of our *own* family, but not of that dreadful family next door. More important, the static 'building block' image actually obstructs our understanding of the relationship between household and community, because it tells us very little about how each is *continually remaking the other*. Whatever we may wish, societies are, like the relations of reproduction which sustain them, continually in flux. That is what history is all about, and that is why the dynamics of reproduction are so important in explaining both social continuity and social change.

The fate of 'the family' continues to arouse our deepest moral passions. While this is in part a measure of our own subjective involvement in home and hearth, the more truly moral question is how and why our notions of 'the family' should loom so large in our collective understandings of modern society. My conclusion is that it is our poor but best effort to comprehend the social relations of reproduction, a process which is difficult to grasp mentally because it has become so pervasive and is so much more extensive than our own short lives. The political and economic dimensions of reproduction still converge in our households, the social unit most usually implied by our discourse on 'the family'. This is why we so often explain our anxieties about its survival in terms of the relentless intrusion of material forces into our private lives (money versus love). Although it may be no less serious a cause for moral concern, the *ex*trusion of reproductive processes out into society seems very much more difficult to conceptualize.

These issues are kept alive mainly because people in each new generation must be 'socialized', and must then adapt their own lives according to the moral standards they have learned and what the real world has to offer. In periods of historical change whole societies have to come to terms not only with the reorganization of economic and political affairs, but also of reproduction ('family affairs'). Thus the industrial revolution launched an epoch of moral debate, which has given us new religions and new philosophies, new schools of social science and new ways of interpreting ourselves. Speculation about how we ought to organize reproduction has been heavily implicit in all of these.

## American dreams

The moral fervour of the European migrants to North America is striking. Their dissatisfaction with the old social order and their concern with the new, soon established the moral triad of Family, God and State as a permanent feature in the discourse about the making of America. On the frontier, where society may seem least structured, the moral dilemmas are often keenest, and the dual force of reproductive and productive issues most starkly evident. Vogt tells us that among twentieth-century settlers in New Mexico:

> there are only two points at which there is rigid compliance with the county and state laws: (a) marriage and divorce, and (b) the ownership and transfer of land and other property, such as cattle and automobiles. These facts underlie the crucial significance of the nuclear family and of the institution of property, especially the ownership of land, in the social structure. The position of the nuclear family is further buttressed by the strong taboo against adultery. . . When cases of adultery do occur (we know of only four cases in the history of Homestead), they are promptly and unequivocally dealt with – first with 'fist fights' and later (in all four cases) with divorce. (Vogt 1955: 157)

More obviously than in the 'old countries' of Europe, American society did not simply evolve, it was constructed. Accordingly, American history is notable for the degree of explicitness with which issues of reproduction were confronted, and new solutions sought. Nineteenth-century legislation seems startlingly intrusive today: in New Jersey even a married couple could get three years in jail for masturbating each other in private.[3] Moral codes developed pluralistically, often bringing civil authority and public interest into conflict. Throughout the nineteenth century, radical attempts were made to produce new designs for living. These 'utopian' experiments aroused great fear and hostility, most particularly in the extent to which they departed from conventions about the organization of reproduction. Although generally suspected of advocating promiscuity, most of these communities in fact placed their adherents under rigid moral discipline. Confronting the dilemmas of reproduction they pursued a wide range of tactics: some, like the Amish and Hutterites, sought to conserve old family structures against the current of economic and political change; others, like the Shakers, viewed reproduction as a source of vice and disruption, and sought to suppress it altogether; but most tried to reconfigure reproduction as a social force, sometimes in very innovative ways. If their endurance is a measure of their success. those which lasted more than a decade had managed to find some means of *material* survival; those which lasted more than a *generation* had cracked the problem of reproduction.[4]

Early in the nineteenth century, George Rapp led some three hundred German migrants to the New World in pursuit of a remedy for their political, economic and religious discontents. Their Harmony Society near Pittsburgh quickly established a successful industrial and horticultural enterprise. With their material base secure, the spiritual and moral structure of their community became a pressing issue. They idealized Adam as the whole, asexual man, and blamed woman for his fall and for the disruptive force of sexuality. Believing that the return of Christ and the Day of Judgment were imminent they decided that reproduction was, like smoking, an unnecessary evil, and abolished both. By 1870, when they were visited by their biographer Charles Nordhoff, the Harmony Society consisted of about 110 robust, elderly people organized into 'households' of approximately equal numbers of men and women. The order and restraint in the community was very striking, as was the appearance in their dress and manners that time had passed them by. By reproductive abstinence they had become a geriatric settlement, evocative of the Malaysian land development schemes described in chapter 6. As their strength and numbers dwindled, they, too, were obliged to hire labour to sustain their enterprise. As they went into collective domestic decline without heirs, their property was reckoned to be worth more than two and a half million dollars.

The central premise of Rappist social organization was the imminence of their own immortality. This confronts us with the familiar counterfactual notion of what Heaven, as a society of immortals in which time stands still, is all about. One of the topsy-turvy aspects of our notions of heaven is that people are 'born' into it by *death*, not by the usual human processes of sexual intercourse (which is why, for some people, heaven seems rather dull). But this is a reminder of the fact that our own mortality, our short lifespan, is actually a function of the way we reproduce. With reproduction subtracted from our experience, life (if that is what we would call it) would be unimaginably different. While we would forgo the pleasures of reproduction, we would be released from the persistent need to deal with its destabilizing effects. For the 'Holy Apostles' who were its members, the remarkable community of Aiyetoro in the coastal swamps of Nigeria *was* Heaven, 'a land of happiness and plenty, where there would be neither darkness nor death' (Barrett 1977: 45).[5] Alas, the human community is not a heavenly state, it is an earthly *process*. As with the Harmony Society, sex and conjugal relations were abolished, but the recurring reality of death presented them with a special problem. Corpses were disposed of secretly at night, and any expression of grief was punished as a major sin.

The way we are obliged to reproduce creates what might best be called 'constructive disruption'. It makes and breaks the beloved family, and unites the sexes and the generations in bonds of affection and antagonism. Our happiest festivities and a large proportion of the nastiest murders are strictly family affairs. To many social reformers the *power* of the reproductive process is inescapable; the challenge is to harness it for our collective welfare. John Humphrey Noyes set about this task with remarkable innovative zeal. Believing that the second coming of Christ had already occurred unnoticed in AD 70, and that since then the way had been cleared for the perfection of life on earth, he and his followers set up a progressive commune in Central New York in 1848. Like the Harmony Society and Aiyetoro, the Perfectionists at Oneida established a very successful industrial enterprise, which survives today as a major manufacturing corporation. In addition to being a spiritual leader of great charisma, Noyes brought his enthusiasm for science and technology to bear on all aspects of Oneida life, from education and diet to management techniques and the reorganization of reproduction.

Inspired by the evolutionism of Charles Darwin and the eugenics of Francis Galton, he invented *stirpiculture*, 'a concerted effort to select those couples whose spiritual and physical qualities most fitted them to reproduce. Members of the community signed an agreement to abide by the decision of a committee as to who should conceive the stirpicults, and between 1869 and 1879 fifty-eight children were born at Oneida' (Lockwood 1965: 409–10). Conjugal relations were reorganized as 'complex marriage', a variant of polygamy in which Noyes hoped to dissolve the domination of women by (individual) males. In his own way an ardent feminist (one of his published tracts is on *Slavery and Marriage*) he saw a direct connection between sexual prudery and the social subordination of women. He sought a rational scientific distinction between the gratifications of *'amative'* intercourse, and the serious business of *'propagative'* intercourse on which the perpetuation and perfection of society so radically depended. The latter was a proper subject for serious committee meetings, and it was the personal duty of men in particular to keep the disruptions of amative intercourse within the bounds of restraint.

Needless to say Noyes and his Perfectionists were the object of public scandal. People in 'mainstream' American society were engaged in their own serious but less overt struggle to devise a new society, and perhaps because of this they were often very hostile to these utopian 'threats' to morality. This outrage is testimony to the public importance of the organization of reproduction, and the resistance to attempts to tinker with it. Almost any experiment of this kind, throughout human history, has been suspected as a motive for releasing the animal forces of 'free love', which 'decent' society has for so long struggled to contain. The moral majority fails to understand that many of these experiments with the organization of reproduction have involved rigorous moral discipline; and that an inherent purpose is to arrange more comfortable and congenial *material* lives for their people.

No utopian commune has survived more than a few months without building a firm economic base for itself. In all the cases mentioned here, spiritual fervour was directed by charismatic leaders to heroic feats of building, self-denial and communal investment.[6] They approached the interrelated problems of production and reproduction with essentially the same innovative zeal, and their communistic economies were often regarded by the wider public with as much suspicion as their sexual codes. Their quest for material equity in tune with the spiritual equality of human souls was usually expressed in the abolition of private property, and the ethic that members should contribute according to their ability and be rewarded according to their needs. This tacit acceptance of the imbalance of needs and capacities built into the reproductive process (see chapter 5) has proved very difficult to sustain. The long-term pattern of give and take is hard to reconcile with the short-term inequity of some members consuming more than they produce. A common tactic is to award 'points' for labour which can be cashed in for consumption needs and privileges. But most communes have found it impossible to keep accounts in the (reproductive) long term, rather than the (economic) short term. The struggle to sustain material 'equality' can demand some heavy authoritarian controls, and the old vices of currency, property and political domination start to creep back in. In short, these material failures put the perpetuation of the commune as a whole in jeopardy.

Unlike families and households, which have been dealing with reproductive pressures since time immemorial, communes are associations of individuals, impatient in their pursuit of absolute spiritual, economic and social equity. Many communes have struggled to operate like extended family households, but it seems that not even the most passionate insistence on 'brotherhood' or the most detailed contract can substitute for the material and emotional interests of the *'real'* transgenerational relations of reproduction.[7] The problems of many communards have been compounded by their passionate rejection of the reproductive and family *process*, and their belief (like the Aiyetoro Apostles or the Rappists) that they have achieved a new spiritual *state* of being. We might say, using the terminology suggested in chapter 2, that they were preoccupied with a new *apical* ideal, and much less attentive to *procedural* norms. This was expressed in their most fundamental problem, how to maintain their own modes of reproduction within the context of a larger, developing society. Lockwood (1965) has made the point that for many of them sustaining their sectarian differences became pointless, because early twentieth-century society had become a kind of rival utopia, accommodating and incorporating many of the moral principles which they had pioneered. Even the 'stirpiculture' of Oneida lost some of its peculiarity (this was a society moving relentlessly towards such things as computer dating and the biological screening of mates) and the new generation of stirpicults themselves showed more interest in the grander American Dream than in the constricted life of the commune.

This makes the successful *social* reproduction of the Hutterite and Amish communities in North America all the more remarkable. Their survival has depended on sustaining the viability of small-scale forms of production which admit technical innovations very sparingly – in marked contrast to the Oneida Perfectionists. This sort of conservatism must not be mistaken for inertia: keeping the modern world at bay involves tough policy-making and firm government. The 'clannishness' of groups like the Old Order Amish is a vital part of this strategy. This self-sufficiency is sustained by an extended pattern of domestic reproduction, marriages within the Order, and some fairly stern policing of the *Regel und Ordnung*, the Amish Constitution, by the elder men. Nevertheless, 'Amish history is a history of divisions' (Hostetler 1968: 158) reflected in sectarian departures from religious orthodoxy. The Hutterites seem to have devised a more effective system for sustaining control of their own reproduction and demographic expansion. This involves lineage-like segmentation into *Leute* in which growth is strictly limited to a hundred persons, whereupon a subgroup must 'hive off' and establish a new colony. Groups of *Leute* remain bonded into Hutterite *Federations*.[8]

## Reproduction – modern and post–modern

Those of us who live in the mainstream of industrial society have fewer occasions to consider the peculiarities of our own principles of reproductive organization. When we do, we are more likely to have in mind the physiology of sex rather than the growth and division of communities. As we saw in chapter 7, after the turbulent epoch of industrialization, family life in the early decades of this century settled into a fairly steady routine. The American (or British, or French) family was regarded as something more than just 'normal' or 'ideal': it was *natural*. Media images reinforced the moral pattern which in turn (polished up by sociologists and psychologists) became the basis for social *therapy*.[9] Confidence in any such 'natural' pattern of family development, typically an insistence on a chronological arrangement of proper 'tasks' for family members, has undoubtedly been shaken by the diversification of 'family' forms and functions in recent decades, and by a growing awareness of the influence of ethnic and class distinctions. While therapists strive to treat such traumas as divorce as 'an interruption or dislocation in the traditional family life cycle' (McGoldrick and Carter 1982: 188), the notion of a single 'proper' way to organize marriage is being eroded rapidly.

We continue doggedly to speculate about the fate of 'the family' rather than about the organization of reproduction, peering inwards at its vestiges in domestic organization, rather than surveying the broadening range of institutions in which it has been constituted.[10] This is partly because we are still inclined to see reproduction as a fundamentally unalterable fact of life. Our very evident success in transforming the material world around us is certainly in marked contrast to our apparent reluctance to transform our own physical selves. But today the organization of reproduction has become the subject of intense moral debate because of a series of startling technical innovations: *in vitro* fertilization, surgical implants, the banking of Nobel prizewinners' sperm, the application of genetic engineering developed in botany and livestock management to human populations. The legal system is now being called on to judge such issues as which 'parent' shall have custody over a frozen embryo.[11] It is hardly surprising that feminists have expressed a keen moral and political interest in these matters. While some have relished the political and economic prospects of liberating women altogether from the processes of childbirth, others fear that new reproductive technology will remain in male control, reinforcing patriarchy.[12]

'The historical/material base of contemporary feminism', says O'Brien, '. . . is the transformation wrought in the hitherto biologically defined process of birth' (1989: 65). However, technical progress in the protraction of life and postponement of death by costly organ transplants and medical apparatus has also stimulated moral debate. A few are so confidant that science will eventually find a cure for death that they arrange to have their corpses put in cold storage ('cryogenics'). Others have the deepest misgivings about whether science has any business at all interfering in human reproduction. At times we have burned our fingers quite severely: the nineteenth- and early twentieth-century enthusiasm for 'eugenics', changing biologically the structure of human beings, culminated in the notorious experiments of Nazi Germany, and little has been heard of it since. If science fact is not enough, science fiction has regaled us with the horrors. Ever since Mary Shelley explored these dilemmas as long ago as 1818, her story of Dr Frankenstein's experiments with surgery, electricity and body-parts have provided a durable moral warning about this sort of scientific megalomania.

Science, Ernest Gellner tells us, 'is the form of cognition of industrial society' (1964: 72). It is the basis of modern philosophy and ideology, our principal means of judging *truth*. But science is a historical innovation, a frame of mind which enabled us to make the technical transformations of our material world in the last two centuries. Its success has given us boundless faith in its powers; we have used it to explain and evaluate matters far beyond the compass of material production. People have stretched the scientific creed to the frontiers of knowledge, explaining things which we shall probably never be able to know, from extrasensory perception to the origins of the universe. Some of these acts of faith make religious challenges to the absolute truth of science look like healthy scepticism.

The technical means to change the physical processes of reproduction, which trouble us so much, are simply the tip of a gigantic iceberg. Science has been inextricably involved in the social organization of reproduction in our modern world. If we enjoy the benefits of scientific medicine, scientific schooling or scientific banking, the puzzle is why we should be so squeamish about genetic tinkering or uterine implants. Our moral doubts seem to run deeper than a feeling that science simply has no business in the private domain of reproductive organization. We actually have good reason to believe that a creed which was devised to explain and organize the transformation of our material world *cannot actually tell us the most important things we need to know about reproduction.*

As the epoch of industrialization recedes, and we try to step beyond the ideologies of 'modernity' to make sense of the emerging 'post-industrial' world, the credentials of science are increasingly being called to question. This is especially true of *social* science, which has always been struggling for respectability on the margins of 'hard' science. But perhaps that very marginality is a good position from which to begin a reappraisal of what we know about the meaning of life.

# 10

# Social and analytical constructions of reproduction

I have written this book because I believe that neither social scientists nor lay persons have an adequate understanding of how reproduction is organized in human societies. In particular, I believe that reproduction has been underrated as a force in the making of modern society. This presumption is rather shocking: producing people is, after all, such a very fundamental human activity. If we do not know about that, what *do* we know?

Most people seem to dismiss reproduction rather coyly as 'only natural', a private rather than a public affair. Nevertheless, a little observation and a few questions will soon reveal the extent to which these matters are manipulated by individuals and controlled by society. Yet even social scientists, who should know better, tend to treat it as autonomic and non-rational, which is probably why biologists and demographers have taken the subject over. If we believe that human regeneration is simply a 'natural' process, we are unlikely to go out of our way to seek a social explanation of it. The attitude is 'male chauvinist' to the extent that it implies an inevitable, ineluctable commitment of women to child-rearing.[1] Certainly, accurate knowledge about the physiology of reproduction is still far from complete, and we have barely begun to use this knowledge to control the way we reproduce. Some (notably the 'sociobiologists' or 'Darwinian social scientists') would argue that our ignorance of biological science obstructs our understanding of the social organization of reproduction. There is even the dark implication that if our genes are orchestrating our reproduction efficiently, they would not wish us to know what they were up to.

Here I take a more direct view of our failure to understand. It is not so much physiological or psychological inhibitions which make us ignorant about reproduction, rather it is the kind of knowledge about these matters that we have at our disposal. It is not how we think but what we think, and as individuals we get most of this sort of knowledge from other people, who in turn draw on the grand information pool we call 'culture'. Changing or improving on that shared knowledge – in a sense using it *against* itself – is the fundamental challenge of science. The nineteenth-century philosopher Herbert Spencer insisted that knowledge of our social selves, the knowledge about knowledge, is the most demanding of all branches of science.

In this chapter I shall draw together ten very basic sorts of misunderstanding about the social organization of reproduction, explain how they arose, and suggest how we can improve on what we know. All of these misunderstandings have a history because like all sorts of knowledge they have developed over time. This is conspicuously true of the first item of biased thinking on my list, which dates from the mid-eighteenth century.

### 1   THE OBSESSION WITH MATERIAL PRODUCTION AND EXCHANGE

The sequence of events which we call 'the industrial revolution' marks the most dramatic and farreaching transformation in human history. Not only did it change our economies, it shifted social organization on to a massive scale, generating the modern nation state and drawing the world into one political system. It also, quite literally, remade history by obliging us to consider anew what had been happening to us. Old ideas of society ticking away like a clock or growing like a plant told us little about how and why it was being so thoroughly transformed. Social science is itself a product of this period. While the pioneers (Spencer, Marx, Durkheim, Weber ...) looked back for inspiration as far as the ancient Greek philosophers, they could see all too clearly that the spectacular technological innovations were at the heart of modern social transformations. The first name for these new studies was *political economy*, firmly anchoring social structure to its material base. The subject rapidly expanded and fragmented into disciplinary specializations, with Economics quickly establishing its dominance. Its *scientific* pretensions were also a product of the times, and economists' use of sophisticated mathematics makes them appear more rigorous than sociologists or anthropologists. Of course, this created considerable tension for people still involved in the old magical or religious ways of thinking and explaining things. Indeed, Creationists and other fundamentalists continue to challenge the ideological force of scientific thought.

This materialistic science acquired so much influence because it delivered so many obvious and immediate truths. Only when its powers were stretched to *prediction* did people have serious doubts. A conspicuous case is Marx's science of history, based on a plausible account of how the social system of capitalism developed from the transformation of the basic processes of production. Marx struggled to establish laws like those of Newtonian physics which would explain the future of the world. His ideas about this shifted significantly during the course of his life: would capitalism be blown apart by its victims when they fully understood how they were being exploited? Or would it quietly autodestruct as one capitalist enterprise gobbled up another, turning the economy into one gigantic monopoly effectively owned by everybody? His scientific laws about the forces of material production in history could not, it seems, produce a single, consistent story. Other economists, in opposition to Marx, saw the processes of exchange as more determinant than the processes of production. Today, 'neoclassical' economics focuses on the marketplace, encouraging other social scientists to think of political and other institutions simply as aggregations of numerous individual transactions. Both these materialist doctrines continue to divide the world we live in: there are those (liberals) who believe that efficient societies consist of rational individuals competing in free markets, with the minimum of state intervention; and those (socialists) who believe that equity can only be assured by state-organized cooperation.

As the shock waves of the industrial revolution recede, doubts have arisen about the advantages of basing all social and historical judgements on material production and exchange.[2] In this book I have complained that in social science, 'reproduction' has come to connote historical inertia rather than change; it is seen as a process which sustains social structure rather than one which has a part to play in its transformation. In so far as they are interested in reproduction or the family at all, rigorous Marxists would conclude that because the relations of reproduction have shown little susceptibility to technical development (there has been little or no 'development of the *reproductive* means') they can have little effect on human history.[3] Viewed on the grand scale, human breeding is therefore taken for granted as the provision of the raw material of social formations, which are shaped by economic forces. But why must we assume that reproduction conforms to the same 'laws' as material production? Why should it only have an effect on history if its 'technology' changes? Are we not simply trapped in the materialist ideology of our own industrialized world?

'Biological reproduction always takes place within a determinate structure of relations of production, distribution, and consumption and occurs simultaneously with economic activity' (Arnould 1984: 130). For the vast majority of social scientists this will be a statement of the obvious. It is, however, a mistaken assertion, not a fact. In this book I have argued that reproduction is as likely to determine economic activities as *vice versa*; and that this is largely because economic and reproductive processes are *not* simultaneous, but operate and interact in different timespans. Understanding cause and effect takes time in the historical sense, which puts it beyond the reach of conventional economic analysis. 'As we proceed beyond the stationary economic state, we enter an uncharted frontier,' one economist interested in reproduction has acknowledged. 'Our analytical maps do not tell us how to proceed... The families we observe are seldom if ever in a state of equilibrium. This uncharted frontier is beset with all manner of disequilibria' (T. W. Schultz 1973: S12).

Understanding the reproductive process as an active force in social organization is not a luxury, it is an intellectual and moral necessity. I believe this is why conscientious social scientists have made such heavy weather in analyzing puzzling cases like that of Lesotho, which I described in chapter 3. If we insist on viewing southern Africa as a big marketplace, we cannot hope to explain why blacks are excluded from so many transactions and are forced to sell their labour so cheaply. An alternative, Marxist view would see the South Africans using the relentlessly expanding power of capitalism to squeeze labour out of people like the Basotho in the black hinterland. But this still leaves too much unexplained. Marx's laws of history have little to say about people who remain both 'modern' wage-earning proletarians and poor 'traditional' peasants. The absurd implication, which many modern Marxists have struggled to explain, is that these people are living simultaneously in the present and the past. Efforts to explain precisely *how* the Basotho are kept locked into their very modern misery have at last obliged social scientists to pay closer attention to the organization of reproduction. Basic materialist questions about the supply of cheap labour have shifted from capitalists and mineworkers to those neglected people-who-produce-people, *women*. Already this new perspective is allowing us to connect the material world to the peculiar ideological regime in South Africa – a state which has been based on rigid rules about who may marry whom, and who may rear their children where. If we see the organization of reproduction not as some dependent variable, but as *mediating* between the supply of labour and the ownership of capital, the predicament of the Basotho becomes much clearer and, perhaps, more accessible to reform.[4]

## 2   THE FIXATION ON 'THE FAMILY'

Social scientists have not ignored human reproduction entirely. They have done something rather worse: they have limited their understanding of it to something called 'the family', thus obscuring its pervasive presence in the rest of social organization. In most American and European colleges no sociology or anthropology course is complete without its segments on 'the family'. In the very influential work of Talcott Parsons, for example, 'the family' is represented as a primary *group*, the fundamental building block in social *structure*, performing such *basic functions* as the raising of children, the provision of subsistence and shelter, and the *ascription of social status* to individuals (Parsons 1949: 154). In chapter 2, I have explained why family relations are too relativistic and too dynamic to bear this sort of definition, and that if we are looking for a basic social unit which combines the organization of reproduction with other vital functions, the most likely candidate is the *household*. But the dynamism of the household obliges us to recognize the extension of reproductive processes out into the fabric of community and society. We cannot hope to see this if our understanding of reproduction remains encapsulated in narrow definitions of 'the family'.

There is a double bind in our assumption that reproduction is essentially a family affair. Firstly, it allows us to believe that as the role of 'the family' evidently dwindles in the modern world, reproductive processes likewise lose their significance. There is no place in our modern mythology for the notion that the family has helped to make the wicked world we now inhabit. Rather, it is the demon of industrial society which breaks up our marriages and renders our children unmanageable. With a kind of populist passion, Lasch rails against 'the invasion of the family by the marketplace and the street, the crumbling of the walls that once provided a protected space in which to raise children, and the perversion of the most intimate relationships by the calculating, manipulative spirit that has long been ascendant in business life' (1977: 166). For their part, none of the more radical social scientists who would like to 'deconstruct' or 'disinvent' the Family have given us a coherent idea of what we should put in its place.[5] In dismissing liberal preoccupations with 'the family' as 'bourgeois claptrap', the Marxists have thrown the baby of reproduction out with the bathwater. Which brings us to the second bind: having been robbed by 'the family' of its wider social significance, 'reproduction' has been left to acquire a residual, metaphoric meaning.

### 3   THE METAPHORICAL DISTORTION

In contemporary social science 'reproduction', in its most general usage, has become a convoluted abstraction far removed from its biological frame of reference. If they use the word today at all, sociologists or anthropologists most probably mean something very abstract: the complex processes by which *our ideas about social structure* (rather than about our physical selves) are renewed.[6] When the liberal declares that 'the only function of the family that matters is socialization' (Lasch 1977: 130) it is plain that physical reproduction has been translated into notions of the transfer of culture. On the left, the metaphor is applied very freely in such phrases as 'the reproduction of labour power' or 'the reproduction of ideology' or 'the reproduction of the conditions of production'.[7] We are no longer talking about mothers and babies, or fertility and mortality, but such abstruse things as how our shared ideas about music or the environment or power get perpetuated over time. These matters are undoubtedly important, but it is clear that the authors of these ideas do not associate them with the organization of physical reproduction. This is not a problem until one meaning of reproduction starts to interfere with the other. Today, unless one is a demographer or a biological anthropologist, one must be emphatically explicit if one proposes to discuss social aspects of *physical reproduction*.

Marxist scholars have been particularly prone to this confusion of fact and metaphor.[8] Claude Meillassoux runs into this problem in his admirable efforts to take physical reproduction into historical account. As an anthropologist he is struck very forcibly by its importance in the social organization of primitive societies, but as a Marxist he is convinced that with the emergence of industrial society the reproduction of something completely different, *capital*, matters more: 'The relations of production revolve now around the means of material production and not any more on the means of human reproduction... The structural reproduction of the productive enterprise is not related any more to human reproduction but to the reproduction of capital, as a means of perpetuating and enlarging the relations of production' (1978: 168). In this Marxist scheme, production detaches itself from reproduction in the course of history. It is very important to see that the real change is in the meaning which Meillassoux ascribes to the word 'reproduction'. This lands him in trouble when he tries to figure out what happens to *human* reproduction in capitalist society. Has it simply vanished? Obviously not. His attention is therefore drawn back to the household, and its persisting importance in the 'reproduction of life as a precondition to production' (Meillassoux 1972: 101). Clinging tightly to the Marxist evolutionary scheme, Meillassoux concludes that what he calls variously the domestic 'society', 'community', 'economy' or 'mode of production' (1981: xii, 1983: 50) is some sort of anachronism, a carry-over into the industrial world of a piece of reproductive organization from our primitive past. 'Up to now and for an indefinite future, the domestic relations of production have been organically integrated into the development of each and all the subsequent modes of production' (1981: xiv). This, he tells us, is how traditional domestic organization in places like Lesotho can serve the industrial capitalists in South Africa so well – how one productive system can 'reproduce' another. But what about the 'primitive' households of the industrial capitalists themselves? What are they 'reproducing'? The primitive past or the capitalist present? We are forced to one of two conclusions: either the Marxist scheme cannot, after all, give us a consistent account of social evolution, of how one 'mode of production' yields to another; or it cannot give us a coherent explanation of the organization of human reproduction in modern society.

4 THE RETREAT TO INDIVIDUALISM

At least we can give the Marxists credit for trying to come to terms with these puzzles. The virtue of the grand historical-materialist framework is that it obliges us to 'think big', about the major classes of people which comprise social structure and have a hand in its transformation. From this perspective the activities of individuals matter only in so far as they express these larger interests, which may be another reason why Marxists do not think very much about the 'more personal' business of human reproduction. Liberal social scientists, on the other hand, are profoundly interested in the actions of individuals, but in many cases this produces a shortsightedness in dealing with social processes on the large scale. The analytical assumption that modernization has atomized society into a mass of individual 'rational actors' has fostered the notion that the western democracies are composed of socially featureless decision-makers, devoid even of age and gender. As Louise Tilly (1985) has explained with reference to nineteenth-century France, industrialization did not leave 'the individual' neutered and socially unfettered; it entrenched the gendered division of labour and the subordination of women. If women have failed to negotiate their way out of their political and economic subordination, it is not because of their failings as 'rational individuals', but because they remain tied into the social organization of reproduction in ways which liberal social theory has failed to comprehend. In earlier chapters I have stressed that individuals simply cannot and do not reproduce themselves, physically or metaphorically, which is one reason why analytical commitment to the idea of rational, self-seeking individuals offers too narrow a view of the organization of reproduction. Where individual choices obviously matter (conspicuously in marriage and divorce) it can offer interesting insights.[9] But when it comes to explaining reproductive processes in larger entities like the household, the approach weakens. Analyses of housework and child-rearing in the idiom of marketplace has recourse to such nebulous, individualized categories as 'psychic income' (Gronau 1977: 1122).

In the reckoning of Economics, 'the family' is under threat because it has not passed the test of efficiency. According to Becker, 'individualism replaced familialism because many family functions in traditional societies are more effectively handled by markets and other organizations of modern societies' (1981: 244). The argument of course is circular, because this kind of economics itself proceeds from individualist assumptions: rational individuals find efficient solutions in terms of what is rational to them as individuals. This has fostered two contradictory misapprehensions about the analysis of social processes like culture or reproduction: either they are excluded as irrational or non-rational; or they are translated into entities which *resemble* individual actors. Indeed, economists habitually treat all social groups, whether business firms or whole states, as entities with a single mind of their own ('IBM thinks that . . .' or 'America wants . . .'). This is notoriously the case in dealing with the material interests of 'families'.[10] The implications of this strike very deeply: census and survey data are routinely collected for 'individual families' (that is, 'households') because, as we know, these tend to be residentially separate units of production and consumption. But the combination of choosing this particular unit and treating it as if it were one person obscures the many important processes which go on *between* households (collaboration, credit, etc.) and *within* them – most significantly the organization of reproduction.[11] Feminist scholars in particular have pointed out that this unitary view of the household obscures the discrete interests of women in domestic activities. I know this to my chagrin and cost, having conducted hundreds of interviews with male 'household heads' on the assumption that they can tell me all I need to know about the economic performance of the group.

Attempting to study the social organization of reproduction in such a constricted frame of reference is surely absurd. Nevertheless, studies of mating, fertility, child-rearing and aging all gravitate back to the household as the social and statistical unit of enquiry, reinforcing our fixation with 'the family' and our assumption that other social units (firms, states) have no significant part to play in the organization of reproduction. Recently, social historians and anthropologists have tried to remedy this by 'disaggregating' households to their component individuals, observing the *life course* of each.[12] The approach has proved enlightening, but takes us back to individualism once again, and leaves the problem of reassembling the *relations of reproduction* from these isolated life-lines. Childhood, for example, is intelligible only in relation to parenthood and other, less obvious, relations like siblingship.[13] Moreover, it has been demonstrated that if we are interested in such things as economic performance and social status, the interaction of life-cycles within the domestic group is much more informative than the life-cycle of each individual.[14]

Understanding the need to organize reproduction helps to explain that most puzzling but least understood motive of man-in-history: selfish greed. The urge to accumulate, to pile up wealth against the threat of the future, to put other people in our debt, is as much a social as a selfish reflex. The supposition that capitalists are peculiarly motivated by this human failing, and that public generosity will bring us earthly paradise, denies that ineluctable aspect of our humanity, the material struggle to reproduce.

## 5  THE STATIC BIAS

The theme of reproductive *dynamism* is so basic to this book that my summary here will be brief. Although we like to think of families and households as fixed social modules, at some level of consciousness we must know that they are bunches of interacting life processes which are continually being undermined by time, and which require constant management. We may take comfort in our family portraits secure in their frames, but the sort of static image we like to put on the mantelpiece has very limited use when it comes to analysing the social dynamism of reproduction. Nevertheless, in sociology and anthropology we have used the same sort of family portraits to describe, compare and analyse reproductive groups around the world. We take a snapshot of a particular pattern of people and label it the 'Western nuclear' or 'Hindu joint' or 'African polygynous' family – although it should be plain that at some stage in their development most Hindu or African families are likely to have a 'nuclear' episode. The static classification is easy and convenient, but it tells us as much about reproduction as a sketch of a wing tells us about how a bird flies. Worse, typing families as if they were insects in a glass case can be downright *misleading*. Just as elvers and eels were for long thought to be different animals because they did not look alike, it may be difficult to imagine that a small 'nuclear' family is en route to becoming a large 'joint' household.[15]

Perhaps this is a basic limitation of the human mind: we are simply more adept at picturing structures than comprehending processes. The best we seem able to do is to chop processes up into a series of static pictures, and reckon that 'change' is the difference between one snapshot and the next. If it is difficult enough to explain how this sequence of states amounts to a process, how much more difficult is it to explain how one process helps to make another? Yet this is the purpose of this book – to explain how organizing human reproduction helps to make social history. The point is that each static image on its own will tell us almost nothing about the *process* of which it is a passing moment. Family types will not in themselves tell us how reproduction makes history. Natural scientists are getting quite good at this sort of explanation (for instance, how marine convection currents affect the food chain) but social scientists are still beginners.[16]

### 6  THE MICRO–MACRO BLOCK

If we want to know *why things happen* we have to study processes, because it is dynamic things, not static things, which cause change. Reproduction is unquestionably dynamic, but if we interpret it through fixed family types its active role in the making and remaking of human society will be lost to us. However, no matter how closely we watch the reproductive behaviour of a single group of individuals, it will not tell us all we need to know about history. This is a very old problem for social scientists, sometimes called the 'micro–macro' dilemma: how do we explain how the activities of thousands of individuals add up to that complicated entity we call society? Evolutionary arguments relocating the individual in the modern world have compounded the micro–macro polarity: the estrangement of 'the family' from wider social processes was the basis of the Maine's shift from social status to legal contract, of Durkheim's conception of mechanical and organic solidarities, and of Parsons's distinction between ascribed and achieved social status.

Explaining how static objects like bricks stack up into a building is a relatively easy micro–macro problem. But if we add the dimension of time and change, imagining some 'living' building material which is continually composing into rocks and decomposing into sand, what sense can we make of the whole structure? Explaining how micro *processes* like reproduction stack up into social history is a great deal more complicated even than that. In a sense, every household 'makes society' simply by being there along with every other household. But not every household 'makes history', in the sense that it alters the way all other households behave. Perhaps a major dynasty or revolutionary leader can have this influence, but usually it is the cumulative force of thousands of households making roughly the same sorts of change (raising fertility, adopting monogamy) over a long period which leaves an impression on the structure of society. As I noted in chapter 2, if all households developed simultaneously (all children being born in one year, all parents dying in another) we would see the historical effects of reproduction with startling clarity. We saw in chapter 6 how special projects like the Malaysian land schemes reveal the effects of this synchronizing of generations. But the fact that human reproduction is perennial, and that ordinary communities consist of households in different stages of development, masks their cumulative influence on social organization. Our mistake is to assume that because *only a small proportion at any one time* have raised fertility or adopted monogamy, this is historically insignificant. Today's statistics may be a deceptive guide to the macro significance of a micro process.

I have argued that people's involvement in activities which are cumulatively of great economic importance – investing or divesting, adopting or rejecting technical innovations – is largely determined by the phase they are in the reproductive process. If historical circumstances (boom, good harvests) are right, those households which are, on their own schedule, ready and able to take advantage of investment opportunities will do so, but the large-scale consequences of their actions may not be evident for some years. The challenge is to try to identify such movements in the making, not by identifying a new family *type* ('nuclear') but by noting adjustments to different aspects of the reproductive *process* (delayed marriage, greater longevity). A hundred thousand families, all proceeding differentially through the development cycle, can exert over several decades a massive, cumulative effect on the institutions of society: making demands for new welfare, employment or service institutions.

By the weight of their numbers they also change the ideals of family development themselves: the practical experience of one generation creates a model for the next to follow or reject. Thus the macro dimension of society in turn influences the micro activity of the social cells. Thinking this way can provide a radically different view of social structure at large: social dynamism is not just peculiar to 'the family' or 'the household', it is a vital aspect of *all* social institutions. Banks, schools, governments are all *social processes* of one kind or another, growing, changing, declining because of the particular activities which they contain. At the same time, it is important for governments or banks to put about themselves the appearance of solidity and permanence. However, if we are resolved to take a dynamic view of social organization, we must recognize that each of the various interrelated processes comprising society has a rhythm of its own. In this regard, human reproduction is slower and vaster than any industrial process we know. This is why it is a good deal easier to explain how setting up a factory changes the lives of people in the surrounding community, whereas we need a much broader and more sophisticated sense of the meanings of time to spell out how the social organization of reproduction in a particular locality affects the establishment and operation of a factory. This, as Tamara Hareven (1982) and others have demonstrated, is an analytical challenge of great subtlety, interest and importance.[17]

### 7 THE EMPIRICAL BIASES

These problems of time and scale all point to serious difficulties with the *evidence* which confronts us in our efforts to argue the historical influence of reproduction on society. Once again, it seems that these problems of perception have reinforced our false impressions of what reproduction is and does.

The duration of the reproductive cycle presents a major problem. A 'proper' study of it would involve *longitudinal observation*, that is, tracing particular individuals and their progeny over many decades.[18] This would in itself take time, outpacing the life of the observer as well as the historical context which most interests him or her.[19] If we are impatient and want to press ahead with our investigations *today*, we can try to play a trick on time. This involves taking advantage of the *differential* development of households in a community: if we cannot watch one household go through all its stages of growth and decline, we can pick out *several* households at *different* stages of development *today* and pretend that they represent snapshot images of a single '*typical*' cycle. This technique is well known to economists, demographers and others as 'cross-section analysis'.

In various forms this has been the procedure of everyone who has made a study of family dynamics: Le Play in his worker surveys, Rowntree (1922) in his York studies, Fortes (1949) in Ashanti, Chayanov (1966) in his scrutiny of Russian statistics and Glick (1957) in his work on US Census data. Although it is a great convenience, the trouble with substituting a cross-section for a time series is that it involves manipulations which often pre-empt the very things we may wish to discover – in this case, how the reproductive process relates to the political and economic processes, and the making of history.[20] The evidence of the time series and the evidence of 'real' longitudinal data can diverge significantly.[21] A sample of today's households gives us some clues about what is happening in history, but cannot tell us the whole story. To be more explicit: the household in our sample which represents the stage of establishment will be in the stage of decline many years hence, probably under quite different historical circumstances from the household which is representing the stage of decline in our sample *today*. The 'timeless' cross-section analysis can only presume that households being established today will decline *in the same way* as the older generation, but this has the effect of shutting history out of the analysis.[22]

Our problems with the time-series tactic begin with our selection of reproductive units for study. If we take 'households' how will we define them? The people who live under one roof, or share a budget, or eat from one pot, or sleep behind a single locked door? All these have been used in family studies, but we now know that the programme of domestic development *alters* these production, consumption and residence arrangements (see J. Goody 1972). The static definition once again sets us off to a bad start in our efforts to explain the dynamic process. In collecting data we are usually obliged to focus on a single informant ('the household head'), although reproduction concerns a continually changing ensemble of people. Construing the life of the household as a function of a single person's career produces patterns which diverge significantly from the more complicated and temporally more extensive growth, decline and replacement of the whole group. Although explanations of the domestic cycle have usually been cued to the career of the senior male in the household, it may actually make more sense to focus on the wife/mother at the reproductive core.[23]

Another hazard of time-series analysis is that it can reduce the reproductive process to a crude demographic abstraction.[24] The network of relationships is robbed of its *social* meaning. Worse: social relationships may be deduced by some culturally relative logic: an adult woman in the household census data is presumed to be a 'wife', a female under fifteen years is presumed to be a 'daughter'. Such assumptions mask the farreaching differences between an elderly widower and an elderly bachelor. In this book I have stressed that economic and political meaning attaches not to some demographic configuration of people distinguished by age, sex or residence, but to the social relationships of father, son, daughter-in-law, stepson, cousin, etc. For this reason it is not surprising that even the most sophisticated demographic models of the family cycle have had limited explanatory power. The 'family cycle' is reduced to a rather weak demographic effect rather than a process which shapes social structure.[25] On the other hand, there is the danger that in arranging households in today's community to give an impression of domestic development past, present and future, we may mistake our statistical norm for a moral norm representing the sort of values and cultural ideas discussed in chapter 2. The importance of this error is, of course, that while statistics simply measure historical effects, morals can actually *cause* them.

## 8   THE HISTORIOGRAPHICAL BIAS

If families are deemed to have an existence in time at all, it has been time in a sense far removed from human history. In the homely image, reproduction makes the world go *round*, not forward. To what extent are historians themselves to blame for failing to understand that reproduction matters?

Until recent years historians have regarded 'social history' in general as a soft option, and at least one of them has protested that the historical study of the family and reproduction is an irrelevant fad.[26] They have been much more interested in the flight of time's arrow, rather than other substantive sorts of temporality more associated with continuity than change.[27] Historians have certainly been much more interested in centres of power, in great men and their actions rather than in slow-moving social undercurrents. Since most historians have been from the upper and middle classes it is not surprising that they should have focused on elite affairs. If they have a narrow view of reproduction, that too may be a product of their privileged class status. I have pointed out in chapter 8 that the social organization of reproduction can be manipulated by one social class in its dealings with another. According to Medick, 'Ruling-class perspectives not only determined the way contemporary observers perceived rural artisans; they persisted in the explicit or implicit middle-class bias which still seems enshrined in the conceptual approach and even methodological perspectives of much that is written in the contemporary history and sociology of the family' (1976: 314).

A new historiography has been in the making for some years now, much more concerned with 'micro' studies of common people, and with motives and meanings springing up from the masses. In the vanguard has been the French *Annales* school, followed closely by *History Workshop* in England and similar movements in America. The old historiography was much more interested in capital (property, accumulation, mercantile power) than in labour, especially its production in the domestic domain, and thus ignored the central importance of women in the process. Even radical historians have been insensitive to the cost of producing labour. Although indignant about the moral claptrap surrounding bourgeois visions of 'the family', Marx himself was evidently unaware of the extent to which reproductive dynamism was a particular affliction of the poorest working-class households. It is notable that the new generation of radical historians has been much less intimidated by those material laws of history of which I have complained above.[28]

We can accept it as a simple biological fact that reproduction is the instrument of human *evolution*, but to argue that reproduction is an instrument of human *history* – something closer to our own lifespan – evokes a peculiar scepticism. Until recently, the historical profession has not been altogether sympathetic to scholars who wish to argue that social structure and change emanates from the family. In many cases, this may be with good reason, because the precise mechanisms by which families make history never seem to be specified with sufficient clarity.[29] For a historian like Reuben Hill the outstanding problem is to establish not *whether*, but *how* 'family development' can be conceptualized 'as a dependent variable with sufficient scope and clarity to promote its understanding and suggest its determinants' (1977: 33). The burden of my argument in this book is that 'family', itself a multifarious institution, is indeed a weak instrument of historical change, and that we must look much more closely into the organisation of reproduction, which creates families and much else besides, if we are to understand the impetus for change which wells up from the masses.

### 9   THE DISCIPLINARY PREROGATIVES

Social scientists have never had a firm grip on the study of human reproduction, partly because they have come to regard biological explanation as intellectually hazardous or simply wrong. 'The phrasing of social relations in biological terms is in effect an ideological mechanism to turn social facts into natural and therefore immutable facts' (Stolcke 1981: 167), a tendency made disreputable by the nineteenth-century theories of *race*, and by the ideologies and practices of Nazi Germany. Accordingly, interpretation of human reproduction has gone by default to the biologists and their social science affiliates the demographers. At various points in this book I have insisted that, however valuable their contribution may have been, these disciplines have been able to tell us relatively little about the *social organization* of reproduction. In reading and thinking about this topic I have been struck by the fact that illumination has almost invariably been found by moving imaginatively between disciplines rather than labouring in the traditions of one of them. The main pioneers of the idea of the family and household development cycle are widely dispersed in time and space, but are all notable transgressors of disciplinary boundaries: Le Play the engineer-historian-philosopher; Chayanov the agronomist-political economist; Fortes the psychologist-anthropologist (who once told me how profoundly he was inspired by the biologist D'Arcy Thompson's classic *Growth and Form* (1942)). Many of them faced academic disdain – and worse – for their leaps of imagination.[30]

Recently a new interdisciplinary heresy has emerged, initially labelled 'sociobiology'. The intolerant response among the established social scientists is only partly due to some extravagant claims which the new discipline made for itself in interpreting the origins of social behaviour.[31] Symons (1989) has pointed out that an important deficiency in sociobiological argument is the lack of some clear-cut mechanism by which genetic drives are translated into social behaviour. Precisely how is the evolutionary thrust of 'inclusive fitness' expressed in wealth, power, leadership and so on? If sociobiologists' interest in reproduction remains fixed on the question of how 'to get genes into future generations' (Betzig 1988: 9), they have many bridges to build before they can make plausible arguments about social organization: perhaps from physiology to psychology and thence to sociology, a route marked by some very old and deep disciplinary rifts.[32] Meanwhile the 'respectable' social sciences are left with notions of 'the family' which tell us precious little about the organization of reproduction, and rather too much about cosy middle-class fantasies of home and hearth.

I have found that I have had to spend a lot of time outside the conventional boundaries of my 'own' subject, anthropology, in my efforts to understand the social organization of reproduction. But since reproduction pervades so many aspects of our lives, anthropology, with its notorious eclecticism and its desire to view society 'holistically', may be a better starting point than most.[33]

## 10  HOME TRUTHS AND THE BIAS OF SUBJECTIVE EXPERIENCE

The most fundamental difficulty confronting social scientists is that we are our own subject matter. Indeed, the reason why we have social science at all is because we know that ultimately we cannot depend on the judgement of our own senses, and that there is nothing absolute about what we know and believe. Disciplines like anthropology and sociology are (or should be) engaged in the perpetual struggle for a bit of objectivity. We try to imitate the methods of our more confident colleagues in the natural sciences, making testable hypotheses, watching and counting, and giving ourselves the licence to ask people what would ordinarily be considered impertinent questions. But what we consider useful or interesting to study in the first place remains (as our jargon has it) a 'value judgement'.

Anthropology has made a business of exploring and explaining the ideas of exotic peoples, and has documented the great diversity of understandings of reproduction, family life and social structure. For a Marxist like Meillassoux we have been so preoccupied with 'the level of native representations' (1981: 49) that we have not understood the more absolute and universal nature of reproduction and production. However, I would insist that subjective views are important and interesting because people have to use the ideas at their disposal to come to grips with the destabilizing effects of the reproductive process. Culture is doubtless conservative, providing an assurance of continuity and order in the face of an unpredictable reality. But culture is not (as some materialists seem to suppose) an obstacle to knowledge, it is simply our (and Meillassoux's) best available means of understanding the world around us.

However, by clinging to their belief in an objective science of society and history, Marxists like Meillassoux have challenged our prejudices and convictions about the meanings of reproduction. If science, like primitive magic, offers some possibilities for prediction it may help us to come to terms with a future which often looks unpromising. After a lengthy period in which transformations in production have dominated our lives, are we perhaps on the threshold of a new epoch, a 'post-industrial' world in which the reorganization of *reproduction* is in the ascendant?[34] If so, our present intellectual attitudes are not well disposed to perceive it. Are the economic consequences of surrogate parenthood, or *in vitro* fertilization, not at least as interesting as the economic *causes*? Similarly, an understanding of the impending crises in pensioning and geriatric welfare must surely depend on explaining the patterns of reproduction which have increased the average age of the industrial populations and separated the generations spatially, economically and perhaps politically. For all these reasons, state interest in matters of reproduction (ambiguously regarded as a sacrosanct family affair) is becoming increasingly contentious.

Having listened in fascination to the rhetoric of the most recent US presidential election campaign, I am aware how powerful and complicated the notion of 'the family' has become. It encompasses emotions of parental care, wholesome meals and morals, conjugal eroticism, sibling responsibility – all the things which are written into the scripts of dozens of TV dramas and situation comedies. But ultimately 'the family' is an outrageous simplification of a multitude of highly divergent interests and images. About as far as one can go in defining the Family as an absolute value is that the sentiments it evokes tend to be *strong*. Strong enough to mask many aspects of reproductive dynamism which I have been trying to reveal in this book. To understand their variety and their force we have to recognize that they, like the reality they seek to capture, are dynamic. In earlier chapters I have considered why the family sentiments of middle-aged people are likely to differ radically from those of young adults. Here I would add that our perception of *time itself* develops as our own lives unfold within the domestic context. In childhood the years have an immensity which increases the closer our memories can take us to the immemorial timelessness of the womb. Things that happened only a year or two ago for our parents occurred near the dawn of time for us. Youth and the phase of domestic establishment bring with them plans and investments, and a *prospective* sense of time, a future to be constructed and used. In the child-rearing years there is a sense of immediacy and increased pace, and then of 'lost time'. Unbelievably, the little ones have grown up and gone. With age and grandparenthood comes a more *retrospective* sense of time, with the ephemerality of present and absence of future.

I have made much of the fact that we seem to exclude time from our idealized visions of family life. God and good government willing, there will always be an America, and an American Family. It seems that *because* they are of life-and-death importance to us we have an acute emotional need to think of these basic reproductive groups as stable and permanent. The reality, which is the making of society and history, is a story of relentless and often hectic change in our own lives and in our relationships with those around us. Struggling to deal with provisioning, with growth and sexuality, death and authority, and with the caprices of weather, markets and governments, the Family is at least our pretence of solidarity. And to the wider community on which we try to dump as many of the burdens of reproduction as we can, the Family puts up a front of harmony and stability. There are good reasons to believe that this is more intelligible to poorer people who know the economic and political pinch of reproductive instability than it is to well-heeled academics or Presidential candidates.

Families matter both individually and collectively not because they are 'natural', stable, dependable social bedrock – which they are not. They matter because they are dynamic, and this animation enables us to *live*, continually remaking society, and providing a vital impetus for the making of human history.

# Notes

CHAPTER 1   INTRODUCTION

1   Popenoe (1988: 11ff.) traces the history of these ideas of 'family decline'.
2   See for example Hannan (1982: 65): 'anthropologists have been unable to develop general schemes for explaining variations in family structure in modern societies. Sociologists have supposed that the family has waned in importance as its functions have been assumed by the state and other bureaucratic institutions. The view that the family in modern society fulfills mainly "expressive" or emotional functions seems widely accepted... Until recently, the situation was even worse in economics. Economists have tended to view their subject matter narrowly as involving the production and distribution of valued material goods. The family plays no important role in these theories other than as a unitary consumer and supplier of labor.'
3   I have in mind the 'new household economics' of Gary Becker and his followers; the concern among political sociologists like Myles (1989, 1990) for the influence of the family life-cycle on the structure of the welfare state; the Darwinian revival in a dozen different disciplines; and the historical studies of domestic structure by Laslett, Goody, Hareven and others – to which I shall make frequent reference in this book.

CHAPTER 2   THE SOCIAL DYNAMICS OF REPRODUCTION

1   Olivia Harris (1981) discusses our assumptions about the 'naturalness' of family and household organization. See also Collier et al. 1982.
2   See Lancaster 1985 for a valuable survey of the higher-primate context for understanding the social organization of human reproduction.
3   See Rossi 1985: 176–7. This does not mean that all mothers operate in the same way, because like all other aspects of reproduction, motherhood is socially organized, and depends on what women know as well as on their instincts. See also Yanagisako 1979: 191.
4   Firth et al. (1970: 87ff.) note that their London middle-class informants included very variable sets of 'relatives' within the closer category of 'family'. 'Family' tends to be '*a term of affective significance*, and the inclusion and

exclusion of kin in "family" is a mode of classifying people not so much by degrees of consanguinity and affinity as by the affective quality of their relation to Ego [oneself]' (p. 92).

5   Nevertheless, synchronizing births might also be a great convenience, especially in matters of bureaucratic control (taxation, social service planning, etc.). At the moment schoolteachers, for example, have to contend with classes which often include children of quite widely divergent ages.

6   This is one reason why it has proved difficult to translate the term 'family' from English into other languages, such as Chinese (see Chang 1988: 110).

7   'According to the terminology formulated by the Bureau of the Census in 1947, a "family" is a group of two or more persons who live together and who are related by blood, marriage, or adoption; all such persons living together are regarded as members of the same family. A "subfamily" is a married man and his wife with or without children, or one parent and one or more own children under 18 years old, sharing the dwelling unit of a relative' (Glick 1957: 3).

8   'The utility of the domestic grouping has been great, even though no cross-cultural definition of the nature of activities has ever been worked out to any satisfactory degree' (Buchler and Selby 1968: 47). On the problems of defining and studying the household see Yanagisako 1979, Laslett 1983, Wall 1983 and Netting et al. 1984.

9   Hajnal (1983: 99), for example, uses the organization of consumption, rather than reproduction or residence, as a key to defining the household in his historical studies.

10   See Sieder and Mitterauer 1983 for a somewhat similar attempt (describing 'real' households in nineteenth-century Austria) to diagram domestic development chronologically, from the perspective of headship of a particular (residential) unit.

11   See especially Fortes 1958, J. Goody 1972.

12   *Frérèche* is the French term for a household consisting of two or more married brothers and their families. It has been used to describe similar arrangements in other parts of Mediterranean and Eastern Europe (see for example Czap 1983: 130; Herlihy 1985: 137). It seems possible that some nineteenth-century authors may have mistaken the *frérèche* for a form of 'group marriage' – the sharing of wives (see for example Engels 1958: 220).

13   Hammel describes the extended family pattern in Serbia, from the sixteenth century until quite recent times. 'Division of the household seems to be encouraged more by the growth of sons' families than by any other factor, and brothers whose own sons are approaching maturity tend to hive off' (1972: 371).

14   Czap notes that the extended households he studied in nineteenth-century Russia have a very marked appearance of continuity, which disguises the cyclical changes within them: 'what we find is a family system characterized by an overwhelming proportion of "perennial households", households for which one can determine no beginning or end in a continuous sequence of generations' (1983: 141). See also Hajnal 1983: 135–43.

15   The distinction, closely similar to mine, which Hajnal (1983) makes in his comparison of Europe and Asia is between 'a joint household formation system' and a 'simple household' system. In any pattern of development a household may be reduced to the parent–child nucleus, but we should take care not to mistake a *single stage* in the extended or stem patterns of development for the *compact* pattern. Wheaton (1975: 606) makes the point that an ideal classification of household types would have to be 'based on the development cycle, not

on the individual stage'. See also Berkner 1976.

16 There is something emotionally attractive about the notion of these self-sufficient family corporations. The medieval Florentine author Leon Battista Alberti advocated a large, stable and mutually supportive household, and urged brothers to live together for as long as possible: 'To make of one family two requires double expenses ... I have never been pleased with the division of families, with brothers going out and coming in through more than one door' (Herlihy 1985: 134–5). But sustaining such an enterprise in the face of individual pressures for domestic fission is a major organizational challenge. Even in Alberti's own society few households managed to achieve this level of solidarity, no doubt because the managerial costs of sustaining a large household in the face of sibling rivalry tended to outweigh the material benefits.

17 From *La Réforme sociale* (published in Tours in 1872), quoted in translation by Silver 1982: 80.

18 Quoted from *La Réforme sociale* by Silver 1982: 260–1.

19 While some have questioned both the incidence of the stem family pattern and its analytical usefulness (see Verdon 1979), there are many well documented accounts of it in Europe and Asia. See for example Gibbon and Curtin 1978 on the Irish case; Collomp 1984 on France; Douglass 1984 and Comas d'Argemir 1988 on Spain; Berkner 1976 on eighteenth-century Austria; B. L. Foster 1978 on Thailand; and Kamiko 1977 on modern Japan.

20 Laslett calls these very general, mostly sublime rules 'noumenal normative norms': people may be unable to recite them, but their statistical effect testifies to their power. On the compact pattern which has prevailed for so long in Europe, Laslett remarks that 'I have been hard put to find a single reference to the undesirability of living after marriage with parents or with a spouse's parents in the whole body of English literary output. Yet here was a behavioral rule that seems to have been almost universally obeyed, from the earliest period, until the present day, in all social classes, in all English regions, in the countryside as well as in the towns' (Laslett 1984: 364). We shall consider the historical implications of this basic rule in later chapters.

21 Apical is the adjective derived from *apex*, which I think captures the idea of a household at the height of its powers.

22 American couples in the 1960s were apparently much happier in the earlier stages of domestic development than in the later stages. According to Duvall (1971: 499): 'Both husbands and wives rate highly the beginning marriage, childbearing, and child-rearing stages, and are at a low point in satisfaction with their present stage while launching their children from the home. After the last child has grown and gone, satisfaction of both partners with their present stage in the family life cycle rapidly increases to about the levels reported when the first child was expected.'

23 For a discussion, see Duvall 1971: 127.

24 Bruce W. Brown, who has examined such advertisements over a fifty-year period, discovered that two-thirds of them depicted couples with children, a quarter of them couples in the pre-parental stage, and only a twelfth couples in the post-fission stage (1981: 21).

25 See Ronald Cohen's account (1984) of aging as 'an inner experience' and as 'a causal force that shapes the society'. From this psychological perspective, Strong observes that: 'In each family there are, in reality, two families: the formal family, created by convention and function, and the experiential family, created by feelings and relationships... A man and woman may be legally

married to one another, live in a quiet home with their children, and perform their roles without ever experiencing themselves as being married' (1973: 457).

26 Baxter and Almagor remark, apropos East African societies, on 'the paradox that a man must be a husband before he is a full man and must depend on a wife to be independent' (1978: 12).

27 There are parallel terms for this status everywhere, for example *Etxekojaun* and *Etxekoandrea*: 'Lord/Lady of the Household' in Basque country (Douglass 1984: 113). 'Mrs' is an abbreviation of 'Mistress': 'The female head of a household or family and, by extension, of an establishment of any kind' (Oxford English Dictionary). It is definitely a 'power word', unlike 'Miss' – although that too derives from 'Mistress'.

28 *Harper's Index* (December 1986) reported that in 1957, 80 per cent of Americans regarded an unmarried woman as 'sick' or 'neurotic', and that by 1986 38 per cent still felt that being single was 'not a fully acceptable life style'.

29 The ubiquitous significance of the first-born has been explored by Fortes 1974.

30 Tilly (1985) gives a detailed account of the economic significance of birth order in a linen-producing region of France in the nineteenth century.

31 See Nahemow 1979.

32 See J. Goody 1983 and Mitterauer and Sieder 1982: 161–2.

33 In our societies 'norm' itself has acquired additional statistical meanings which are a source of confusion. Mean, median and mode are various measures of 'central tendency' in a range of numbers – giving us the idea of an 'average' or of the 'greatest frequency'. However, there is no reason why the statistically 'average' family (e.g. a particular combination of males and females of particular ages) should look anything like the 'ideal' household represented in the 'apical norm'. Worse, since it is almost impossible to calculate with any accuracy all the social variables that make an 'average' household, the apical norm is sometimes simply *assumed* to represent a statistical average. Thus, for long the US Bureau of Labour Statistics modelled domestic budgets on two 'typical' family forms: (a) a *'standard'* family comprising a thirty-eight-year-old employed man, his unemployed wife, a son aged thirteen and a daughter aged eight; and (b) a retired couple (Oppenheimer 1974: 229). The first of these is only a 'moment' in a particular pattern of domestic development, represented by only a very small number of households at any time. See also Keller 1980: 69.

34 Larger populations in which distinct strata of rich and poor have emerged over many generations often reveal this relationship between the norms of domestic development and the acquisition (and transmission) of wealth. See, for example, Freedman 1966: 43–5 on south–east China in the prerevolutionary period; and Esther Goody 1973 on the Gonja of northern Ghana.

35 Citing the example that the continued emotional and other dependence of Americans on their children in old age is incompatible with their enthusiasm for fewer children and the likelihood of divorce, Laslett (1984) suggests that the relationship between such norms and actions is 'irrational'. I would prefer to say that there are two distinct rationalizations at odds here, distinguished mainly by the greater uncertainty of the (reproductive) long term over the (economic) short term.

CHAPTER 3   ECONOMIC AND POLITICAL RELATIONS OF REPRODUCTION

1 Sexual dimorphism dictates that with gestation and parturition this prime responsibility falls to women. As Pfeffer (1985: 44) remarks, 'Reproduction . . . is unique in that it is the only bodily function not essential for the maintenance

of an individual's survival; rather . . . it is connected with the furtherance of the human species and as such carries meaning and significance different from say digestion or respiration. Because it is the only bodily function that is different in men and women, it lies at the heart of debates about gender.'

2 See Minge–Kalman (1977) for an account of the dependency ratio. A basic definition of dependency ratio in households is 'the number of dependent aged and children per one hundred persons in the economically active age range' (Reyna 1976: 186). Wrigley and Schofield reckon it as 'the number of those aged 0–14 and 60 or over per 1000 aged 15–59' (1981: 444). I have taken it to be 'the sum of household members aged under 15 and over 65, divided by the sum of those under 15 and between 15 and 65' (Robertson 1987: 171). It will be noted that these calculations ignore sex differences.

3 We can see this in the isolated 'street people' of our societies, or in Colin Turnbull's startling tale of the self-seeking Ik, desocialized through hunger and disaster (1972).

4 See Sahlins 1972.

5 See Meillassoux 1981: 16–17.

6 See Meillassoux's account of 'delayed production' in agriculture (1981: 27).

7 For a discussion of these issues, see James C. Scott's *Moral Economy of the Peasant*, 1976.

8 Nimkoff and Middleton (1960), using Murdock's World Ethnographic Sample of 549 cultures, point to the statistical association of the 'independent family type' with hunter-gatherer societies, and 'extended family type' with agricultural-pastoral societies. Reyna (1976), writing about the Barma people in sub-Saharan Chad, explains how retaining able-bodied adults in a household reduces the dependency ratio and allows higher overall levels of productivity. For further discussion of economic implications of the extended pattern of domestic development see Befu (1968) on Japan; Silverman (1975: 180–1) on Umbria, central Italy; and Fuller (1976) on the Nayar of south India. Wheaton (1975) gives a useful survey of the extended or 'joint' pattern of domestic development and its economic rationales in Europe and Asian history.

9 In a very different context, Barth (1964) explains the demand for shepherding labour among the Basseri nomads of Persia, and how insistence on a compact pattern of domestic development must be accommodated by 'co-operative herding units' of between two and five households ('tents').

10 Gordon Hughes and Malcolm Hall; for details see Robertson and Hughes 1978.

11 On the need to be provident, Ganda say, 'Never lay out a small pen for a breeding goat.' Cain (1978) explains the relationship between the cycle of domestic development, economic security and the accumulation of wealth in Bangladesh. Critical factors are children's net labour contributions, the ability of household resources (especially sons) to withstand periodic crisis (flood, drought), and the ability of the group to survive property attrition on the patriarch's death.

12 The costs of this 'unequal development' have been at the roots of Uganda's political misery over the last thirty years; see Nabudere 1980, and Hansen and Twaddle 1988.

13 It is notable that the compact pattern is characteristic of fisherfolk everywhere and at all times. Fishing is also notoriously difficult to place within any conventional evolutionary schema (hunter – nomadic pastoralist – farmer – urbanite). Fishing, ancient and modern, is a form of hunting-and-gathering but, like pastoralism, is almost invariably integrated with some form of

agriculture, whether directly or through trade, and relations of production (e.g. share-catch arrangements) are remarkably similar on primitive canoe and deep sea trawler. No other way of making a living confronts higher degrees of uncertainty, which is probably why fishermen are typically obsessed with both luck and skill, and seek short-term security in pragmatic forms of collaboration and exchange. Exclusive, property-owning family corporations are much less characteristic of fisherfolk than ramifying family networks which provide people in relatively isolated settlements with very open choices of working association and marriage partner. Fishermen have also been pioneers of cooperative capital, savings and credit organizations, which cut across family ties and, in the form of large-scale unions, work to protect fishermen's trading interests in the wider society. The greatest inhibition on the progress of fishermen is their distance from centres of economic and political power, on which their trading relationships in particular are dependent. (See, for example, Firth 1966.)

14 See for example Gove et al. 1973 and Oppenheimer 1974.

15 See Rowntree 1922. Rowntree was certainly not the *first* to comment on cyclical stress in the compact pattern of domestic development. In a sixteenth-century tract on 'provision for the poor', Henry Arthington identified three stages of hardship, directly similar to Rowntree's; these were the deserving 'impotent poore' (R. M. Smith 1981: 607). The pattern was also noted by French commentators in the nineteenth century (Tilly and Scott 1978: 105–6).

16 We should recognise that the problems of cyclical stress are not confined to urban-industrial settings. For example, in a study which focuses on child malnutrition in north–east Brazil, Tanner shows how people struggle to escape from the cyclical squeeze. 'As they develop, *all* households will pass through a high-risk "Young" phase, and will suffer the trauma of severe malnutrition and possibly losing a child, as a matter of course. . . It is only once this period is past that income-gathering strategies can change to incorporate growing children into the household labour force and raise overall income per capita' (1987: 260). Pressure to buy land in order to expand production adds to the cycle of stress: leaving the farm to earn wages leads to a neglect of subsistence production which in turn causes hunger. Like Rowntree's model, Tanner's helps to show how and *when* diet supplements should be delivered by nutritional programmes.

17 See Wynn 1970. Schorr, for example, points out that welfare services tend to treat families *after* they have become problems, rather than concentrating resources prophylactically at the earlier pressure points in the 'family life cycle squeeze' (1966: 22–3).

18 Laslett (1984: 371) points out that the domestic *economy* is often in the hands of women – the more so, perhaps, in poorer households.

19 The most influential account of this was L. H. Morgan's *Ancient Society*, 1964.

20 A !Kung mother carries each child a total of about five thousand miles during the first four years of its life (Lee 1979: 312).

21 This is discussed by England and Kilbourne 1990.

22 For a useful survey of explanations of the subordination of women see Sanday (1981: 163–83). It is, she says, 'a complex question, for which no one answer suffices' (p. 8). She inclines tentatively to a cultural/ideological account, rather than to the more materialist views of Meillassoux and others. Biological explanations of male supremacy, which usually turn on such issues as anatomical strength or relative vulnerability to illness (see Pfeffer 1985: 31), are much less in favour today.

23 See O. Harris 1981: 151.

24  For example, the Tiv of Nigeria see the household as 'a group of people who work together and share the produce of their work in organized ways. . . Common residence and the jural aspects characteristic of the compound itself, typically reinforced with kinship ties, combine to make it one of the strongest emotional centers of Tiv life, and the phrase "one compound" (*ya mom*) is a strong affective phrase of unity' (Bohannan and Bohannan 1953: 19).

25  Hartmann, for example, has insisted on viewing 'the family as a locus of *struggle* . . . a *location* where production and redistribution take place' (1981: 368).

26  For an illuminating account of this 'knot' of individual interests in the rural Bangladeshi household, see Cain 1978: 431–3.

27  Here is a normative image from the nineteenth century, drawn from *Chambers's Information for the People*: 'The marriage state is the foundation of one of the most sacred and important institutions in society – that of a family. A family is a little commonwealth, jointly governed by the parents, but under the more special guardianship and direction of the husband and father, who is morally and legally the *head of the house*' (Chambers and Chambers 1875: 559). Compare Engels (1958: 218), quoting Marx: 'The modern family . . . contains within itself in *miniature* all the antagonisms which later develop on a wide scale within society and its state.'

28  For a discussion, see Bloch 1973. It is notable that we extend our terms for the relations of reproduction to particularly important friendships and associations ('brother', 'sister', 'godfather', 'mother superior', and so on) rather than vice versa.

29  This is discussed by E. Wolf 1982: 88–99.

30  For an assertive statement of this point of view, see Schneider 1984.

31  Because lineages or clans vary greatly in how they are organized and operate, we should recognize that they can have very different forms and functions in different societies. Simply to declare that a particular society 'has patrilineages' is very uninformative. (See Kuper 1982.)

32  The classic account of this 'genealogical charter' is by Bohannan 1952.

33  Lasch concludes that: 'As business, politics, and diplomacy grow more savage and warlike, men seek a haven in private life, in personal relations, above all in the family – the last refuge of love and decency' (1977: xiii). 'The family has slowly been coming apart for more than a hundred years,' he declares; 'the modern world intrudes at every point' into the family 'and obliterates its privacy' (pp. xiv, xvii). See also Hareven 1987 on the history of domestic privacy.

34  For an ambitious attempt to explain the relationships between the public and the private domains see Commaille's 'political sociology of the family', 1987.

35  Britain has the curious category of 'patrial', a means of discriminating in favour of those immigrants (preponderantly white) whose parents had birthright even if they themselves were born abroad.

36  Notable discussions of the issue of social scale, and its relationship to notions of continuity in society, are Wilson and Wilson 1945 and Barth 1978.

37  Tait, for example, tells us that among the Konkomba of northern Ghana, 'all structures from the family to the clan are unstable, though the major lineages and clans, at least, are conceived as permanent. They have political functions' (1956: 220).

38  For a detailed study based on this adversarial view of family and society, see Sennett 1970.

39  For an illuminating study of the relationships between individual, household and state in Mexican and Filipino urban households, see Hackenberg

et al. 1984.

40 Stoler (1985) has provided an illuminating account of the political, economic and sexual manipulation of women in the context of colonial plantation agriculture in northern Sumatra. 'Servicing the sexual and more general domestic needs of male workers and managers was more of a necessity than a choice, given that women's wages in 1894 were half those of men and were inadequate to meet daily dietary requirements, let alone other necessities.' Stoler concludes that 'women were kept available and "willing" to perform these services by careful design' (p. 31) and that 'estate policies have not only compounded the subordination of women but have ensured the political and economic vulnerability of the work force as a whole' (p. 210).

CHAPTER 4   THE ECONOMIC ORGANIZATION OF REPRODUCTION

1 For a tentative exploration of the link between domestic processes on the one hand, and population structure and social institutions on the other, see B. Foster 1978.

2 Father and son are 'emotional symbols of very great power' for the Irish farmers described by Arensberg and Kimball. 'They cannot be divorced from the pattern of relationships which they symbolise', and 'To separate their social from the economic activities is meaningless ... there is an absolute coincidence of "social" and "economic" factors within single relationships' (1968: 60–1).

3 See Barker-Benfield's fascinating essay (1978) on the 'spermatic economy' in nineteenth-century America. Of course, reproduction provides our basic vocabulary of obscenity and can be applied to virtually anything; but industrial processes in turn provide us with reproductive slang – shafting, grinding, baby-machines, etc.

4 For example, England and Farkas (1986: 74) describe the household as 'a little factory' for all sorts of goods and services, including the production of children. From a robustly neoclassical economic perspective, Gary Becker concludes that 'a kinship group is a reasonably effective "insurance company"'; however, 'kinship is less important in modern than in traditional societies because market insurance is used instead of kin insurance, market schools instead of family schools, and examinations and contracts instead of family certification' (1981: 238, 243). Pollack provides another example of this line of argument, concluding that the larger household may be a relatively efficient insurer in the face of 'old age, separation and divorce, unemployment, or the illness and death of an earner'. It has the advantage of more thorough information, and family ties reduce selfish opportunism. By dispensing with accounts, audits, contracts and other bureaucratic paraphernalia, the family farm is likely to face lower *transaction costs* than the business firm. However, compared with modern firms, households lack scale economies, and are usually unable to select out bad liabilities, refusing to insure the weak, the sick or the stupid (Pollack 1985: 588–91). The effect of these comparisons is to tell us more about the performance of insurance companies than the structure of households.

5 For a review of the feminist commentary on Meillassoux's argument, see H. Moore 1988: 49–54.

6 The social 'institution' of 'marriage by capture' is in fact well known to anthropologists. According to Meillassoux, 'Abduction encapsulates all the elements of the enterprise of the inferiorisation of women and anticipates all others... Made inferior because of their *social* vulnerability, women are put to work under male protection and are given the least rewarding, the most tedious

and, above all, the least gratifying tasks such as agriculture and cooking' (1981: 29).

7    The phrase 'in-laws' seems to signal the *jural* significance of marital relations.

8    J. Goody (1969: 70) quotes the nineteenth-century anthropologist Edward Tylor to the effect that mankind is faced with the alternative of marrying-out or being killed out.

9    See, for example, Brandes's 1976 discussion of '*La solteria*, or why people remain single in rural Spain'; and Schuler 1987: 46–72 on '*non*marriage' in resource-scarce regions of the Himalayas.

10   Fuller 1976: 2–6 discusses accounts of polyandry among the Nayar elite in South India, in the eighteenth century.

11   For discussions of polyandry see Berreman 1962; Mair 1971: 144ff.; Schuler 1987; N. Levine 1987, 1988; and J. Goody 1990: 137–53.

12   See Comaroff 1980 for a critical discussion of various interpretations of marriage payments and their meaning.

13   See J. Goody 1976b: 124.

14   This was brought home to me in Lesotho, where the plough has been used for more than a hundred years. Women whose menfolk were away in the South African mines complained of the physical difficulties in trying to plough.

15   On bridewealth and dowry, see especially Goody and Tambiah 1973.

16   Since the 1960s, the scarcity of children and the increase in divorce rates in our societies has disposed more men to claim paternal rights over children.

17   These, and similar arrangements among the Nuer of the Sudan, are described by Evans–Pritchard (1951: 109–123).

18   For this reason, Marx and Engels took a dim view of monogamy, seeing as its purpose 'the begetting of children of undisputed paternity; this paternity being required in order that the children may in due time inherit their father's wealth as his natural heirs' (Engels 1958: 221). As society evolved, men 'invented' patrilinearity and the patriarchal monogamous family to guarantee inheritance to 'their own' children (pp. 213–16). See also Stolcke 1981: 161.

19   I have described my experiences of these domestic arrangements in Uganda (Robertson 1978: 85–92).

20   The same point is made by R. M. Smith (1986: 46), viewing marriage in English history over many centuries: 'marriage may be more appropriately considered as a *process* than a status.' Francis Bacon wryly observed that 'Wives are young men's mistresses; companions for middle age; and old men's nurses' (Macfarlane 1978a: 110). For their part, husbands may complain that the winsome lass they married is transformed all too quickly into the authoritative matron and then into the elderly shrew. Adapting to these changes usually requires some effort (or divorce), and the experience undoubtedly affects our moral judgements and the advice we give to others.

21   See Robertson 1973: 248–51.

22   Cain (1981: 36–8) points out that the nuclear family/modernization hypothesis, stated most clearly by Goode, still leads observers to expect the imminent demise of 'joint' households in South Asia. Given the underdevelopment of alternative welfare institutions, such a development is very unlikely.

23   See Oppong and Bleek 1982 for an illuminating discussion of birth control in one particular West African context.

24   This trick was noted by Nicholas Culpeper, the seventeenth-century physician and herbalist (McLaren 1984: 41).

25   An interesting example is 'woman marriage' or 'gynaegamy', in which an

infertile woman 'marries' another woman, paying the costs and completing appropriate ceremonies. 'The man cohabiting with the "wife" of such a marriage is only the "genitor" of the children, who are considered the lawful children of the woman who has contracted the marriage with the mother; in some ethnic groups she even pays bridewealth for her' (Schott 1988: 98–9). Evans–Pritchard (1951: 111) reports that occasionally a Nuer woman may undertake this sort of marriage to raise patrilineal heirs for a dead kinsman.

26 Petchesky (1981) examines the political and economic pressures – domestic and national – which force women to 'opt for' sterilization. She cites the case of four women workers at the American Cyanamid chemical plant in West Virginia, who 'chose' sterilization, to avoid losing jobs which were officially regarded as a threat to their reproductive functions.

27 Engels, who took a very dim view of bourgeois ideals of the 'patriarchal monogamous family', noted that the Napoleonic Code of nineteenth-century France allows conjugal infidelity to the husband 'as long as he does not bring his concubine into the conjugal home' (1958: 221).

28 Anthropologists have shown considerable interest in the regulation of intercourse and pregnancy in the period during which a woman is breastfeeding her child. Lactation is known to reduce fertility, and deferring weaning for two or three years longer than strictly necessary may be an institutionalized form of birth-control. More explicitly, sexual relationships may be tabooed until a child stops feeding at the breast. Richard Lee has examined the practicalities of these controls among the !Kung San. With food and equipment to carry, !Kung women have good reason to minimize the number of children under four years old. They say 'A woman who gives birth like an animal to one offspring after another has a permanent backache.' Breastfeeding until the child is as old as four or five helps to reduce fertility so effectively that there is little evidence of abortion or infanticide (Lee 1979: 312). One implication of this, according to Lee, is that when !Kung settle down to an agricultural way of life, birth spacing is likely to be reduced and the population will increase (pp. 17–8).

29 The classic survey of penis sheaths is by Ucko 1970.

30 See the survey of infanticide by Scrimshaw 1984. Schulte (1984: 77) reports that infanticide was 'an event occurring within the everyday circumstances of life and work' in nineteenth-century Bavaria, especially among farm servant-girls. After their two to seven year official sentences, such girls were often reincorporated in local communities with little disgrace.

31 In recent decades the plight of the refugee has become distressingly common, political and ecological disasters putting entire populations, young and old, on the move.

32 For discussion of the 'demographic transition' see Watkins 1986: 421–2, Simmons 1985 and Coale and Watkins 1986.

33 See Simmons 1985 for a helpful survey of diverse theories of fertility, the overall message of which is that clear, comprehensive and intellectually rigorous explanations are not yet within our reach.

34 'Marxist theories of fertility see little independent role to be played by cultural or biological factors' (Simmons 1985: 28).

35 For example, Becker declares that a market for children would not work because 'parents would be more likely to put their inferior children rather than their superior children up for sale or adoption if buyers were not readily able to determine quality' (Becker 1981: 98–9).

36 Meillassoux's argument that women have little competitive interest in men as

a scarce resource may partly explain why women are unlikely to refer to their valued property (jewellery? domestic appliances?) as 'he'.

37 The capital debt on Hong Kong's Mass Transit underground railway system extends well into the next century, long after the return of the territory to the Peoples' Republic of China. Tomorrow's uncertainties affect our calculations much less than today's.

38 See Espenshade 1977 for an illuminating survey of discussions of the economic value of children.

39 *Los Angeles Times*, 3 June 1990.

40 Children's insurance was introduced in the late nineteenth century, but was sternly resisted by many as pricing the priceless, and placing temptation before unscrupulous parents (Zelizer 1985: 117ff.)

41 See Zelizer 1985: 201ff.

42 There has been a keen debate about the direction in which the benefits flow – up from children or down from parents – in different kinds of economy, and how this affects decisions about child-rearing. Caldwell (1981) has argued that pre-industrial modes of production are characterized by a net flow of resources from the junior to the senior generation, which puts a premium on high fertility; and that the shift towards industrial capitalism reverses the net flow and reduces the 'value' of children. Commenting on this, Macfarlane notes that in West African societies *becoming a parent* is the focal interest in getting married, because benefits 'flow up' to them from children; whereas in our industrial societies, where benefits 'flow down', *becoming a spouse* matters more (1986: 40). Others have pointed out that both the compact pattern of domestic development and the net flow of resources from parents to children were prevalent in England many centuries before the industrial revolution (Laslett 1984: 40; and R. M. Smith 1981). However, these arguments about the 'net flow' of resources tend to overlook the fact that resources are moving both 'up' to parents and 'down' to children *at different stages* in the domestic and life cycles.

43 See Demos 1978 for an account of the aging process in colonial New England. In this land-rich, labour-poor environment, with extensive patterns of neighbourhood and kin cooperation, the elderly fared surprisingly well.

44 See also Hajnal 1983; and Cain 1985: 149.

45 Gaunt gives some graphic illustrations of the familial tensions involved: 'A classic example tells of a [Swedish] farmer who had turned over his property to his grown son and daughter-in-law and was being treated badly. Eventually he hit upon an ingenious plan and told the young couple that he hadn't given them all his wealth, but that he had more hidden away in a chest which he would leave to them when he died. From that moment his treatment became much better and continued good up to death. After burial the son and his wife rushed to open the chest, but the only thing they found was a long-handled club on which a verse was written: He who gives so that he must beg / Ought to be clubbed until he lies out flat' (Gaunt 1983: 260).

46 See for example Clark's study (1982) of East Anglia in the fourteenth century; and Gaunt 1983: 270.

47 'Today, young people form a horizontal group which feels above them the weight of two generations. The adults have the jobs and the old people have the wealth. Many a young household is devoting thirty per cent of its meager income to its small dwelling whilst their parents only devote five per cent' (Alfred Sauvy, quoted by Wynn 1970: 137). These concerns may have inspired

the recent surge of interest among social scientists in aging and its social organization. Hitherto we seem to have been squeamish about this topic, perhaps because none of us likes to get old, or die. See also Halperin 1984: 160.

48  See Rosenzweig and Wolpin 1979; Becker 1981: 239.

49  See Hochschild 1978: 16ff. However, Shanas (1973) seeks to dispel the 'social myth' that elderly people in modern societies are typically isolated: in the US, Denmark, UK, Poland, Yugoslavia and Israel, most still depend fundamentally on family ties.

50  See especially the work of Mead Cain 1978, 1981, 1985 on rural India and Bangladesh, where long-term survival strategies depend on a gamble with high fertility. 'Neither rural India nor Bangladesh maintains public or community-based institutions to provide for the needs of the elderly.' In such circumstances 'reproductive failure' – for the 17 per cent or 18 per cent who have no surviving son when they are over sixty – poses a grave threat to older people, conspicuously for the poor and for women (1981: 26).

51  Sex preferences in children find expression in the 'survival' rate for girls or boys: on male–female discrimination in infanticide and child mortality see Johansson 1984.

52  Macfarlane 1986; J. Goody 1976a: 90ff.

53  'It has often been pointed out that in many societies the alternatives to investing in children are either non-existent or unattractive. There are no banks, no stocks and shares, no pension schemes, and no other forms of long-term storage for temporary profits. . . Although children may for a while be a burden, as is all saving, they are at least one way of accumulating resources against times when they will be needed' (Macfarlane 1986: 70).

54  'One of each' seems to be the norm in our societies; if the boy is older than the girl in this family portrait it may be a memory of our European/Asian preferences.

55  See especially Becker 1964.

56  The rising middle classes are very clearly the pioneers of fertility reduction in the western world; in the bourgeoisies and aristocracies of sixteenth- and seventeenth-century Italy, the late age (of men) at marriage and the high rate of those never married are very striking (Livi–Bacci 1986). Rapid economic development in recent years has had much the same effect on fertility patterns in countries like the Philippines, Korea, or Taiwan.

57  The extent to which pets have become a cheap substitute for children in family life has often been remarked upon. In a recent American TV film (30 August 1988) about pet cemeteries (animals are now given the obsequies due to close kin) a proprietor who claimed to 'know all about it' pointed out that people in three phases of family life need pets: children who lack other siblings; couples who have deferred child–rearing and need 'something to hug'; and old people who don't have *grandchildren* to hug.

58  In Philadelphia in 1880, Irish children living with both their parents contributed between 38 per cent and 46 per cent of their household's earnings (Zelizer 1985: 58, quoting C. Goldin). Mamdani (1972, 1981) discusses the relative value of children in pre-capitalist rural 'families', and in the 'proletarianized masses' of Third World urban slums where 'it is not unusual to find whole families who are supported by the children' (1981: 48). The 'rationality' of the bourgeois, propertied classes, critical of this profligate breeding, is simply out of context: 'Exploitation is viewed merely as poverty, and the explanation of poverty becomes the poor themselves' (p. 49).

59    In his novel about Spain, *Voices of the Old Sea*, Norman Lewis writes: 'In many areas of Mediterranean poverty – a poverty I had become familiar with – large families are the thing, and it is a proud, although almost everyday accomplishment for a woman to have borne ten children by the time she is thirty-five. The economic facts are that children in a city offering endless opportunities for low-grade, low-paid employment, are an insurance against economic disaster, and from the age of eight upwards many of them work to contribute small sums to the family budget.

'In an impoverished fishing village the sea is the only employer and the resources it provides are strictly finite. A family of fifteen children in Naples may be something to boast about. In Farol where many families remained voluntarily childless, one-child families were common, and any number of children in excess of two was rare and to be deplored. [They] kept their families down by postponing marriages until the late twenties, by sexual abstinence – many couples infrequently occupied the same bed – and by the devices furnished by the Curandero. Every time he arrived he took time off to go on a hunt for the small, densely-textured local variety of sponge to be hooked out of fairly shallow water, thereafter cleaning, and shaping, and offering each specimen with a supply of prophylactic ointment made up from lard impregnated with crushed hemlock' (Lewis 1985: 23).

60    Becker and Tomes (1976: S143) argue that in our societies, compared with the demand for quality in children, the demand for quantity is more responsive to increases in parental income. See also Becker and Lewis 1973; T. W. Schultz 1973; De Tray 1974. In the western media we are once again seeing the association of larger families with more affluent lifestyles.

61    Efforts to take account of a household's *long-run* reckoning of utilities include various 'life cycle' and 'permanent income' hypotheses (see for example M. B. Johnson 1971: 66ff.). Models based on 'bargaining theory' are probably least sensitive to the reproductive calculus, although they have been applied with great enthusiasm (see particularly the work of Becker 1981).

62    'Parents are viewed as deciding in a single period on the appropriate number of births needed to yield them an optimal lifetime number of children.' However, 'Reproductive behavior occurs sequentially, and the constraints on childbearing exert diverse influences on many other areas of economic and demographic decision making in the household sector' (T. P. Schultz 1974: 273).

63    See T. W. Schultz 1973, 1974; J. P. Smith 1977. Rejecting the notion that the female wage is a sound indicator of opportunity cost of child–rearing, Montgomery and Trussell note, 'There are many examples in which predicted female wages are shown to vary negatively with cumulative fertility.' They conclude that: 'Much of the work in the areas of marital status and childbearing has proceeded by analogy. Theories of age at first marriage have been (loosely) informed by theories of search in the labor market. Household production models have their origins in the standard theorems of international trade. The simpler models of fertility treat childbearing as fully analogous with the purchase of durable goods at known prices. We think it appropriate to ask just how much has been and can be learned about marital status and childbearing from the relentless pursuit of such analogies' (Montgomery and Trussell 1986: 264).

CHAPTER 5    THE REPRODUCTIVE ORGANIZATION OF THE ECONOMY

1    Douglass (1984) describes various 'mechanisms to accommodate vagaries in the

development cycle of the domestic group' in the Basque country of north–west Spain. A long-range strategy for augmenting an 'understaffed' stem household was full adoption of a nephew or niece from an 'overexpanded' household, or from an orphanage. A solution for the medium term was 'to contract the live-in services of an adolescent drawn from an overstaffed household. The servant received little more than room and board, and the arrangement often lasted for several years. At its conclusion he/she might be given a lump sum payment, a dowry, or passage to the New World' (p. 112). Hajnal (1983) makes the point that there was a similar circulation of servants, relatives and lodgers in the north–west European compact pattern of development but that this was *not* characteristic of the extended pattern ('joint' in Hajnal's term). On the 'balancing' exchanges of personnel in various European contexts, see also Wall 1983: 13ff.; Sieder and Mitterauer 1983.

2   Parkinson 1957.
3   See Becker 1964. T. W. Schultz (1973: S5) explains that investment in human capital 'rests on the proposition that there are certain expenditures (sacrifices) that are made deliberately to create productive stocks, embodied in human beings, that provide services over future periods. These services consist of producer services revealed in future earnings and of consumer services that accrue to the individual as satisfactions over his lifetime.'
4   For a nice account of how different kinds of interest in the land (ownerships sharecropping, wage-earning) affect the *quality* of work performed, see Martinez–Alier 1971: 180–1.
5   From scrutiny of his own and other people's survey data Chayanov could see that cyclical changes in the composition of the household had a profound effect on the operation of the Russian family farm: the kinds of crops it grew, the amount of land it used, the yields, and so on. To explain what was going on, Chayanov constructed a simple model based on a series of rather narrow assumptions. Households depended on their own supply of labour, but had access to extra land if and when they needed it. They were little affected by such external factors as money, markets, landlords and tax collectors. In Chayanov's modal household a peasant couple produced a baby every third year until they had nine children. In the early stages of this sequence the large proportion of little children meant that there were more people in the household consuming than there were producing. Only when the children were old enough to take an active role in farm work did the balance change, so that the household as a whole could produce more food that it actually needed for basic subsistence. Chayanov was able to express this as a changing *dependency ratio* (see chapter 3), basically the consumer demand of the household divided by the producer capability. This he illustrated in a graph which is comparable with the diagrams of Wynn (figure 3.2) and Rowntree (figure 3.3).
6   Barlett (1980: 140–5) uses Chayanov's model to illuminate the agricultural strategies of households in Costa Rica. See also Herring 1984 on Chayanov in the Asian context.
7   See especially the study by Donham 1985 on *Work and Power in Maale, Ethiopia*; and also Erasmus 1956.
8   This issue is discussed by Bloch 1973. On these ambiguous feelings about close kin, Firth et al. 1970: 93 quote a middle-class Londoner: 'One may *love* one's connections, but one has a *duty* to one's relations.' 'Relations' here are basically consanguineal kin, and 'connections' are in-laws.
9   Skinner 1968 gives an illuminating account of this alienation among fathers,

sons and brothers among the Mossi of West Africa.

10   The domestic stresses of property devolution in the stem pattern in early modern Haute–Provence, France, are described vividly by Collomp (1984). The all-important wedding 'match' in County Clare, Ireland, ideally assembles a *balance* of movable and fixed assets – 'farm and fortune', land and working capital (Arensberg and Kimball 1968: 106).

11   We could say that while a European or Asian woman brings capital into her marriage, an African woman brings labour.

12   From her own family the pastoral Fulani bride brings 'female property . . . the objects of a wife and a dairymaid' into her marriage – pots, calabashes, etc (Stenning 1958: 96).

13   Beauroy (1986: 33) has noted the significance of 'female property' in wills in late thirteenth- and early fourteenth-century England.

14   See A. Cohen 1969 67–8. Kirby notes that in northern Ghana, 'The tremendous influx of goods which come under the general category of cookware, domestic articles and women's clothing, together with the freedom in commerce, which has been traditionally given to women, has, in effect, put them in control of great stores of capital goods and most of the commerce.' An intriguing development in one area 'is that women entrepreneurs are now acquiring their own "wives" so that they can devote themselves full time to trading' (1987: 69).

15   On the practicalities of these scale economies, see Czap 1983 and Poni 1978.

16   See Robertson 1987.

17   See Bray and Robertson 1980; Robertson 1987: 19.

18   See Firth and Yamey 1964 for a collection of essays on the relations among capital, savings, credit and peasant social organization.

19   For an exemplary study of the political economy of consumption, see Sidney Mintz's (1985) history of sugar.

20   See J. Goody 1982: 192. I once made a fool of myself in a polygynous Ganda household by remarking to one of the wives that it was evidently her turn to make supper. The sexual innuendo made her flee in embarrassment (Robertson 1978: 90). Women produce food, men consume it; which is perhaps why a Ganda monarch was said to 'eat' the country on his accession. See also Stenning 1958: 109 on feeding and sleeping rotas among the pastoral Fulani.

21   See for example Tilly and Scott (1978: 43–60) on the importance of women in the organization of consumption in early modern England and France.

22   George Foster (1973) argues that peasants commonly behave as though they believe that economic good is limited and unexpandable. The implication is that if people believe that one person's gain must equal another person's loss, there are major social disincentives for economic development. However, if gains and losses vary over the domestic cycle, it is very hard to understand the subjective logic of Foster's idea of 'limited good'. People have to draw a *variable* share of the *fixed* good as their domestic needs and capacities change over several decades. How do they take account of this, as one generation gradually succeeds another? Foster's model, like so many others, does not take us into the flexible mind of the peasant so much as into the static mental frame of the economist.

23   Thus R. M. Smith (1981: 618) notes that for several centuries the English seem to have had an idea of 'a basic minimum living standard below which individuals were loath to descend when marrying and forming new households'. This welfare assessment (part of what Smith calls a 'culturally determined moral economy') found expression in upward or downward drifts in fertility statistics.

24   'Conspicuous consumption' of goods is a very common means of building

prestige. The 'potlatch' of the Northwest American Indians, the ceremonial destruction of property, is a famous example. Commenting on competitive giving in Melanesia, Young (1971) concludes that happiness is inflicting 'your' yams on someone else before they rot.

25 In his account, inspired by the work of Chayanov, Marshall Sahlins (1972) concludes that the 'domestic mode of production' is an 'impediment' to agricultural development. However, we must be careful not to confuse level of productivity with technical development. Average production of households across the domestic cycle will always be less than that of the most productive household, and enthusiasm for improvements may well be dampened by the demands of landlords and others; but none of this necessarily prevents households in the stage of expansion from seeking new and more efficient means of production, nor does it mean that the family farm is inherently less efficient than the agricultural firm. Friedmann (1978), for example, explains how 'simple commodity producers' on the family farm (especially in Europe), with their lower productive and reproductive overheads, could compete successfully against capitalist firms in the production of wheat for world markets. See also Reyna 1976: 193.

26 For a discussion of these issues see Friedland and Robertson 1990.

27 Marxists emphasize the political and historical significance of production for *use* and for *exchange*. Engels remarks, for example, that: 'When the producers no longer directly consumed their product, but let it go out of their hands in the course of exchange, they lost control over it' (1958: 267).

28 Gaunt (1983: 277) explains how European peasant farms came to be valued less in terms of their capacity to sustain a particular number of people, and more in terms of a dissociated 'speculative, free-market value'.

29 See Usher 1943: 5ff.; J. Goody 1986: 45ff.

30 The hostility of the medieval Christian church to banking, and especially the taking of interest on deposits, may be related to the fact that it was engaged in a vigorous campaign of its own to extract wealth in the form of endowments from private individuals (see J. Goody 1983).

31 See Usher 1943: 156.

32 For accounts of the early history of banking see Lopez 1979, Usher 1943, Hoggson 1926, and R. D. Richards 1958.

33 Venice did not, however, get around to forming its own state bank until 1587 (Hoggson 1926: 61).

34 See Lopez 1979: 11.

35 The moral justification for the scheme was that it would guide women towards 'an honorable and praiseworthy life' (Kirshner 1977: 193). Among the moral objections to the Monte was that it involved 'committing usury', and was a gamble, a kind of 'negative insurance' on a daughter's life and reproductive progress: when it was set up, funds were not payable if the daughter died or failed to marry and conceive. A more material criticism of the Monte was that it distracted resources from other forms of public investment.

36 See R. D. Richards 1958: 110ff.

37 'The engines of the Industrial Revolution, which made England so rich and powerful ... were moved by the oil of finance; and at the heart of the English financial system stood the Bank' Fisher 1936: 774.

38 Plumb 1950: 147.

39 These developments are discussed in chapter 7. See also Wolff 1919.

40 On the emergence of these 'banking' institutions in modern Third World

development, see Banton 1957, Geertz 1966, Little 1965 and Fallers 1967. Metge (1964) gives an excellent example of the extension of the *social* banking system of kinship and community into the money-and-market complex, by the creation of a formal 'transitional' institution: the New Zealand Maori *Komiti* (Committee), based on family networks but using formal credit-club organization to generate cash savings, mainly to finance funerals and maintain public assembly places. Papanek and Schwede (1981: 91–5) describe *Arisan* savings clubs in Jakarta, Indonesia, and their importance in providing women with some freedom from male control of domestic budgets.

CHAPTER 6 GENERATION, GENDER, AND SOCIAL CLASS

1  See Shanin 1972, Littlejohn 1977, Harrison 1977, Friedmann 1978.

2  The Chayanovian point of view may be at something of a disadvantage, because the whole idea of continuity is rather boring. Change is much more exciting. At any rate, Lenin and the Bolsheviks prevailed in Russia – at colossal cost to the peasantry.

3  On the complementarity of Chayanovian and Marxist explanations of social differentiation Banaji insists: 'We must not ask which of these tempos or tendencies adequately describes the dynamics of peasant farm-composition, but rather, *how they are related*' (1976: 1606). See also Herring 1984 with reference to Asia, and Deere and De Janvry 1981 with reference to Peru.

4  I have discussed this in more detail in Robertson (forthcoming).

5  In daily usage, the vocabulary of material and reproductive relations are quite freely mixed. We often use the language of generation and gender as a metaphor for class matters: 'patron', 'brother'; and variously 'brothers', 'sons and daughters' and 'mothers' of the revolution. If economic class is less often used as a metaphor for reproductive categories, it is probably because the latter have preceded the former historically.

6  The problem of reconciling ego-centred generational categories with broader social categories is illustrated by a quirk noted by Fortes: a young Tallensi man may be obliged to call a small boy 'Father' because the child is the junior sibling of his father, and thus technically of a different generation (1984: 102). In our society we sometimes get the same effect with the category 'uncle' or 'aunt'. Interestingly, precise chronological *age* matters much more to us than to people in other societies.

7  On May 1968 in Paris and the political meaning of generation, see Kriegel 1978.

8  In a remarkable study begun in 1932, Elder (1974) traces the influence of the childhood and adolescent experience of the Great Depression on the adult life courses of a generation which went on to become veterans of the Second World War, and 'baby boom' parents. 'Countless Americans who were born before 1929 are convinced, in retrospect, that the experiences of the Depression have had an enduring impact either on their lives or on the lives of persons living in their age group. And their children, now of college age or older, share this causal view when they assume that a childhood of scarcity accounts for outmoded parental conduct and priorities' (p. 150). Cain makes a similar observation of the impact of historical events on domestic development in Bangladesh. In one case, 'just as the process of household expansion through reproduction was getting under way, the 1971 war of liberation intervened, causing serious interruption of the agricultural cycle and a series of poor harvests.' This left the subsequent development of the household, and

presumably many others like it, severely impaired (1978: 428–30).

9   In an article in the *Los Angeles Times* (16 October 1988) Edward L. Schneider observes: 'the aging of America ... will produce burdens society has not yet come to terms with ... Unless major changes are made in both public and private medical and social services in this country, there will not be adequate housing, sufficient transportation or appropriate and affordable medical care to support most members of the baby boom generation in their final years of life.'

10   I have described the Felda project in Robertson 1984: 232ff.

11   As one bemused economist put it: 'There is an inherent conflict between the demographic growth path of the household and that of the yield profile of the production function. What is crucial is that the period of low yield, and thus low return, coincides with the latter stage of the life cycle of the family' (Chan 1982: 4).

12   The same dilemma confronts development projects of all kinds around the world – for example, the famous Gezira scheme in the Sudan, which was built in two phases, with two successive age cohorts (Robertson 1987: 80–127). My own first experience of this phenomenon was in Uganda, in an area which had been cleared of insect-borne diseases and was colonized very rapidly by large numbers of people (Robertson 1978). Quite reasonably, it was the young, not the old, who had migrated in search of new opportunities and who therefore constituted the bulk of the population of newly settled villages. When I lived there they were thriving, but I suspect that latterly they have become geriatric settlements, rather like the Malaysian schemes. Like the age cohorts in our housing tracts, communities in many societies have generational emphases: the 'age villages' of the Nyakyusa in Tanzania are well known to anthropologists (see Wilson 1951, and also Abrahams 1977). The moral, which accords with the experience of most 'ordinary' communities, must be that a mixture of households at different stages of development provides a more stable pattern of economic and political life in the long term. In *reality*, however, human history is often made by our pursuit of profits in the short term.

13   The American version of this saying seems to be 'shirtsleeves to shirtsleeves in three generatons', suggesting a faster turnaround.

14   It is worth noting that Rey himself was part of that youthful 'class' which unleashed generational war in Paris in May 1968.

15   Generations, for Meillassoux, are distinguished by 'anteriority and posteriority', particularly important in the long-term 'cycle of advances and returns' which characterizes agricultural and pastoral production. 'In the domestic community elders are such because they themselves have invested their own labor-energy in breeding juniors intended to reproduce the same cycle of advances and returns' (1981: 46–7, 80).

16   Of husbands in capitalist society, Engels (1958) blithely observes: 'within the family he is the bourgeois; and the wife represents the proletariat.' The problem with these historical materialist interpretations is their inability to explain why the subordination of women is essentially unaltered with the transformation of one system of production into another (e.g. feudalism to capitalism). Women's predicament did not *originate* with the expansion of capitalism, and the purpose of reproduction is not *simply* to 'reproduce class relations'. We must therefore doubt, as a remedy, 'the elimination of hereditary class privilege and forms of domination for whose persistence the subordination of women is as fundamental as the exploitation of labour' (Stolcke 1981: 175).

17   'In developing a Marxist-feminist analysis of the family', says Hartmann, 'I

concentrate on the nature of the work people do in the family and their control over the products of their labour' (1981: 368). In contrast, Stolcke has insisted that: 'To propose that women have first to become like men in order to become free is almost like suggesting that class exploitation might be ended by making it possible for workers to become capitalists ... The subordination of women is not resolved by depriving women of their procreative capacity or by converting women into workers' (Stolcke 1981: 175). See also England and Kilbourne 1990.

18  Asserting the importance of matters of heredity as well as of environment in understanding gender, Rossi declares that 'persistent differences between men and women and variations in the extent to which such differences are found along the life line are a function of underlying biological processes of sexual differentiation and maturation as well as social and historical processes' (1985: 162). From a more radical perspective, Mackintosh concludes that 'gender-typing is most rigid in areas crucial to the social relations which I have called the relations of human reproduction, and which generally incorporate male dominance and control of women's sexuality' (1984: 13). See also Pfeffer 1985: 44.

19  'Class relations', Meillassoux reminds us, 'are created, not out of *categories* like 'elders' and 'juniors', but through the dominance of entire, organically constituted communities which endow *all their members*, irrespective of age or sex, with prerogatives and privileges, over *all* the members of the dominated communities' (1981: 81).

20  There are numerous ethnographic examples of this, sometimes startling to a western observer. A mature Nuer woman, for example, can *marry* another woman if she has the resources to pay bridewealth, the offspring being raised as members of her own patrilineage (Evans–Pritchard 1951: 108–9). Brodsky (1986) gives a graphic account of the 'emancipation' of widows in Elizabethan London. Elsewhere, I tell the tale of an encounter in Uganda with a transvestite wife, whose husband told me he had liberated her with a 'Jubilee' celebration. 'In this unusual way he had chosen to formalize a transition which many Ganda women achieve less spectacularly. After twenty-five years her independence and authority had been recognised, and she had become, in a very real sense, another man about the house' (Robertson 1978: 88).

21  It might be said that there is a change of emphasis as the domestic cycle proceeds: in the early stages of marriage and childbearing, distinctions of *gender* are most at issue; but with maturation of children, the distinctions of *generation* come to the fore.

22  One expression of this corporate male chauvinism is that age-mates in eastern Africa may be allowed sexual access to a man's wife – a right which can cause a young husband considerable anguish (Baxter and Almagor 1978: 17–18).

23  See Bernardi 1985: 132ff.

24  See for example Boserup 1970, P. Roberts 1979, Obbo 1985.

25  The extent to which income is pooled domestically has become an important issue in gender studies in the Third World. See for example Smith, Wallerstein and Evers 1984; H. Moore 1988: 54–6.

26  See Collier et al. 1982.

CHAPTER 7   REPRODUCTION AND THE RISE OF INDUSTRIAL CAPITALISM

1   See Wall 1983, Macfarlane 1986: 334–5 and Macfarlane 1978b. Herlihy (1985) has found elements of the compact pattern in the early medieval period in

western Europe. A ninth-century survey of the lands of the monastery of St Germain des Prés in France reveals a median household size of six persons (p. 69), with lateral expansion but 'very little evidence of vertical extension, that is, over generations' (pp. 70–1). Herlihy believes that the biblical 'religious culture' of the Middle Ages reinforced the compact pattern: 'Marriage is monogamous and permanent; the family itself, stable and cohesive. Parents must be honored and obeyed, and their children must aid and support them in old age and illness. The wise father will retain control over the patrimony until his death, but his patriarchal power is not absolute. A son or daughter may leave father and mother and cleave to a spouse... In imposing the same sexual morality on all social classes, the teachings helped in the early Middle Ages to make households similar and commensurable, as we have argued. In giving precedence to the family of marriage over family of origin, they blocked the development of a full-blown patriarchal system in Europe' (pp. 133–4).

2  See also Hareven: 'Historical studies have revealed that the role of the family was in fact that of an active agent, fostering social change and facilitating the adaptation of its members to new social and economic conditions' (1978: 58).

3  Czap 1983: 122; Gaunt 1983: 276.

4  See Herlihy 1985: 11–12. The church was certainly not out to prevent reproduction, rather to control it: for example, 'Prolonged or permanent celibacy did not have the approval of the Church – as one might think – when it was not accompanied by vows of chastity' (Flandrin 1976: 188).

5  See J. Goody 1983; Macfarlane 1986; Ozment 1983: 25ff.

6  For example, examining the wills of the burgers of Bishop's Lynn, England, Beauroy (1986) sees evidence of the companionate, compact style of family organisation in the late 13th and early 14th centuries.

7  Macfarlane 1986: 336–7; Laslett 1969: 218.

8  R. M. Smith (1981: 615) ascribes considerable historical force to this 'highly distinctive cultural situation which demanded economic independence for the newly married couple', seeing it as more important than major transformations in the mode of economic production in controlling the aggregate pattern of fertility in England from the mid-sixteenth to mid-nineteenth centuries.

9  Laslett 1983: 532.

10  See D. Levine 1977: 118.

11  Historians now see the 'preventive check' of marriage as more important than the 'positive check' of disease and mortality in accounting for demographic trends since the sixteenth century (see Ohlin 1961; Wrigley and Schofield 1981; Herlihy 1985: 145). R. M. Smith (1981: 597) offers this summary account of changing fertility patterns in England, in terms of gross reproduction rate:

1550: high (*c.*2.8)
1650: low (*c.*1.9)
1750: med. (*c.*2.3)
1816: high (*c.*3.1)
1850: med. (*c.*2.4)
1900: low (*c.*1.8)

This pattern correlates with the proportion of people marrying for the first time (pp. 600–1), which in turn seems to reflect, with a thirty-year time lag, changes in the trend in real wages (p. 602; and see Wall 1983: 493). Economic constraints meant that right up to about 1940, a high proportion of people did not marry at all (Hajnal 1965: 101). Hajnal speculates that strategic timing of marriage is more important in the compact than in the extended pattern of domestic development: 'In Europe it has been necessary for a man to defer marriage until he could establish an independent livelihood adequate to support a family; in other societies the young couple could be incorporated in a larger economic unit, such as a joint family. This, presumably, is more easily achieved and does not require such a long postponement of marriage' (p. 133).

12  Flandrin (1976: 55) has traced the following average household sizes in seven European and one North American locality: 4.16 in Italy (1782); 4.95 in Serbia (1733–4); 5.05 in France (1788); 5.25 in Scotland (1779); 5.4 in Poland (1720); 5.77 in Germany (1687); 5.85 in Bristol, Rhode Island (1689).

13  See Hajnal 1983; R. M. Smith 1981: 603; and for the early medieval period, Herlihy 1985: 69.

14  See Lesthaeghe 1980; R. M. Smith 1981: 606–11. Smith emphasizes the importance of the domestic cycle in the operation of these mutual welfare funds: 'Obviously, the affluent would be likely to contribute to the communal fund throughout their life-cycle, while the "middling sorts" might well contribute more heavily as their children left home, after which they might be excused again later in life as their declining strength brought a further drop in income' (1981: 608). According to Cain, 'While particular institutional arrangements have varied over time – with the source of relief, for example, shifting from the manor and guild to parish and then to the state – there has nevertheless been a remarkable consistency in the extrafamilial locus of welfare institutions' (1985: 148). Cain makes the point that our own historical habits of *non*-familial dependence have led us to misjudge the different parenting strategies in modern developing countries.

15  Medick 1976: 312.

16  Flandrin 1976: 4–5.

17  Ozment 1983: 49, 132.

18  Stone 1977; Ozment 1983.

19  Lasch (1977: 1, 15) relishes the observation that in our modern world social scientists and welfare professionals have replaced clergymen as the moderators and definers of familial ethics.

20  Hajnal (1983) identifies three distinctive features of household formation in the north–west European cradle of industrialization: late marriage for both sexes, the circulation of unmarried people to other households as servants, and the shift away from the parents' household on marriage. He contrasts these features of the compact pattern of development with the 'joint household systems' of India and China, characterized by earlier marriage, co-residence with spouse's parents, later fission and the frequent consolidation of complex households.

21  See Medick 1976: 301–2.

22  Watt transformed the meaning of 'horsepower' and in due course the electrical unit was named after him.

23  E. P. Thompson 1968: 341.

24  See Mendels 1972: 252.

25  D. Levine 1977: 147.

26  'The changing organization of production and reproduction interacted to produce a proletariat that grew more than 23-fold in 12 generations, from 600,000 in 1524–1525 to around 14 million by the middle of the nineteenth century' (D. Levine 1984: 104).

27  See B. Moore 1967.

28  As Aries puts it, 'the moral ascendancy of the family was originally a

middle-class phenomenon... There is therefore a connection between the concept of the family and the concept of class' (1962: 413–14).

29  The 'family wage' purported to take account of the needs not just of the individual worker but of his whole household. It was in essence a crude measure to alleviate absolute poverty, not a system of rewards geared to the domestic cycle. For example, in 1795 the Berkshire magistrates ruled that the weekly agricultural wage should include a supplement linked to the current price of a one-gallon loaf of bread for each member of the worker's household (Chambers and Chambers 1895: 503).

30  See Lazonick 1978; also Foucault 1979 and Minge–Kalman 1978: 459–60.

31  See the classic study of 'family and kinship in East London' by Young and Willmott (1962).

32  All being well, I shall receive a pension from a large and powerful organization which still proudly declares its origins in nineteenth-century providence: the Scottish Widows Life Assurance.

33  The great actuarial pioneer William Farr helped to translate the principles of the early voluntary mutual funds into the pensioning and life insurance corporations of today. For example, the new vital statistics made it clear that a sixty-year-old was four times more likely than a thirty-year-old to be incapacitated. This drew official censure to an 'inequity' in the Friendly Societies: by extracting fixed contributions from young and old alike, the senior generation was arranging a subsidy for itself at the expense of the junior (Chambers and Chambers 1875: 517). For an illuminating account of the development of life insurance in the US, see Zelizer 1979.

34  See E. P. Thompson 1968.

35  See Thomson 1950: 200.

36  As late as 1948, the Act which set up the UK National Health Service was opposed by the medical profession.

37  See Hareven 1978 and Wall 1986 on 'the *adaptive family economy*', especially in nineteenth century England.

38  On the 'homogenization of experiences of growing up' in Britain in the 1960s–1970s, Anderson notes, 'Most people indeed, it seems, planned their lives on the assumption that they would follow the "normal" pattern at about the "normal" age' (1985: 81, 69–70). On the strength of 1970 US Census data, Spanier et al. (1979) note the close correlation of age and domestic cycle stage.

39  Hareven 1978: 61.

40  Glick 1957: 66.

41  Average household size in England, where households were already small, dropped by a third to about three persons during the nineteenth century (Laslett 1969: 218).

42  'Husband, wife, and their children until maturity live in the same home. Other relatives may live with them but this is regarded as undesirable' (Folsom 1934: 16). This is in contrast to the nineteenth-century pattern in which a period in service very commonly interceded between leaving the parental home and marrying (see D. Levine 1984: 92). Wall notes 'the virtual elimination from the household of resident labour, represented by servants' by the mid-twentieth century (Wall 1983: 496).

43  Glick 1957: 193.

44  Goode 1980: 41–2.

45  In the US in the 1940s and 1950s, 'household formation took place at an unusually high rate, the proportion of persons married climbed to new heights,

the median age at marriage declined more than a year, birth rates rose to the level of a generation ago, and divorce rates fluctuated within a range well above those recorded before 1940' (Glick 1957: 192). See also Davis 1985, Anderson 1985. The total number of households has subsequently been increased by the proportion of people who now live alone: 25 per cent in 1960; 35 per cent in 1975; and a projected 45 per cent by 1990. Among the causes of this are postponement of marriage, increased divorce and more prolonged widowhood (Rossi 1985: 166).

46    'Implicit in our analysis of family dynamics is the view that the modern family acts as a deployment agency regulating the participation of its members in many institutional sectors. This regulation should be particularly clear with regard to participation in the labour market, in financial institutions (insurance, savings, investment, and credit granting agencies), and in the consumer market (housing, transportation, clothes, etc.) as well as with regard to such things as the education of children' (Gove et al. 1973: 190).

47    Rossi points out that relative *overall* sex ratio balance in our societies is achieved because 'Mortality reduction that produces a *female surplus* in old age is balanced by mortality reduction in infancy and childhood that produces a *male surplus* in the younger years' (1985: 163). Medical developments have enhanced the survival of males, who are more vulnerable than females to aberration in foetal development. Rossi also points out that increased longevity protracts the reproductive capacities of men, but not of women (p. 164). The significance of the gender imbalance in later life should not be underrated. Hess, for example, argues that social policy and welfare services for the elderly 'have been consistently framed in terms of the male life course and concerns, despite the rather obvious facts that the majority of elderly are women, and that whatever problems are associated with advanced age in our society are overwhelmingly experienced by women'. Health services should, for example, take more account of (typically female) chronic illness rather than (typically male) emergency treatment (1985: 319).

48    See Anderson 1985: 69–73.

49    With the low tendency for people to move to smaller accommodation when their children leave home, these people are holding a disproportionately high share of available housing (Glick 1957: 2, 50, 197)

50    Since the Second World War, there is an increasing number of people living 'in institutions', including the armed forces: 7.1 per cent of all census units in 1953 (Glick 1957: 2).

51    Opinions vary about the extent to which older people in the US are severed from wider family ties. Once again, the key factor is public provision for this phase of the reproductive process. Gaunt reports that 'In countries like the United States, where institutional care for the elderly has not been given priority, more than one-third of all aged single people live with relatives, usually adult children. In Sweden, however, the number of old people's homes has rapidly expanded since the Second World War. In the early 1970s only 7% of 70-year-olds in the large city of Gothenburg lived with relatives, and of those living alone and needing help only 9% received such help from their own children' (1983: 250).

52    As the increasing proportion of older people in the population of our societies threatens the viability of pensioning arrangements, it is possible that four-generation 'extended' households may come into vogue in the twenty-first century. I am indebted to Michael Whyte for this interesting speculation.

53  See, for example, Shorter 1975 and Lasch 1977.
54  See for example Sennett's (1970) account of 'families against the city' in nineteenth-century Chicago: an image of the 'intense' compact pattern of domestic development, and the insecurity generated by urban industrial employment.
55  See especially the radical critique of Hartmann 1981.
56  See Easterlin 1962; England and Farkas 1986.
57  A headline in the business section of *Los Angeles Times*, 13 August 1989, read: 'Sales of Children's Books Soar as Baby Boomers Become Parents.' Television situation comedies have traced the collective life-cycle of the boomers: a current success is called *Thirty-something*.
58  A more conventional account of women's 'invasion' of the labour market sees it as the result of postwar economic expansion, creating a *demand* for labour which *attracted* women to jobs outside the home, and which in turn reduced their enthusiasm for child-rearing (see for example Tilly and Scott 1978: 230). A 'supply-side' reckoning of domestic pressures makes much better sense of the timing of the economic and demographic events. Accordingly, Marvin Harris insists that it was economic necessity which *drove* married women out to work: 'As all the polls and surveys of the 1950s showed, the baby boom mothers had no intention of giving up their homebody role' (1981: 90–1).
59  Glick 1957: 90–1, England and Farkas 1986: 14. In 1950 33.9 per cent of women were in the labour force, in 1976 47.3 per cent; in 1950 women constituted 29.6 per cent of the total labour force, in 1976, 40.5 per cent (US Department of Labour 1977: tables 1–3).
60  England and Farkas 1986: 11.
61  Radical economic views of the old issues of housework have raised some intriguing questions. Hartmann notes that 'it is the wife who, with respect to housework at least, does all the adjusting to the family life cycle' (1981: 385). 'The rather small, selective, and unresponsive contribution of the husband to housework raises the suspicion that the husband may be a net drain on the family's resources of housework time – that is, husbands may require more housework than they contribute' (p. 383). With this negative appraisal of the costs of 'husband care' comes the call for 'housechildren' – to reclaim the labour of children for domestic chores (Zelizer 1985: 223).
62  According to Hartmann, 'Women are resisting doing housework and rearing children, at least many children; the majority of women increasingly perceive their economic security to lie primarily in being self-supporting. Therefore, they are struggling with men to get out of the house and into decent jobs in the labour market' (1981: 390–1).
63  'As married women poured into the labour force, all the dire warnings that procreation and employment outside the home were incompatible suddenly came true. The baby boom collapsed, and the fertility rate began its historic plunge, reaching zero population growth levels in 1972 and falling still further to an average of 1.8 children per woman by 1980' (M. Harris 1981: 89).
64  In the 1980s roughly 18 per cent of American births were 'illegitimate' (Rossi 1985: 165). See also Espenshade 1985 on the 'decline of American marriage'.
65  See England and Kilbourne 1990, who make the interesting point that while a man can borrow while he seeks another job, there are as yet no financial institutions which allow women to borrow while they seek another mate.
66  Rossi (1985: 169) reports an English study which indicates that 12 per cent of single parents raising their children are men.

67　Child allowances are long-established in the industrial states, but to the extent that they come as income supplements and tax breaks they are of greatest benefit to the salaried classes.

68　See D. Thomson 1986: 365, and Benda–Beckmann et al. 1988.

69　It is interesting to note how often allusion is made in such discussion to the dominant anxiety of our times, the spread of the AIDS virus. Not for the first time in history, the economic and political dangers to society of 'free' women – and aberrant men – are given sexual overtones.

70　See Popenoe 1988.

71　The future bodes ill in a country like Korea, which has not developed state social security systems but has experienced massive economic and demographic expansion. Kim Choong Soon (1988: 132–3) agonizes about the prospects for an aging population in a mobile society which is rapidly losing its traditions of filial piety.

CHAPTER 8　WAGES, SALARIES AND THE POLITICAL ECONOMY OF REPRODUCTION

1　Goode puts it this way: 'The *different* adjustment of families in *different* classes to the industrial system emphasizes the *independence* of the two sets of variables, the familial and the industrial, as well as the presence of some "disharmonies" between the two' (1980: 49–50 – emphasis in the original).

2　People in the wage-earning category with dependent children in their households may well prefer stable employment to the risks of job-shopping. Sennett's study of Chicago in the late nineteenth century indicates that *married* men were in more *steady* employment than unmarried – especially men in their twenties. Sennett wonders whether this was because employers were more inclined to consider men with family responsibilities 'not just as "a pair of hands" but as social creatures'; or whether such men were obliged by their domestic responsibilities to be better or more docile workers (1970: 132).

3　See Bowey 1982. On life insurance, see especially Zelizer (1979) who traces its origins in the US to 'husbands and fathers of middle-class families' in the latter part of the nineteenth century.

4　'Men in occupations with peak median earnings of $7,000 or more in 1959 are much more likely to have experienced earnings increases over time that roughly parallel increases in the cost of maintaining a family' (Oppenheimer 1974: 241). See also Lydall 1955: 141–2.

5　Lydall 1955: 141.

6　H. F. Clark 1937: 8–9, 122. Sensing the indignant cries of the librarians, I would note that, like so many other middle-class occupations, they have had some success in dignifying their profession and salarizing the structure of their rewards during the course of this century.

7　Schorr (1966: 20) makes the point that it is the 'life cycle squeeze', rather than income level per se, which obliges wage-earners to 'moonlight'.

8　'Out' here is taken to include industrial home-work, the 'putting out' of tedious manual tasks to people self-employed in the home.

9　See J. P. Smith 1977: 213–6, especially his figure 1f.

10　The pressures on mothers to work is notorious among the urban underclass in developing countries. Papanek and Schwede (1981: 86–7) note that among lower and lower-middle class women in Jakarta, Indonesia, those with young children are *most* likely to be out to work, rather than not working or self-employed. 'This directly contradicts the conventional assumption that the time pressures of child care keep women out of the labour force' (p. 86).

11 The fact that married women can count on health-care and pensioning provided through their husbands' employment has been encouraging the dramatic expansion of forms of 'temporary' or 'casual' employment for women which do not include such perquisites. Professional couples receive double benefits, an inducement for many middle-class women to compete with men to sustain their own professional careers. The salary structure of man and woman allows ample resources for buying child-care from wage-dependent households. See Haines 1979, Oppenheimer 1974.

12 Wynn 1970: 141–5. In the US the most usual approach to measuring class difference has been by ethnic comparisons of black and white populations. The figures are revealing: overall, the life earnings pattern for black men peaks earlier and is 'flatter' than for whites (J. P. Smith 1977: 214). The proportion of women out to work is notoriously higher for blacks than for whites (Glick 1957: 92, J. P. Smith 1977: 220). On an analysis of American data (1960–70) J. P. Smith concludes that 'the life cycle behavioral patterns of black women more closely parallel those of white men than of white women', in that black women are more *continuously* out to work than white women (1977: 205). Smith supposes that this is because the reproductive activities of black women are spread out over a longer period than whites, and black women must confront the insecurity of higher divorce rates (p. 236).

13 See, for example, Becker 1964, Rosen 1976. According to T. P. Schultz, 'the human capital framework postulates that investments occur that augment the productive capacity of the human agent, while other processes, such as depreciation and obsolescence, may work to diminish that capacity over time' (1976: 259).

14 On the 'institutional' approach within economics, see especially Williamson 1981, and Oberschall and Leifer 1986.

15 See for example Ben–Porath 1967, Heckman 1976, and Lupton and Bowey 1983.

16 In Britain, banks and building societies (the principal source of mortgages) rank professions according to career security, and are notoriously unsympathetic to wage-earners – unless they have contrived to bank substantial savings with the society.

17 Wynn remarks that: 'It has never, of course, been the aim of trade unions to seek wages for their members that bear any relation to differing family responsibilities. However, some of the more old-fashioned systems of wage-payment show a quite unnecessary disregard of the normal demands of the family cycle – those wage agreements that provide for a maximum wage at age 21 or 25, without provision for further increments throughout a working life, being particularly inefficient socially... It would seem that the trade unions could do something to promote a better relationship between age and reward, a relationship that is already much more satisfactory for salary earners than for workmen earning a weekly wage' (Wynn 1970: 150).

18 See Garbarino 1962, Lupton & Bowey 1983: 133ff.

19 See Ballon 1982.

20 See Gordon et al. 1982. I am indebted to Christian Zlolniski for pointing this out to me.

CHAPTER 9    MORAL CRISES AND UTOPIAN EXPERIMENTS

1 Lasch (1977: 189) complains that: 'Today the state controls not merely the individual's body but as much of his spirit as it can preempt; not merely his

outer but his inner life as well; not merely the public realm but the darkest corners of private life, formerly politically inaccessible to political domination. The citizen's entire existence has now been subjected to social direction, increasingly unmediated by the family or other institutions to which the work of socialization was once confined. Society itself has taken over socialization or subjected family socialization to increasingly effective control.' Lasch concludes that the effects of this on 'personal and political freedom' must be 'devastating'.

2    A. S. Makarenko, quoted in Bronfenbrenner 1972: 125–6.

3    M. Harris 1981: 85.

4    Those which made no serious efforts in either regard, like the Brook Farm commune portrayed in Nathaniel Hawthorne's *Blithedale Romance*, very quickly lost their sense of purpose, and collapsed. Like many subsequent experiments, they had the appearance of romantic, middle-class summer camps.

5    Aiyetoro is rendered as 'Olowo' in Stanley Barrett's account.

6    By contrast, the majority of latter-day communes in Europe and America seem to have subsisted off middle-class savings and subscriptions, or welfare checks.

7    We might count among the many examples of economic associations which have explicitly taken family or household structure as their model the industrial 'dynasties' of Europe and America: see for example McDonogh (1986: 59ff.) on the industrial elite of Barcelona. Examining the commercial dynasties of Texas, Marcus (1980) has revealed how family relations imprint themselves on the corporate structure of the firm; and how, in the course of time, the financial and legal organization of the firm segments and restructures family relations.

8    See Bennett 1967, 1975.

9    See for example the influential work of Evelyn Millis Duvall (1971).

10    Popenoe, for example, picks over the fragments of the 'postnuclear' family: 'the pattern of association between intimate pair-bonding (with or without marriage), sexual activity, and the procreation of children is being abandoned. These functions of the bourgeois nuclear family are becoming differentiated into separate spheres of life that are dissociated from one another' (1988: 300). I would propose that the decline of 'the family' is much less interesting than how these fragments are being reconstituted in the broader realms of social organization.

11    A husband in Knoxville, Tennessee, challenged his ex-wife's decision to donate seven frozen embryos to a childless couple, declaring, 'I don't want a child out there to be mine if I can't be a parent to it.' Awarding custody to the mother, the judge ruled that 'life begins at conception' and that, as children, it would be in the embryos' best interests to remain with their mother (*Los Angeles Times*, 27 May 1990).

12    For a discussion of moral and ethical issues in reproductive technology see Whiteford and Poland 1988. See also Lewin 1985 on the meanings of 'motherhood' in the light of new reproductive technologies, labour markets, etc. According to O'Brien, 'The changes in reproductive process are both grounds of and challenge to the feminist movement.' Women must move 'to wrest control of reproductive process from the corporate scientific elite, and to reconstruct a caring and shared notion of parenthood in an assault on patriarchal power' (1989: 26, 68). While authors like Firestone (1979) and O'Brien have seen the technical synthesis of the reproductive process as an avenue to true female emancipation, others (see Corea et al. 1985) fear that development of reproductive technologies will only serve to reduce further women's control over their bodies. Stolcke, too, is sceptical: 'the proposition

that only by abolishing biological differences can sex hierarchies be eliminated is much like proposing that racism will only end once people are all of the same phenotype' (1981: 174). I would warn against the misleading notion that reproduction is only about pregnancy and parturition; the emancipation of women will concern their engagement in *all* aspects of the reproductive process, including maturation, aging and death.

CHAPTER 10   SOCIAL AND ANALYTICAL CONSTRUCTIONS OF REPRODUCTION

1   See Stolcke 1981.
2   For a fuller discussion of these issues, see Friedland and Robertson 1990.
3   See C. Harris 1983: 181. On how Marxists have failed to take direct account of reproduction – despite Engels's early insistence on its historical importance – see Hartmann 1981: 370–1.
4   See Murray 1981, Robertson 1987.
5   See for example Rapp 1987.
6   See for example Giddens 1984.
7   See for example Althusser 1971.
8   See for example the attempt by Evers et al. (1984) to distinguish between 'primary' or 'subsistence' reproduction, and 'secondary' reproduction.
9   See England and Kilbourne 1990; Becker et al. 1977.
10   'The traditional theory of consumer and household behavior developed by economists ignores cooperation and conflict among members, in essence assuming that each household has only one member' (Becker 1981: 4). The point has been pursued forcefully by radical feminists like Hartmann, who explains how notions of the 'privatization' and 'unitary' nature of the family accompanied the rise of industrial capitalism (1981: 368, 376). For Guyer, who urges 'the importance of documentation by individual and that of tracing interactions over time', the unitary view 'renders women invisible. It also renders invisible the structural, cyclical, and historical processes determining rural consumption, investment, and long-term change' (1981: 172).
11   See especially Laslett 1984 on these dangers of regarding the household as a single unitary economic interest.
12   Kertzer and Keith (1984: 50–61) provide an extensive range of references on the life-course approach. For example, Hogan has essayed 'a life course perspective on individual behavior' (1985: 72) to interpret 'the synchronization of life transitions', and thus to establish a link between social norms and demographic change (pp. 72, 75).
13   Laslett (1983) has sought to distinguish between the *life course* of the individual, the *cycle* of the family, and *history* of the household. I would object only to his understanding of 'family', and would focus instead on the underlying cycle of *reproduction*.
14   See Lansing and Kish 1957; Robertson & Hughes 1978: 432. On the other hand, Spanier et al. (1979), using 1970 US Census data, conclude that 'family life cycle stages' are no better than 'marriage cohort' or 'age cohort' in interpreting the economic variance associated with 'family development'. Allowing for a multitude of problems in analysing the limited variables and the cross-sectional data, this explanatory equivalence may reflect the close correlation of age and domestic development, and the relative stability of marriage, achieved during the first half of this century. It seems improbable that the authors could draw the same conclusion from current census data.
15   The commonplace sociological distinction between 'family of orientation' and

'family of procreation' (see Parsons and Bales 1955) is a familiar example of the reduction of family process to static types. What is missing is an explanation (no simple matter!) of how and why one of these family 'types' is succeeded by the other.

16   I have explored this problem more fully elsewhere (Robertson, forthcoming). Social science has a remarkably feeble grip on the very basic idea that families and households are dynamic. A symptom of this is the periodic 'rediscovery' of the idea, each author having rather little awareness of his predecessor. The discontinuity is striking: In his seminal essays, Fortes (1949, 1958) makes no mention of Le Play, Rowntree, Chayanov, Sorokin, Glick or Duvall. In his investigation of *The Domestic Mode of Production* Sahlins (1972) is preoccupied with Chayanov, and does not mention other proponents of the idea. Although sharing his concern for domestic fission, Goody (1958) does not refer to Sorokin. More surprisingly, Roy H. Rodgers, commissioned to trace the history of the 'family life cycle concept' for Jean Cuisinier's collection of European studies (1977) has nothing to say about Chayanov, Fortes, Goody or Sahlins; he begins with Rowntree and mentions Le Play, but his conspectus is very much that of American sociology – Sorokin, Glick, Duvall and others. It is the name of Chayanov which provides some tenuous continuity, but the reader needs sharp eyes: In French he is 'Cajanov'; Sorokin et al. (1931: 12, 144ff.) cite 'Tschaianov'; Loomis (1936) 'Tschajanow'; and Eric Wolf (1966: 14) 'Chaianov'; before Thorner et al. (1966) give currency to 'Chayanov'. The convolutions of this last rediscovery are very telling: Thorner, the radical expatriate American scholar working in Paris, was encouraged by a Russian-educated Indian scholar who had worked with the German text to collaborate with French and British colleagues on an English translation of Chayanov's *Theory of Peasant Economy* published in 1966.

17   According to Hareven, 'family time is autonomous in certain areas. Historical changes in the family are slower than in other social institutions, and the accepted historical "stages" and "periods" in the study of Western society may or may not fit historical change in the family. The next assignment for social and cultural historians, particularly for family historians, should be the sorting of the relationship between family time and social time, family process and social process' (Hareven 1977: 347).

18   See R. Hill 1977, Goode 1977, Sieder and Mitterauer 1983 and Carter 1984 on the problems and strategies for longitudinal studies of households, and on techniques for reconstructing the domestic cycle from historical data.

19   John Barnes tells me: 'I always like to think of forestry as the discipline where this difficulty is most widespread. A forester often has to start an experiment merely in the hope that long after he is dead some successor will be sufficiently interested in the results to publish them.'

20   For example, R. M. Smith makes the point that a cross-sectional study would not reveal the social/demographic significance of the chronological relationship *between* households ('replacement' in Fortes's terms): 'Any study conducted on cross-sectional evidence for any period in these three centuries [mid- sixteenth to mid-nineteenth] would fail to detect that it was the initiation of new households, not what went on in the households of birth of the married couple or the latter's conjugal household, that powered the demographic motor in early modern England' (1981: 602).

21   See Loomis and Hamilton 1936; also Otterbein 1970 for a study of the discontinuity between historical recollections of the domestic cycle, cross-

section analysis and diachronic observation over seven years on a Bahamian island. J. P. Smith (1977: 217–22) makes an illuminating effort to show the differences and relationships between time-series and cross-section data on married women's participation in the US labour force, 1947–74. Browning draws attention to the interesting discrepancy that time-series analyses tend to reveal a positive correlation between fertility and income, while cross-section analyses reveal a negative correlation (1985: 150–1). He also makes the observation that time-series data (typically extending over a decade or two) are more likely to reveal short-run cyclical changes, while cross-section data are more likely to express 'variations which are longstanding in nature'. The problem is that we have no accurate way or reasonable means of translating these gross cross-sectional differences into historical explanations.

22 Thus, in his efforts to explain fertility in Taiwan, T. P. Schultz laments that 'lags and adjustments of a biological and behavioral nature interpose themselves between the observed environment characterized in the model and the observed birth rate the model seeks to predict' (1974: 266).

23 For examples of this approach see Hammel 1961, Glick and Parke 1965, Yanagisako 1979: 190, Gay 1980.

24 This was the effect of Chayanov's model (see chapter 5). It can also be seen very clearly in Loomis and Hamilton 1936: 226ff.

25 See, for example, Glick 1957.

26 See, for example, the review of Ozment (1983) by Geoffrey Elton in the *New York Review of Books*, 14 June 1984.

27 'Those who have a unilinear view of time cannot come to terms with the idea of cyclic time: it creates a moral vertigo since all their morality is based on cause and effect' (Berger 1985: 201).

28 Progress in connecting the short-term reckoning of economics with the long term reckoning of reproduction has come, appropriately enough from historians: see for example Michael Anderson's efforts (1971) to adduce 'social exchange theory' to a view of the instrumentality of domestic group relations in history; and see the painstaking efforts of David Levine (1984), from a thoroughly materialist perspective, to take a long-term view of the transition to industrialization, incorporating the influence of reproductive organization.

29 Those seeking a determinate role for the family in history have done so mainly at the level of ideological, cultural, psychic or affective factors. In a much-discussed study, Banfield (1958) argued that an ethic of 'amoral familism' was responsible for the inability of southern Italian peasants to lift themselves collectively out of their poverty and misery. More recently, Medick and Sabean (1984) have sought to rehabilitate *interest and emotion* in the study of family and kinship. Arguments about normative structure are victim to an uneasy circularity: family ideas affect social ideas which affect family ideas. Shorter's thesis that a 'surge of sentiment' in matters of courtship, maternity and domestic privacy 'helped to dislodge the traditional family' (1975: 5) leaves him with no firmer grip on causation than the prognosis that the family is heading into 'the unknown' (pp. 5, 255ff., 269). See also Wall's conclusions about 'cultural factors' in family history (1983: 63), and Thadani (1978: 461–4) on the 'nuclear family' as historical cause or consequence. Perhaps the boldest essay along these lines is Todd's (1985) proposal that distinct types of family structure explain international differences in political ideology.

30 Le Play was ignored by such founding fathers of modern social science as Marx, Weber and Parsons. Durkheim refers to him (in an essay first published in 1915)

with disparaging brevity as one 'completely outside the movement of ideas which gave birth to sociology' (1960: 382; and see Silver 1982: 6, 10, 126). For his departure from Marxist orthodoxy, Chayanov paid the heaviest price: in 1930 he was arrested and accused of counterrevolutionary conspiracy. He died in 1939.

31   In an effort to kick over the traces, some sociobiologists have relabelled themselves 'evolutionary anthropologists' or 'Darwinian social scientists' (see Symons 1989).

32   See discussion in Alexander 1988.

33   There has been much fruitful collaboration between the fields of anthropology and history. See for example the interpretation of European kinship 1500–1900 by Plakans (1984).

34   Mackintosh (1984: 14), for example, has commented on the significance of such a change in our mode of reproduction.

# References

Abrahams, R. G. 1977: Time and village structure in Northern Unyamwezi. *Africa* 47(4), 372–85.

Alexander, Richard D. 1988: Evolutionary approaches to human behavior: what does the future hold? In L. Betzig, M. Borgerhoff Mulder and P. Turke (eds), *Human Reproductive Behavior: A Darwinian perspective*, Cambridge University Press, Cambridge, 317–41.

Althusser, Louis 1971: Ideology and ideological state apparatuses. In Ben Brewster (ed.), *Lenin and philosophy*, New Left Books, London, 123–73.

Anderson, Michael 1971: *Family Structure in Nineteenth Century Lancashire*. Cambridge University Press, Cambridge.

——1978: Family, household, and the industrial revolution. In Michael Gordon (ed.), *The American family in social-historical perspective* (2nd edn), St Martin's Press, New York, 38–50.

——1985: The emergence of the modern life cycle in Britain. *Social History* 10(1), 69–87.

Arensberg, Conrad M. and Kimball, Solon T. 1968: *Family and Community in Ireland*. Harvard University Press, Cambridge, Mass.

Aries, Philippe 1962: *Centuries of Childhood: A History of Family Life*. Alfred Knopf, New York.

Arnould, Eric J. 1984: Marketing and social reproduction in Zinder, Niger Republic. In R. McC. Netting, R. R. Wilk and E. J. Arnould (eds), *Households*, University of California Press, Berkeley/Los Angeles, 130–62.

Ashley, Maurice 1952: *England in the Seventeenth Century*. Penguin, Harmondsworth.

Bailyn, Lotte 1980: Accommodation of work to family. In A. Skolnick and J. Skolnick (eds), *Family in transition* (3rd edn), Little, Brown & Co., Boston, 566–79.

Ballon, Robert J. 1982: *Salaries in Japan: The System*. Business Series Bulletin 91, Institute of Comparative Culture, Sophia University, Tokyo.

Banaji, Jairus 1976. Chayanov, Kautsky, Lenin: considerations towards a synthesis. *Economic and Political Weekly* (Bombay), 2 October, 1594–607.

Banfield, Edward C. 1958: *The Moral Basis of a Backward Society*. Free Press, New

York.

Banton, Michael 1957: *West African City: A Study of Tribal Life in Freetown.* Oxford University Press, London.

Barker–Benfield, G. J. 1978: The spermatic economy: a nineteenth century view of sexuality. In Michael Gordon (ed.), *The American Family in Social-historical Perspective* (2nd edn), St Martin's Press, New York, 374–402.

Barlett, Peggy 1980: Cost–benefit analysis: a test of alternative methodologies. In P. F. Barlett (ed.), *Agricultural Decision Making*, Academic Press, New York, 137–59.

Barrett, Stanley R. 1977: *The Rise and Fall of an African Utopia: A Wealthy Theocracy in Comparative Perspective.* Wilfrid Laurier, Waterloo, Ontario.

Barth, Fredrik 1964: Capital, investment and the social structure of a pastoral nomad group in South Persia. In R. Firth and B. S. Yamey (eds), *Capital, Saving and Credit in Peasant Societies*, Allen & Unwin, London, 69–81.

——1966: *Models of Social Organization.* Occasional paper 23, Royal Anthropological Institute, London.

——(ed.) 1969: *Ethnic Groups and Boundaries.* Allen & Unwin, London.

——(ed.) 1978: *Scale and Social Organization.* Universitetsforlaget, Oslo.

Baxter, P. T. W. and Almagor, Uri 1978: *Age, Generation and Time: Some Features of East African Age Organisations.* C. Hurst, London.

Beauroy, Jacques 1986: Family patterns and relations of Bishop's Lynn will-makers in the fourteenth century. In Lloyd Bonfield, Richard M. Smith and Keith Wrightson (eds), *The World We Have Gained*, Basil Blackwell, Oxford, 23–42.

Becker, Gary S. 1964: *Human Capital: A Theoretical and Empirical Analysis, with Special Reference to Education.* National Bureau of Economic Research, New York.

——1981: *A Treatise on the Family.* Harvard University Press, Cambridge, Mass.

Becker, Gary S. and Lewis, H. Gregg 1973: On the interaction between the quantity and quality of children. *Journal of Political Economy* 81(2), part II, S279–88.

Becker, Gary S. and Tomes, Nigel 1976: Child endowments and the quantity and quality of children. *Journal of Political Economy* 84(4), part II, S143–62.

Becker, Gary S., Landes, Elisabeth M. and Michael, Robert T. 1977: An economic analysis of marital instability. *Journal of Political Economy* 85(6), 1141–87.

Befu, Harumi 1968: Ecology, residence, and authority: the corporate household in Central Japan. *Ethnology* 7, 25–42.

Belshaw, Cyril S. 1976: *The Sorcerer's Apprentice: An Anthropology of Public Policy.* Pergamon, New York.

Benda–Beckman, F. von, Benda–Beckman, K. von, Casino, E., Hirtz, F., Woodman, G. R. and Zacher, H. F. (eds) 1988: *Between Kinship and the State: Social Security and Law in Developing Countries.* Foris, Dordrecht.

Beneria, Lourdes and Roldan, Martha 1987: *The Crossroads of Class and Gender: Industrial Homework, Subcontracting, and Household Dynamics in Mexico City.* University of Chicago Press, Chicago.

Bennett, John W. 1967: *Hutterian Brethren.* Stanford University Press, Stanford.

——1975: The Hutterian colony: a traditional voluntary agrarian commune with large economic scale. In P. Dorner (ed.), *Cooperative and commune*, University of Wisconsin Press, Madison.

Ben–Porath, Yoram 1967: The production of human capital and the life cycle of earnings. *Journal of Political Economy* 75(4), part I, 352–65.

Berger, John 1985: *Pig Earth.* Chatto & Windus, London.

Berkner, Lutz K. 1972: The stem family and the developmental cycle of the peasant household: an eighteenth-century Austrian example. *American Historical Review*, 77, 398-418.

— —1975: The use and misuse of census data for the historical analysis of family structure. *Journal of Interdisciplinary History* 5(4), 721-38.

— —1976: Inheritance, land tenure and peasant family structure: a German regional comparison. In J. Goody, J. Thirsk and E. P. Thompson (eds), *Family and Inheritance: Rural Society in Western Europe, 1200-1800*, Cambridge University Press, Cambridge, 71-95.

Bernardi, Bernardo 1985: *Age Class Systems: Social Institutions and Polities Based on Age*. Cambridge University Press, Cambridge.

Berreman, Gerald 1962: Pahari polyandry: a comparison. *American Anthropologist* 64, 60-75.

Betzig, Laura 1988: Mating and parenting in Darwinian perspective. In L. Betzig, M. Borgerhoff Mulder & P. Turke (eds), *Human Reproductive Behavior: A Darwinian Perspective*, Cambridge University Press, Cambridge, 3-20.

Bielby, Denise and Bielby, William 1988: She works hard for the money: household responsibilities and the allocation of work effort. *American Journal of Sociology* 93, 1031-59.

Binswanger, Hans P. and Rosenzweig, Mark R. 1986: Behavioural and material determinants of production relations in agriculture. *Journal of Development Studies* 22(3), 503-39.

Bloch, Maurice 1973: The long term and the short term: the economic and political significance of the morality of kinship. In Jack Goody (ed.), *The character of kinship*, Cambridge University Press, Cambridge, 75-87.

— —1987: Descent and sources of contradiction in representations of women and kinship. In Jane F. Collier and Sylvia Yanagisako (eds), *Gender and kinship*, Stanford University Press, Stanford, 324-37.

Bohannan, Laura 1952: A genealogical charter. *Africa* 22(4), 301-15.

Bohannan, Laura and Bohannan, Paul 1953: *The Tiv of Central Nigeria*. Ethnographic Survey of Africa: Western Africa, part 8. International African Institute, London.

Bonfield, Lloyd 1986: Normative rules and property transmission: reflections on the link between marriage and inheritance in early modern England. In Lloyd Bonfield, Richard M. Smith and Keith Wrightson (eds), *The World We Have Gained*, Basil Blackwell, Oxford, 155-76.

Boserup, Ester 1970: *Woman's Role in Economic Development*. Allen & Unwin, London.

— —1981: *Population and Technological Change: A Study of Long-term Trends*. University of Chicago Press, Chicago.

Bowey, Angela (ed.) 1982: *Handbook of Salary and Wage Systems* (2nd edn). Gower Press, Aldershot.

Brandes, Stanley H. 1976: *La solteria*, or why people remain single in rural Spain. *Journal of Anthropological Research* 32(3), 205-33.

Bray, Francesca and Robertson, A. F. 1980: Sharecropping in Kelantan, Malaysia. *Research in Economic Anthropology* 3, 209-44.

Brodsky, Vivien 1986: Widows in late Elizabethan London: remarriage, economic opportunity and family orientations. In Lloyd Bonfield, Richard M. Smith and Keith Wrightson (eds.), *The World We Have Gained*, Basil Blackwell, Oxford, 122-54.

Bronfenbrenner, Uri 1972: The changing Soviet family. In M. Gordon (ed.), *The Nuclear Family in Crisis*, Harper & Row, New York, 119-42.

Brown, Bruce W. 1981: *Images of Family Life in Magazine Advertising: 1920–1978*. Praeger, New York.

Brown, Donald E. 1988: *Hierarchy, History, and Human Nature: The Origins of Historical Consciousness*. University of Arizona Press, Tucson.

Browning, Mark 1985: Time-series, cross-sections and pooling. In Ghazi M. Farooq and George B. Simmons (eds), *Fertility in Developing Countries* St Martin's Press, New York, 149–70.

Buchler, Ira R and Selby, Henry A. 1968: *Kinship and Social Organization: An Introduction to Theory and Method*. Macmillan, New York.

Cain, Mead T. 1978: The household life cycle and economic mobility in Bangladesh. *Population and Development Review* 4(3), 421–38.

— —1981: The material consequences of reproductive failure in rural South Asia. In D. Dwyer and J. Bruce (eds), *A Home Divided: Women and Income in the Third World*, Stanford University Press, Stanford, 20–38.

— —1985: Fertility as an adjustment to risk. In Alice S. Rossi (ed.), *Gender and the life course*, Aldine, New York, 145–59.

Caldwell, J. C. 1981: The mechanisms of demographic change in historical perspective. *Population Studies* 35(1), 5–27.

Carter, Anthony T. 1984: Household histories. In R. McC. Netting, R. R. Wilk and E. J. Arnould (eds), *Households*, University of California Press, Berkeley/Los Angeles, 44–83.

Chambers, William and Chambers, Robert (eds) 1875: *Chambers's Information for the People* (5th edn). W. & R. Chambers, London.

Chan, Paul 1982: A comment on the FELDA model and a suggestion for another. *CCSEAS-ISEAS Joint International Conference on Village-level Modernization*, Singapore, June 1982.

Chang Chih–Ming 1988: Changing relations between traditional and state social security in Taiwan. In F. von Benda–Beckman et al., *Between Kinship and the State*, Foris Dordrecht, 109–24.

Chayanov, A. V. 1966: Peasant farm organization. In Daniel Thorner, Basile Kerblay and R. E. F. Smith (eds), *A. V. Chayanov on the Theory of Peasant Economy*, Irwin, Homewood, Ill., 29–269.

Clark, E. 1982: Some aspects of social security in medieval England. *Journal of Family History* 7, 307–20.

Clark, Harold F. 1937: *Life earnings. In Selected Occupations in the United States*. Harper, New York.

Clarke, Edith 1966: *My Mother Who Fathered Me: A Study of the Family in Three Selected Communities in Jamaica* (2nd edn). Allen & Unwin, London.

Coale, Ansley J. 1986: The decline of fertility in Europe since the eighteenth century as a chapter in human demographic history. In Ansley J. Coale and Susan C. Watkins (eds), *The Decline of Fertility in Europe*, Princeton University Press, Princeton NJ, 1–30.

Coale, Ansley J. and Watkins, Susan Cotts (eds) 1986: *The Decline of Fertility in Europe*. Princeton University Press, Princeton NJ.

Cohen, Abner 1969: *Custom and Politics in Urban Africa: A Study of Hausa Migrants in Yoruba Towns*. University of California Press, Berkeley/Los Angeles.

Cohen, Ronald 1984: Age and culture as theory. In D. I. Kertzer and J. Keith (eds), *Age and Anthropological Theory*, Cornell University Press, Ithaca, 234–49.

Collier, Jane F. and Yanagisako, Sylvia J. (eds) 1987: *Gender and Kinship: Essays Toward a Unified Analysis*. Stanford University Press, Stanford.

Collier, Jane, Rosaldo, Michelle Z. and Yanagisako, Sylvia 1982: Is there a family? New anthropological views. In B. Thorne and M. Yalom (eds), *Rethinking the Family: Some Feminist Questions*, Longmans, New York, 25–39.

Collomp, Alain 1984: Tensions, dissensions, and ruptures inside the family in seventeenth- and eighteenth-century Haute–Provence. In Hans Medick and David W. Sabean (eds), *Interest and Emotion: Essays on the Study of Family and Kinship*, Cambridge University Press, Cambridge, 145–70.

Comaroff, J. L. 1980 Introduction. In J. L. Comaroff (ed.), *The Meaning of Marriage Payments*, Academic Press, London, 1–47.

——(ed.) 1980: *The Meaning of Marriage Payments*. Academic Press, London.

Comas d'Argemir, Dolors 1988: Household, family, and social stratification: inheritance and labour strategies in a Catalan village (nineteenth and twentieth centuries). *Journal of Family History* 13(1), 143–63.

Commaille, Jacques 1987: Ordre familial, ordre social, ordre légal. Éléments d'une sociologie politique de la famille. *Année Sociologique* 37, 265–90.

Corea, Gena et al. (eds) 1985: *Man-made Women: How New Reproductive Technologies Affect Women*. Hutchinson, London.

Cox, Terry 1979: Awkward class or awkward classes? Class relations in the Russian peasantry before collectivisation. *Journal of Peasant Studies* 7(1), 70–85.

Cuisinier, Jean (ed.) 1977: *The Family Life Cycle in European Societies*. Mouton, The Hague.

Czap, Peter 1983: 'A large family: the peasant's greatest wealth': serf households in Mishino, Russia, 1814–1858. In R. Wall, J. Robin and P. Laslett (eds), *Family Forms in Historic Europe*, Cambridge University Press, Cambridge, 105–51.

Davenport, William 1968: The family system of Jamaica. In Paul Bohannan and John Middleton (eds), *Marriage, family, and Residence*, Natural History Press, New York, 247–84.

Davin, Anna 1984: Working or helping? London working-class children in the domestic economy. In J. Smith, I. Wallerstein and H- D. Evers (eds), *Households and the World-economy*, Sage, Beverly Hills, 215–32.

Davis, Kingsley 1985: The future of marriage. In Kingsley Davis (ed.), *Contemporary Marriage: Comparative Perspectives on a Changing Institution*, Russell Sage Foundation, New York, 25– 52.

Deere, Carmen D. and de Janvry, Alain 1981: Demographic and social differentiation among Northern Peruvian peasants. *Journal of Peasant Studies* 8(3), 335–66.

Demos, John 1978: Old age in early New England. In Michael Gordon (ed.), *The American Family in Social-historical Perspective* (2nd edn), St Martin's Press, New York, 220–56.

De Tray, Dennis N. 1974: Child quality and the demand for children. In Theodore W. Schultz (ed.), *Economics of the Family*, University of Chicago Press, Chicago, 91–116.

Donham, Donald L. 1985: *Work and Power in Maale, Ethiopia*. University Microfilms International (UMI) Research Press, Ann Arbor, Michigan.

Donzelot, Jacques 1979: *The policing of Families*. Pantheon, New York.

Dore, Ronald 1973: *British Factory – Japanese Factory: The Origins of National Diversity in Industrial Relations*. Allen & Unwin, London.

Douglas, Mary 1966: Population control in primitive groups. *British Journal of Sociology* 17(3), 263–73.

Douglass, William A. 1984: Sheep ranchers and sugar growers: property transmission in the Basque immigrant family of the American West and Australia. In R. McC.

Netting, R. R. Wilk and E. J. Arnould (eds), *Households*, University of California Press, Berkeley/Los Angeles, 109–29.

Dunn, John and Robertson, A. F. 1984: *Dependence and Opportunity: Political Change in Ahafo*. Cambridge University Press, Cambridge.

Durkheim, Emile 1960: Pragmatism and sociology. In K. H. Wolff (ed.), *Essays on Sociology and Philosophy*, Harper Row, New York, 386–436.

Duvall, Evelyn Millis 1971: *Family Development* (4th edn). J. B. Lippincott, Philadelphia.

Dyson–Hudson, Neville 1966: *Karimojong Politics*. Clarendon Press, Oxford.

Easterlin, Richard A. 1962: *The American Baby Boom in Historical Perspective*. National Bureau of Economic Research, occasional paper 79.

Elder, Glen H. 1974: *Children of the Great Depression: Social Change in Life Experience*. University of Chicago Press, Chicago.

——1985: Perspectives on the life course. In G. H. Elder (ed.), *Life Course Dynamics*, Cornell University Press, Ithaca, 23–49.

Engels, Frederick 1958: The origin of the family, private property and the state (first edition 1884). In Karl Marx and Frederick Engels, *Selected works*, Foreign Languages Publishing House, Moscow, vol. 2, 170–327.

England, Paula and Farkas, George 1986: *Households, Employment, and Gender*. Aldine, New York.

England, Paula and Kilbourne, Barbara 1990: Markets, marriages, and other mates. In R. Friedland and A. F. Robertson (eds), *Beyond the Marketplace*, Aldine de Gruyter, New York, 163–88.

Erasmus, Charles 1956: The occurrence and disappearance of reciprocal farm labour in Latin America. *Southwestern Journal of Anthropology* 12, 444–69.

Espenshade, Thomas. J 1977: The value and cost of children. *Population Bulletin* 32(1), 1–47.

——1985: The recent decline of American marriage: blacks and whites in comparative perspective. In Kingsley Davis (ed.), *Contemporary Marriage: Comparative Perspectives on a Changing Institution*, Russell Sage Foundation, New York, 53–90.

Evans–Pritchard, E. E. 1940: *The Nuer: A Description of the Modes of Livelihood and Political Institutions of a Nilotic People*. Clarendon Press, Oxford.

——1951: *Kinship and Marriage among the Nuer*. Clarendon Press, Oxford.

Evers, Hans–Dieter, Clauss, Wolfgang and Wong, Diana 1984: Subsistence reproduction: a framework for analysis. In J. Smith, I. Wallerstein and H–D. Evers (eds), *Households and the World-economy*, Sage, Beverly Hills, 23–36.

Fallers, Lloyd A. (ed.) 1967: *Immigrants and Associations*. Mouton, The Hague.

Firestone, Shulamith 1979: *The Dialectic of Sex: The Case for Feminist Revolution*. Women's Press, London.

Firth, Raymond, 1957: *We, the Tikopia: A Sociological Study of Kinship in Primitive Polynesia* (2nd edn). Allen & Unwin, London.

——1966: *Malay Fishermen: Their Peasant Economy* (2nd edn). Routledge & Kegan Paul, London.

Firth, Raymond and Yamey, B. S. (eds) 1964: *Capital, Saving and Credit in Peasant Societies: Studies from Asia, Oceania, the Caribbean and Middle America*. Allen & Unwin, London.

Firth, Raymond, Hubert, Jane and Forge, Anthony 1970: *Families and their Relatives: Kinship in a Middle-class Sector of London*. Routledge & Kegan Paul, London.

Fisher, H. A. L. 1936: *A History of Europe*. Edward Arnold, London.

Flandrin, Jean–Louis 1976: *Families in Former Times: Kinship, Household and Sexuality*. Cambridge University Press, Cambridge.

Folsom, Joseph Kirk 1934: *The Family: Its Sociology and Social Psychiatry*. John Wiley, London.

Forde, C. Daryll 1934: *Habitat, Economy and Society: A Geographical Introduction to Ethnology*. Methuen, London.

——1950: Double descent among the Yakö. In A. R. Radcliffe–Brown and Daryll Forde (eds), *African Systems of Kinship and Marriage*, Oxford University Press, London, 285–32.

Fortes, Meyer 1949: Time and social structure: an Ashanti case study. In M. Fortes (ed.), *Social Structure: Studies Presented to A. R. Radcliffe–Brown*, Clarendon Press, Oxford.

——1950: Kinship and marriage among the Ashanti. In A. R. Radcliffe–Brown and Daryll Forde (eds), *African Systems of Kinship and Marriage*, Oxford University Press, London, 252–84.

——1953: The structure of unilineal descent groups. *American Anthropologist* 55, 17–41.

——1958: Introduction. In J. Goody (ed.), *The Developmental Cycle in Domestic Groups*, Cambridge University Press, Cambridge, 1–14.

——1969: *Kinship and the Social Order: The Legacy of Lewis Henry Morgan*. Routledge & Kegan Paul, London.

——1974: The first born. *Journal of Child Psychology and Psychiatry* 15, 81–104.

——1984: Age, generation and social structure. In D. I. Kertzer and J. Keith (eds), *Age and Anthropological Theory*, Cornell University Press, Ithaca, 99–122.

Foster, Brian L. 1978: Domestic development cycles as a link between population processes and other social processes. *Journal of Anthropological Research* 34(3), 415–41.

Foster, George M. 1973: *Traditional Societies and Technological Change* (2nd edn), Harper and Row, New York.

Foucault, Michel 1979: *Discipline and Punish: The Birth of the Prison*. Vintage Books, New York.

Fox, Robin 1983: *Kinship and Marriage: An Anthropological Perspective* (2nd edn). Cambridge University Press, Cambridge.

Freed, Stanley A. and Freed, Ruth S. 1983: The domestic cycle in India: natural history of a will-o'-the-wisp. *American Ethnologist* 10(2), 312–27.

Freedman, Maurice 1966: *Chinese Lineage and Society: Fukien and Kwangtung*. Athlone Press, London.

Friedland, Roger and Robertson, A. F. 1990: Beyond the marketplace. In R. Friedland and A. F. Robertson (eds), *Beyond the Marketplace: Rethinking Economy and Society*, Aldine de Gruyter, New York, 3–49.

Friedmann, Harriet 1978: World market, state, and family farm: social bases of household production in the era of wage labour. *Comparative Studies in Society and History* 20(4), 545–86.

Fuller, C. J 1976: *The Nayars Today*. Cambridge University Press, Cambridge.

Furstenberg, Frank F. 1966: Industrialization and the American family: a look backward. *American Sociological Review* 31(3), 326–37.

Garbarino, Joseph W. 1962: *Wage Policy and Long-term Contracts*. The Brookings Institution, Washington.

Gaunt, David 1983: The property and kin relationships of retired farmers in northern and central Europe. In R. Wall, J. Robin and P. Laslett (eds), *Family Forms in Historic Europe*, Cambridge University Press, Cambridge, 249–79.

Gay, Judith S 1980: Basuto women's options: a study of marital careers in rural Lesotho. PhD dissertation, Cambridge University.

Geertz, Clifford 1966: The rotating credit association: a 'middle rung' in development. In I. Wallerstein (ed.), *Social Change: The Colonial Situation*, Wiley, New York, 420–46.

——1973: *The Interpretation of Cultures*. Basic Books, New York.

Geertz, Hildred and Geertz, Clifford 1968: Teknonymy in Bali: parenthood, age-grading and genealogical amnesia. In Paul Bohannan & John Middleton (eds), *Marriage, Family, and Residence*, Natural History Press, New York, 355–76.

——1975: *Kinship in Bali*. University of Chicago Press, Chicago.

Gellner, Ernest 1964: *Thought and Change*. Weidenfeld & Nicolson, London.

General Synod of the Church of England 1965: *The Threshold of Marriage*. Church Information Office, London.

Gibbins, H. de B. 1912: *Industry in England: Historical Outlines*. Charles Scribner's Sons, New York.

Gibbon, P. and Curtin, C. 1978: The stem family in Ireland. *Comparative Studies in Society and History* 20(3), 429–53.

Giddens, Anthony 1984: *The Constitution of Society: Outline of the Theory of Structuration*. University of California Press, Berkeley/Los Angeles.

Glick, Paul C. 1957: *American families*. John Wiley, New York.

Glick, Paul C. and Parke, Robert 1965: New approaches in studying the life cycle of the family. *Demography* 2, 187–202.

Gluckman, Max 1950: Kinship and marriage among the Lozi of Northern Rhodesia and the Zulu of Natal. In A. R. Radcliffe–Brown & Daryll Forde (eds), *African Systems of Kinship and Marriage*, Oxford University Press, London, 166–206.

Goode, William J. 1963: *World Revolution and Family Patterns*. Free Press, New York.

——1977: Family cycle and theory construction. In Jean Cuisinier (ed.), *The Family Life Cycle in European Societies*, Mouton, The Hague, 59–74.

——1980: World revolution and family patterns. In A. Skolnick and J. Skolnick (eds), *Family in Transition* (3rd edn), Little, Brown, Boston, 41–51.

Goody, Esther N. 1973: *Contexts of Kinship. An Essay in the Family Sociology of the Gonja of Northern Ghana*. Cambridge University Press, Cambridge.

——(ed.) 1982: *From Craft to Industry: The Ethnography of Proto-industrial Cloth Production*. Cambridge University Press, Cambridge.

Goody, Jack 1958: The fission of domestic groups among the LoDagaba. In J. Goody (ed.), *The Developmental Cycle in Domestic Groups*, Cambridge University Press, Cambridge, 53–91.

——1969: Inheritance, property, and marriage in Africa and Eurasia. *Sociology* 3(1), 55–76.

——1972: *Domestic Groups*. Addison–Wesley, Reading, Mass.

——1973: Bridewealth and dowry in Africa and Eurasia. In Jack Goody and S. J. Tambiah, *Bridewealth and Dowry*, Cambridge University Press, Cambridge, 1–58.

——1976a: *Production and Reproduction: A Comparative Study of the Domestic Domain*. Cambridge University Press, Cambridge.

——1976b: Aging in non-industrial societies. In J. R. Birren, E. Shanes and R. Binstock (eds), *Handbook of Aging and the Social Sciences*, Van Nostrand Reinhold, New York, 117–29.

——1976c: Inheritance, property and women: some comparative considerations. In J. Goody, J. Thirsk and E. P. Thompson (eds), *Family and Inheritance: Rural*

*Society in Western Europe, 1200–1800*, Cambridge University Press, Cambridge, 10–36.

——1982: *Cooking, Cuisine and Class. A Study in Comparative Sociology*. Cambridge University Press, Cambridge.

——1983: *The Development of the Family and Marriage in Europe*. Cambridge University Press, Cambridge.

——1986: *The Logic of Writing and the Organization of Society*. Cambridge University Press, Cambridge.

——1990: *The Oriental, the Ancient and the Primitive: Systems of Marriage and the Family in the Pre-industrial Societies of Eurasia*. Cambridge University Press, Cambridge.

Goody, Jack and Tambiah, S. J. (eds) 1973: *Bridewealth and Dowry*. Cambridge University Press, Cambridge.

Gordon, David M., Edwards and Reich, Michael 1982: *Segmented Work, Divided Workers: The Historical Transformation of Labor in the United States*. Cambridge University Press, Cambridge.

Gove, Walter R., Grimm, James W., Motz, Susan C. and Thompson, James D. 1973: The family life cycle: internal dynamics and social consequences. *Sociology and Social Research* 57(2), 182–95.

Greenhalgh, Susan 1985: Is inequality demographically induced? The family cycle and the distribution of income in Taiwan, 1954–1978. *American Anthropologist* 87, 571–94.

Gronau, Reuben 1974: The effect of children on the housewife's value of time. In Theodore W. Schultz (ed.), *Economics of the Family*, University of Chicago Press, Chicago, 457–88

——1977: Leisure, home production, and work – the theory of the allocation of time revisited. *Journal of Political Economy* 85(6), 1099–123.

Gulliver, P. H. 1964: The Arusha family. In R. F. Gray and P. H. Gulliver (eds), *The Family Estate in Africa*, Routledge & Kegan Paul, London, 197–229.

Guyer, Jane 1981: Dynamic approaches to domestic budgeting: cases and methods from Africa. In D. Dwyer and J. Bruce (eds), *A Home Divided: Women and Income in the Third World*, Stanford University Press, Stanford, 155–72.

Hackenberg, Robert, Murphy, Arthur D. and Selby, Henry A. 1984: The urban household in dependent development. In R. McC. Netting, R. R. Wilk and E. J. Arnould (eds), *Households*, University of California Press, Berkeley/Los Angeles, 187–216.

Haines, Michael R. 1979: Industrial work and the family life cycle, 1889–1890. In Paul Uselding (ed.), *Research in Economic History*, 4, JAI Press, Greenwich, Connecticut, 289–356.

——1985: The life cycle, savings, and demographic adaptation: some historical evidence for the United States and Europe. In Alice S. Rossi (ed.), *Gender and the Life Course*, Aldine, New York, 43–63.

Hajnal, J. 1965: European marriage patterns in perspective. In D. V. Glass and D. E. C. Eversley (eds), *Population in History: Essays in Historical Demography*, Aldine, Chicago, 101–43.

——1983: Two kinds of pre-industrial household formation system. In R. Wall, J. Robin and P. Laslett (eds), *Family Forms in Historic Europe*, Cambridge University Press Cambridge, 65–104.

Halperin, Rhoda 1984: Age in cultural economics: an evolutionary approach. In D. I. Kertzer and J. Keith (eds), *Age in Anthropological Theory*, Cornell University Press, Ithaca, 159–94.

Hammel, E. A. 1961: The family cycle in a coastal Peruvian slum and village. *American Anthropologist* 63(5), part 1, 989–1005.

——1972: The Zadruga as a process. In Peter Laslett and Richard Wall (eds), *Household and Family in Past Time*, Cambridge University Press, Cambridge, 335–73.

Hannan, Michael T. 1982: Families, markets, and social structures: An essay on Becker's *A Treatise on the Family*. *Journal of Economic Literature* 20(10), 65–73.

Hansen, Holger B. and Twaddle, Michael (eds) 1988: *Uganda Now: Between Decay and Development*. James Currey, London.

Hareven, Tamara K. 1977: The family cycle in historical perspective: a proposal for a developmental approach. In Jean Cuisinier (ed.), *The Family Life Cycle in European Societies*, Mouton, The Hague, 339–52.

——1978: Family time and historical time. In A. S. Rossi, J. Kagan and T. K. Hareven (eds), *The Family*, W. W. Norton, New York, 57–70.

——1982: *Family Time and Industrial Time: The Relationships between the Family and Work in a New England Industrial Community*. Cambridge University Press, Cambridge.

——1986: Historical changes in the social contruction of the life course. *Human Development 29(3), 171–80*.

——1987: Family history at the crossroads. *Journal of Family History* 12(1–3), ix-xxiii.

——1990: Family strategies: social change and economic change. In Roger Friedland and A. F. Robertson (eds), *Beyond the Marketplace*, Aldine de Gruyter, 215–44.

Harris, C. C. 1983: *The Family in Industrial Society*. Allen & Unwin, London.

Harris, Marvin 1981: *America Now: The Anthropology of a Changing Culture*. Simon and Schuster, New York.

Harris, Olivia 1976: Women's labour and the household. Discussion paper presented at the British Sociological Association Conference workshop on the Peasantry, 13 March.

——1981: Households as natural units. In K. Young, C. Wolkowitz and R. McCullagh (eds), *Of Marriage and the Market*, Routledge and Kegan Paul, London, 136–55.

Harison, Mark 1977: The peasant mode of production in the work of A. V. Chayanov. *Journal of Peasant Studies* 4(4), 323–36.

Hartmann, Heidi 1981: The family as the locus of gender, class, and political struggle: the example of housework. *Signs: Journal of Women in Culture and Society* 6(3), 366–94.

Hausfater, Glenn and Hrdy, Sarah Blaffer (eds) 1984: *Infanticide: Comparative and Evolutionary Perspectives*. Aldine, New York.

Heady, Earl O. and Kehrberg, Earl W. 1952: Relationship of crop share and cash leasing systems to farming efficiency. *Research Bulletin* 386, Agricultural Experiment Station, Iowa State College, Ames, Iowa, 634–83.

Heckman, James J. 1976: Estimates of a human capital production function embedded in a life-cycle model of labour supply. In Nestor E. Terleckyj (ed.), *Household Production and Consumption*, National Bureau of Economic Research, New York, 227–64.

Herlihy, David 1985: *Medieval Households*. Harvard University Press, Cambridge, Mass.

Herring, Ronald J. 1984: Chayanov versus neoclassical perspectives on land tenure and productivity interactions. In E. Paul Durrenberger (ed.), *Chayanov, Peasants and Economic Anthropology*, Academic Press, Orlando, 133–49.

Hess, Beth B. 1985: Aging policies and old women: the hidden agenda. In Alice S.

Rossi (ed.), *Gender and the Life Course*, Aldine, New York, 319–31.

Hewlett, Sylvia Ann 1986: *Lesser Life: The Myth of Women's Liberation in America*. Warner Books, New York.

Hill, Polly 1972: *Rural Hausa: A Village and a Setting*. Cambridge University Press, Cambridge.

Hill, Reuben 1970: *Family Development in Three Generations*. Schenkman, Cambridge, Mass.

——1977: Social theory and family development. In Jean Cuisinier (ed.), *The Family Life Cycle in European Societies*, Mouton, The Hague, 9–38.

Hobsbawm, E. J. 1959: *Primitive Rebels*. Manchester University Press, Manchester.

Hochschild, Arlie Russell 1978: *The Unexpected Community: Portrait of an Old Age Subculture* (revised edn). University of California Press, Berkeley/Los Angeles.

Hogan, Dennis P. 1985: The demography of life-span transitions: temporal and gender comparisons. In Alice S. Rossi (ed.), *Gender and the Life Course*, Aldine, New York, 65–78.

Hoggson, Noble Foster 1926: *Banking throuah the Ages*. Dodd, Mead, New York.

Hostetler, John A. 1968: *Amish Society* (revised edn). Johns Hopkins Press, Baltimore.

Hunt, Diana 1978: Chayanov's model of peasant household resource allocation and its relevance to Mbere Division, Eastern Kenya. *Journal of Development Studies* 15(1), 59–86.

Hunt, Robert 1965: The developmental cycle of the family business in rural Mexico. In J. Helm (ed.), *Essays in Economic Anthropology*, University of Washington Press, Seattle, 54–80.

Hunter, L. C. and Robertson, D. J. 1969: *Economics of Wages and Labour*. Augustus M. Kelley, New York.

Ingold, Tim 1976: *The Skolt Lapps Today*. Cambridge University Press, Cambridge.

Johansson, Shiela Ryan 1984: Deferred infanticide: excess female mortality during childhood. In G. Hausfater and S. B. Hrdy (eds), *Infanticide: Comparative and Evolutionary Perspectives*, Aldine, New York, 463–85.

Johnson, M. Bruce 1971: *Household Behaviour: Consumption, Income and Wealth*. Penguin, Harmondsworth.

Jones, Jeffrey R. 1984: Chayanov in Bolivia: changes in potato productivity among Cochambamba peasants. In E. Paul Durrenberger (ed.), *Chayanov, Peasants and Economic Anthropology*, Academic Press, Orlando, 151–66.

Kamiko, Takeji 1977: The internal structure of the three- generation household. In Jean Cuisinier (ed.), *The Family Life Cycle in European Societies*, Mouton, The Hague, 157–74.

Keller, Suzanne 1980: Does the family have a future? In A. Skolnick and J. Skolnick (eds), *Family in Transition* (3rd edn), Little, Brown, Boston, 66–79.

Kertzer, David I & Keith, Jennie (eds) 1984: *Age in Anthropological Theory*. Cornell University Press, Ithaca.

Kim, Choong Soon 1988: An anthropological perspective on filial piety versus social security. In F. von Benda–Beckmann et al. (eds), *Between Kinship and the State*, Foris, Dordrecht, Holland, 125–35.

Kirby, Jon P. 1987: Why the Anafo do not eat frogmeat: the importance of taboo-making for development work. *African Affairs* 86(342), 59–72.

Kirkpatrick, Clifford 1955: *The Family: As Process and Institution*. Ronald Press, New York.

Kirshner, Julius 1977: Pursuing honor while avoiding sin: the *Monte delle doti* of Florence. *Studi Senesi* 87, 177–258.

Kirshner, Julius and Molho, Anthony 1978: The dowry fund and the marriage market in early *quattrocento* Florence. *Journal of Modern History* 50, 403–38.

Kriegel, Annie 1978: Generational difference: the history of an idea. *Daedalus* 107, 23–38.

Kuper, Adam 1982: Lineage theory: a critical retrospect. *Annual Review of Anthropology* 11, 71–95.

Kusnesof, Elizabeth A. 1980: Household composition and headship as related to changes in mode of production: Sao Paulo 1765 to 1836. *Comparative Studies in Society and History* 22(1), 78–108.

Lancaster, Jane B. 1985: Evolutionary perspectives on sex differences in the higher primates. In Alice S. Rossi (ed.), *Gender and the Life Course*, Aldine, New York, 3–27.

Lansing, John B. and Kish, Leslie 1957: Family life cycle as an independent variable. *American Sociological Review* 22, 512–19.

Lasch, Christopher 1977: *Haven in a Heartless World: The Family Besieged*. Basic Books, New York.

Laslett, Peter 1969: Size and structure of the household in England over three centuries. *Population Studies* 23(2), 199–223.

——1972: Introduction: the history of the family. In P. Laslett & R. Wall (eds), *Household and Family in Past Time*, Cambridge University Press, Cambridge, 1–89.

——1983: Family and household as work group and kin group: areas of traditional Europe compared. In R. Wall, J. Robin and P. Laslett (eds), *Family Forms in Historic Europe*, Cambridge University Press, Cambridge, 513–63.

——1984: The family as a knot of individual interests. In R. McC. Netting, R. R. Wilk, and E. J. Arnould (eds), *Households*, University of California Press, Berkeley/Los Angeles, 353–79.

Lazonick, William 1978: The subjection of labour to capital: the rise of the capitalist system. *Review of Radical Political Economics* 10(1), 1–31.

Lee, Richard Borshay 1979: *The !Kung San: Men, Women and Work in a Foraging Society*. Cambridge University Press, Cambridge.

Lenin, V. I 1899: *The Development of Capitalism in Russia* (2nd revised edn). Progress Publishers, Moscow.

Le Play, Frédéric 1895: *L'Organisation de la famille selon le vrai modèle signalé par l'histoire de toutes les races et de tous les temps* (4th edn). Alfred Mame et fils, Paris.

Lesthaeghe, Ron 1980: On the social control of human reproduction. *Population and Development Review* 6(4), 527–48.

Levine, David 1977: *Family Formation in an Age of Nascent Capitalism*. Academic Press, New York.

——1984: Production, reproduction, and the proletarian family in England, 1500–1851. In D. Levine (ed.) *Proletarianization and Family History*, Academic Press, Orlando, 87–127.

Levine, Nancy E. 1987: Fathers and sons: kinship value and validation in Tibetan polyandry. *Man (N.S.)* 22(2), 267–86.

——1988: *The Dynamics of Polyandry: Kinship, Domesticity, and Population on the Tibetan Border*. University of Chicago Press, Chicago.

Lewin, Ellen 1985: By design: reproductive strategies and the meaning of motherhood. In Hilary Homans (ed.), *The Sexual Politics of Reproduction*, Gower, London, 123–38.

Lewis, Norman 1985: *Voices of the Old Sea*. Penguin, Harmondsworth.

Little, Kenneth 1965: *West African Urbanization: A Study of Voluntary Associations in Social Change*. Cambridge University Press, Cambridge.

Littlejohn, Gary 1977: Peasant economy and society. In B. Hindess (ed.), *Sociological Theories of the Economy*, Macmillan, London, 118–56.

Livi–Bacci, Massimo 1986: Social-group forerunners of fertility control in Europe. In Ansley J. Coale & Susan C. Watkins (eds), *The Decline of Fertility in Europe*, Princeton University Press, Princeton NJ, 182–200.

Lockwood, M. 1965: The experimental Utopia in America. *Daedalus* 94(2), 410–18.

Loomis, Charles P. 1936: The study of the life cycle of families. *Rural sociology* 1, 180–99.

Loomis, Charles P. and Hamilton, C, Horace 1936: Family life cycle analysis. *Social Forces* 15(2), 225–31.

Lopez, Robert S. 1979: The dawn of medieval banking. In Center for Medieval and Renaissance Studies, University of California, Los Angeles (ed.), *The Dawn of Modern Banking*, Yale University Press, New Haven, 1–23.

Lupton, Tom & Bowey, Angela 1983: *Wages and Salaries* (2nd edn). Gower Press, Aldershot.

Lydall, Harold 1955: The life cycle in income, saving, and asset ownership. *Econometrica* 23(2), 133–50.

McCulloch, John Herries and Stirling, Kenneth J. 1936: *The Edinburgh Savings Bank: A Review of its Century of Service 1836–1936*. Pillans & Wilson, Edinburgh.

McDonogh, Gary Wray 1986: *Good Families of Barcelona: A Social History of Power in the Industrial Era*. Princeton University Press, Princeton NJ.

Macfarlane, Alan 1978a: Modes of reproduction. *Journal of Development Studies* 14(4), 100–20.

— —1978b: *The Origins of English Individualism: The Family, Property and Social Transition*. Basil Blackwell, Oxford.

— —1986: *Marriage and Love in England 1300–1840*. Basil Blackwell Oxford.

McGoldrick, Monica and Carter, Elizabeth A. 1982: The family life cycle. In Froma Walsh (ed.), *Normal Family Processes*, Guildford Press, New York, 167–95.

Mackintosh, Maureen 1984: Gender and economics: the sexual division of labour and the subordination of women. In K. Young, C. Wolkowitz and R. McCullagh (eds), *Of Marriage and the Market: Women's Subordination Internationally and its Lessons* (2nd edn), Routledge & Kegan Paul, London, 3–17.

McLaren, Angus 1984: *Reproductive Rituals: The Perception of Fertility in England from the Sixteenth Century to the Nineteenth Century*. Methuen, London.

Mair, Lucy 1971: *Marriage*. Penguin, Harmondsworth.

Majumdar, D. N. 1962: *Himalayan Polyandry: Structure, functioning and Culture Change: A Field Study of Jaunsar-Bawar*. Asia Publishing House, London.

Malthus, Robert Thomas 1970: *An Essay on the Principle of Population* (first published 1798). Penguin Books, Harmondsworth.

Mamdani, Mahmood 1972: *The Myth of Population Control: Family, Caste and Class in an Indian Village*. Monthly Review Press, New York.

— —1981: The ideology of population control. In Karen L. Michaelson (ed.), *And the Poor Get Children: Radical Perspectives on Population Dynamics*, Monthly Review Press, New York 39–49.

Marcus, George E. 1980: Law in the development of dynastic families among American business elites: the domestication of capital and the capitalization of family. *Law and Society Review* 14(4), 859–903.

Martinez–Alier, Juan 1971: *Labourers and Landowners in Southern Spain*. G Allen

& Unwin, London.

Marx, Karl and Engels, F. 1967: *The Communist Manifesto*. Penguin, Harmondsworth.

Mauss, Marcel 1954: *The Gift: Forms and Functions of Exchange in Archaic Societies*. Free Press, Glencoe, Ill.

Medick, Hans 1976: The proto-industrial family economy: the structural function of household and family during the transition from peasant society to industrial capitalism. *Social History* 3, 291–315.

Medick, Hans and Sabean, David W. (eds) 1984: *Interest and Emotion: Essays on the Study of Family and Kinship*. Cambridge University Press, Cambridge, 371–413.

Meillassoux, Claude 1972: From reproduction to production: A Marxist approach to economic anthropology. *Economy and Society* 1(1), 93–104.

——1978: The social organisation of the peasantry: the economic basis of kinship. In D. Seddon (ed.), *Relations of Production: Marxist Approaches to Economic Anthropology*, Frank Cass, London, 159–69.

——1981: *Maidens, Meal and Money: Capitalism and the Domestic Community*. Cambridge University Press, Cambridge.

——1983: The economic bases of demographic reproduction: from the domestic mode of production to wage- earning. *Journal of Peasant Studies* 11(1), 50–61.

Mendels, Franklin F. 1972 Proto-industrialization: the first phase of the industrialization process. *Journal of Economic History* 32(1), 241–61.

Metge, Joan 1964: Rural local savings associations (Maori Komiti) in New Zealand's far north. In R. Firth and B. S. Yamey (eds), *Capital, Saving and Credit in Peasant Societies*, Allen and Unwin, London, 207–29.

Miller, R. A. 1974: Are familists amoral? A test of Banfield's amoral familism hypothesis in a south Italian village. *American Ethnologist* 1, 515–35.

Mincer, Jacob and Polachek, Solomon 1974: Family investments in human capital: earnings of women. In Theodore W. Schultz (ed.), *Economics of the Family*, University of Chicago Press, Chicago, 397–429.

Minge–Kalman, Wanda 1977: On the theory and measurement of domestic labour intensity. *American Ethnologist* 4(2), 273–84.

——1978: The industrial revolution and the European family: the institutionalization of childhood as a market for family labour. *Comparative Studies in Society and History* 20(3), 454–68.

Mintz, Sidney W. 1985: *Sweetness and Power: The Place of Sugar in Modern History*. Penguin, Harmondsworth.

Mitterauer, Michael and Sieder, Reinhard 1982: *The European Family: Patriarchy to Partnership from the Middle Ages to the Present*. Basil Blackwell, Oxford.

Modell, John and Hareven, Tamara K. 1973: Urbanization and the malleable household: an examination of boarding and lodging in American families. *Journal of Marriage and the Family* 35, 467–79.

Montgomery, Mark and Trussell, James 1986: Models of marital status and childbearing. In O. Ashenfelter and R. Layard (eds), *Handbook of labor Economics*, vol. 1, Elsevier, New York, 205–71.

Moore, Barrington 1967: *Social Origins of Dictatorship and Democracy: Lord and Peasant in the Making of the Modern World*. Penguin, Harmondsworth.

Moore, Henrietta L. 1988: *Feminism and Anthropology*. Polity Press, Cambridge.

Morgan, Lewis H. 1964: *Ancient Society* (edited edn). Harvard University Press, Cambridge, Mass.

Mumford, Lewis 1923: *The Story of Utopias: Ideal Commonwealths and Social*

*Myths.* Harrap, London.

Murray, Colin 1981: *Families Divided: The Impact of Migrant Labour in Lesotho.* Cambridge University Press, Cambridge.

Myles, John 1989: *Old Age and the Welfare State: The Political Economy of Public Pensions* (revised edn). University of Kansas Press, Lawrence, Kansas.

— —1990: States, labour markets and life cycles. In Roger Friedland and A. F. Robertson (eds), *Beyond the Marketplace,* Aldine de Gruyter, 271–98.

Nabudere, D. Wadada 1980: *Imperialism and Revolution in Uganda.* Onyx Press, London.

Nahemow, Nina 1979: *Residence, kinship and social isolation among the aged Baganda. Journal of Marriage and the Family* 41(1), 171–83.

Nash, June 1979: *We Eat the Mines and the Mines Eat Us: Dependency and Exploitation in Bolivian Tin Mines.* Columbia University Press, New York.

Netting, Robert McC., Wilk, Richard R. and Arnould, Erik J. (eds) 1984: *Households.* University of California Press, Berkeley/Los Angeles.

Newbery, David 1989: Agricultural institutions for insurance and stabilization. In P. Bardhan (ed.), *The Economic Theory of Agrarian Institutions,* Clarendon Press, Oxford, 267–98.

Nimkoff, M. F. and Middleton, Russell 1960: Types of family and types of economy. *American Journal of Sociology* 66(3), 215–25.

Obbo, Christine 1985: Development and women: critical issues. In W. Derman and S. Whiteford (eds), *Social Impact Analysis and Development Planning in the Third World,* Westview Press, Boulder, 199–215.

Oberschall, Anthony and Leifer, Eric M. 1986: Efficiency and social institutions: uses and misuses of economic reasoning in sociology. *Annual Review of Sociology* 12, 233–53.

O'Brien, Mary 1989: *Reproducing the World: Essays in Feminist Theory* Westview Press, Boulder.

Ohlin, G. 1961: Mortality, marriage, and growth in pre-industrial populations. *Population Studies* 14(3), 190–7.

Oppenheimer, Valerie K. 1974. The life cycle squeeze: the interaction of men's occupational and family life cycles. *Demography* 11(2), 227–45.

Oppong, Christine and Bleek, Wolf 1982: Economic models and having children: some evidence from Kwahu, Ghana. *Africa* 52(4), 15–33.

Otterbein, Keith F. 1970: The developmental cycle of the Andros household: a diachronic analysis. *American Anthropologist* 72(6) 1412–19.

Ozment, Steven 1983: *When Fathers Ruled: Family Life in Reformation Europe.* Harvard University Press, Cambridge, Mass.

Papanek, Hanna and Schwede, Laurel 1981: Women are good with money: earning and managing in an Indonesian city. In D. Dwyer and J. Bruce (eds), *A Home Divided: Women and Income in the Third World,* Stanford University Press, Stanford, 71–98.

Parkinson, C. Northcote 1957: *Parkinson's Law, and Other Studies in Administration.* Houghton Mifflin, Boston.

Parsons, Talcott 1949: The social structure of the family. In R. N. Anshen (ed.), *The Family: Its Function and Destiny,* Harper, New York, 173–201.

Parsons, Talcott and Bales, Robert F. 1955: *Family, Socialization and Interaction Process.* Free Press, Glencoe, Ill.

Pasternak, Burton 1972: The sociology of irrigation: two Taiwanese villages. In W. E. Willmott (ed.), *Economic Organization in Chinese Society,* Stanford University Press, Stanford, 193–213.

Pasternak, Burton, Ember, Carol R. and Ember, Melvin 1976: On the conditions favoring extended family households. *Journal of Anthropological Research* 32(2), 109–23.

P'Bitek, Okot 1972: *Song of Lawino and Song of Ocol*. East African Publishing House, Nairobi.

Petchesky, Rosalind Pollack 1981 'Reproductive choice' in the contemporary United States: a social analysis of female sterilization. In Karen L. Michaelson (ed.), *And the Poor Get Children: Radical Perspectives on Population Dynamics*, Monthly Review Press, New York, 50–88.

Pfeffer, Naomi 1985: The hidden pathology of the male reproductive system. In Hilary Homans (ed.), *The Sexual Politics of Reproduction*, Gower, London, 30–44.

Plakans, Andrejs 1984: *Kinship in the Past: An Anthropology of European Family Life, 1500–1900*. Blackwell, Oxford.

Plumb, J. H. 1950: England in the Eighteenth Century. Penguin, Harmondsworth.

Pollack, Robert A. 1985: A transaction cost approach to families and households. *Journal of Economic Literature* 23(2), 581–608.

Poni, Carlo 1978: Family and 'podere' in Emilia Romagna. *Journal of Italian History* 1, 201–34.

Popenoe, David 1988: *Disturbing the Nest: Family Change and Decline in Modern Societies*. Aldine de Gruyter, New York.

Poster, Mark 1978: *Critical Theory of the Family*. Seabury Press, New York.

Rapp, Rayna 1987: Toward a nuclear freeze? The gender politics of Euro–American kinship analysis. In Jane F. Collier and Sylvia Yanagisako (eds), *Gender and Kinship*, Stanford University Press, Stanford, 119–31.

Rex, John 1961: *Key Problems in Sociological Theory*. Routledge and Kegan Paul, London.

Rey, Pierre Phillipe 1979: Class contradictions in lineage societies. *Critique of Anthropology* 4(13/14), 41–60.

Reyna, S. P. 1976: The extending strategy: regulation of the household dependency ratio. *Journal of Anthropological Research* 32(2), 182–98.

Richards, A. I. 1950: Some types of family structure amongst the Central Bantu. In A. R. Radcliffe-Brown and Daryll Forde (eds), *African Systems of Kinship and Marriage*, Oxford University Press, London, 207–51.

Richards, R. D. 1958: *The Early History of Banking in England*. Frank Cass, London.

Roberts, Pepe 1979: The integration of women into the development process: some conceptual problems. *Institute for Development Studies Bulletin* 10(3), 60–6.

Roberts, Penelope A. 1988: Rural women's access to labour in West Africa. In Jane Parpart and Sharon Stichter (eds), *Patriarchy and Class in Africa*, Westview Press, Boulder, 97–114.

Roberts, Robert 1973: *The Classic Slum: Salford Life in the First Quarter of the Century*. Penguin, Harmondsworth.

Robertson, A. F. 1973: Bugerere – a county case history: the successful farmer in an immigrant society. In A. I. Richards, F. Sturrock and J. M. Fortt, eds, *From Subsistence to Commercial Farming in Present-day Buganda*. Cambridge University Press, Cambridge, 232–68.

— —1978: *Community of Strangers: A Journal of Discovery at the Source of the Nile*. Scolar Press, London.

— —1984: *People and the State: An Anthropology of Planned Development*. Cambridge University Press, Cambridge.

——1987: *The Dynamics of Productive Relationships: African Share Contracts in Comparative Perspective.* Cambridge University Press, Cambridge.

——(forthcoming): Reproduction and the making of history: time, the family, and modern society. In R. Friedland and D. Boden (eds), *Time, Space and Modernity.*

Robertson, A. F. and Hughes, G. A. 1978: The family farm in Buganda. *Development and Change* 9(3), 415–38.

Rodgers, Roy H. 1977: The family life cycle concept: past, present, and future. In Jean Cuisinier (ed.), *The Family Life Cycle in European Societies*, Mouton, The Hague, 39–57.

Rosen, Sherwin 1976: A theory of life earnings. *Journal of Political Economy* 84(4), part II, S45–67.

Rosenzweig, Mark R and Wolpin, Kenneth L. 1979: *An Economic Analysis of the Extended Family in a Less Developed Country: The Demand for the Elderly in an Uncertain Environment.* Discussion Paper 317, Economic Growth Center, Yale University, August.

Rossi, Alice S. (ed.) 1985: *Gender and the Life Course.* Aldine, New York.

Rowntree, B. Seebohm 1922: *Poverty: A Study of Town Life* (first published 1901). Howard Fertig, New York.

Sahlins, Marshall 1972: *Stone Age Economics.* Aldine Atherton, Chicago.

Sanday, Peggy Reeves 1981: *Female Power and Male Dominance.* Cambridge University Press, Cambridge.

Schneider, David M. 1984: *A Critique of the Study of Kinship.* University of Michigan Press, Ann Arbor.

Schorr, Alvin L. 1966: The family cycle and income development. *Social Security Bulletin* 29(2), 14–25.

Schott, Rüdiger 1988: Traditional systems of social security and their present-day crisis in West Africa. In F. von Benda–Beckman et al. (eds), *Between Kinship and the State: Social Security and law in developing countries* Foris, Dordrecht, 89–107.

Schuler, Sidney Ruth 1987: *The Other Side of Polyandry: Property, Stratification, and Nonmarriage in the Nepal Himalayas.* Westview Press, Boulder.

Schulte, Regina 1984: Infanticide in rural Bavaria in the nineteenth century. In Hans Medick and David W. Sabean (eds), *Interest and Emotion: Essays on the Study of Family and Kinship*, Cambridge University Press, Cambridge, 77–102.

Schultz, T. Paul 1974: Birth rate changes over space and time: a study of Taiwan. In Theodore W. Schultz (ed.), *Economics of the Family*, University of Chicago Press, Chicago, 255–91.

——1976: Comments on 'Estimates of a human capital production function embedded in a life-cycle model of labor supply' [by James J. Heckman]. In Nestor E. Terleckyj (ed.), *Household Production and Consumption*, National Bureau of Economic Research, New York, 259–264

Schultz, Theodore W. 1973: The value of children: an economic perspective. *Journal of Political Economy* 81(2), part II, S2–13.

——(ed.) 1974: *Economics of the Family: Marriage, Children, and Human Capital.* National Bureau of Economic Research, University of Chicago Press, Chicago.

Scott, James C. 1976: *The Moral Economy of the Peasant: Rebellion and Subsistence in Southeast Asia.* Yale University Press, New Haven.

Scrimshaw, Susan C. M. 1984: Infanticide in human populations: societal and individual concerns. In G. Hausfater and S. B. Hrdy (eds), *Infanticide: Comparative and Evolutionary Perspectives*, Aldine, New York, 439–62.

Segalen, Martine 1984: Nuclear is not independent: organization of the household in the Pays Bigouden Sud in the nineteenth and twentieth centuries. In R. McC. Netting, R. R. Wilk and E. J. Arnould (eds), *Households*, University of California Press, Berkeley/Los Angeles, 163–86.

Sen, Amartya 1981: *Poverty and Famines*. Clarendon Press, Oxford.

Sennett, R. 1970: *Families against the City*. Harvard University Press, Cambridge, Mass.

Shanas, Ethel 1973: Family-kin networks and aging in cross-cultural perspective. *Journal of Marriage and the Family*, 35(3), 505–11.

Shanin, Teodor 1972: *The Awkward Class: Political Sociology of Peasantry in a Developing Society: Russia 1910–1925*. Clarendon Press, Oxford.

Shorter, Edward 1975: *The Making of the Modern Family*. Basic Books, New York.

Sieder, Reinhard and Mitterauer, Michael 1983: The reconstruction of the family life course: theoretical and empirical results. In R. Wall, J. Robin and P. Laslett (eds), *Family Forms in Historic Europe*, Cambridge University Press, Cambridge, 309–45.

Silver, Catherine B. 1982: *Frédéric Le Play: On Family, Work, and Social Change*. University of Chicago Press, Chicago.

Silverman, Sydel F. 1968: Agricultural organization, social structure, and values in Italy: amoral familism reconsidered. *American Anthropologist* 70(1), 1–19.

——1975: *The Three Bells of Civilization: The Life of an Italian Hill Town*. Columbia University Press, New York.

Simmons, George B. 1985: Theories of fertility. In Ghazi M. Farooq and George B. Simmons (eds), *Fertility in Developing Countries*, St Martin's Press, New York, 20–55.

Skinner, Elliott P. 1968: Intergenerational conflict among the Mossi: father and son. In Paul Bohannan and John Middleton (eds), *Marriage, Family, and Residence*, Natural History Press, New York, 237–45.

Skynner, Robin and Cleese, John 1984: *Families and How to Survive Them*. Oxford University Press, New York.

Skolnick, Arlene and Skolnick, Jerome (eds) 1980: *Family in Transition: Rethinking Marriage, Sexuality, Childrearing and Family Organization*. Little, Brown, Boston.

Smith, James P. 1977: Family labour supply over the life cycle. *Explorations in Economic Research* 4(2), 205–76.

Smith, Joan, Wallerstein, Immanuel and Evers, Hans–Dieter (eds.) 1984: *Households and the World-economy*. Sage, Beverly Hills.

Smith, Richard M. 1981: Fertility, economy, and household formation in England over three centuries. *Population and Development Review* 7(4), 595–622.

——1986: Marriage processes in the English past: some continuities. In Lloyd Bonfield, Richard M. Smith and Keith Wrightson (eds), *The World We Have Gained*, Basil Blackwell, Oxford, 43–99.

Sorokin, Pitirim, Zimmerman, Carle C. and Galpin, Charles J. 1931: *A Systematic Source Book in Rural Sociology*. Russell and Russell, New York.

Spanier, G. B., Sauer, W. and Larzelere, R. 1979: An empirical evaluation of the family life cycle. *Journal of marriage and the Family* 41(1), 27–38.

Spilerman, Seymour 1977: Careers, labour market structure, and socioeconomic achievement. *American Journal of Sociology* 83(3), 551–93.

Spiro, Melford E. 1968: Is the family universal? In Paul Bohannan and John Middleton (eds), *Marriage, Family, and Residence*, Natural History Press, New York, 221–35.

Stenning, Derrick J. 1958: Household viability among the pastoral Fulani. In Goody, Jack (ed), *The Developmental Cycle in Domestic Groups*, Cambridge University Press, Cambridge, 92–119.

Stolcke, Verena 1981: Women's labours: the naturalisation of social inequality and women's subordination. In K. Young, C. Wolkowitz and R. McCullagh (eds), *Of Marriage and the Market*, Routledge and Kegan Paul, London, 159–77.

Stoler, Ann Laura 1985: *Capitalism and Confrontation in Sumatra's Plantation Belt, 1870–1979*. Yale University Press, New Haven.

Stone, Lawrence 1975: The rise of the nuclear family in early modern England: the patriarchal stage. In C. E. Rosenberg (ed.), *The Family in History*, University of Pennsylvania Press, 13–57.

— —1977: *The family, Sex and Marriage in Enqland 1500–1800*, Weidenfeld and Nicolson, London.

Strong, Bryan 1973: Toward a history of the experiential family: sex and incest in the nineteenth century family. *Journal of Marriage and the Family* (35)3, 457–66.

Symons, Donald 1989: A critique of Darwinian anthropology. *Ethnology and Sociobiology* 10, 131–44.

Tait, David 1956: The family, household and minor lineage of the Konkomba. *Africa* 26(3), 219–49; 26(4), 332–42.

Tanner, Christopher 1987: Malnutrition and the development of rural households in the Agreste of Paraiba State, North-east Brazil. *Journal of Development Studies* 23(2), 242–64.

Thadani, Veena N. 1978: The logic of sentiment: the family and social change. *Population and Development Review* 4(3), 457–99.

Thompson, D'Arcy Wentworth 1942: *Growth and Form*. Cambridge University Press, Cambridge.

Thomson, David 1950: *England in the Nineteenth Century (1815–1914)*. Penguin, Harmondsworth.

— —1986: Welfare and the historians. In Lloyd Bonfield, Richard M. Smith and Keith Wrightson (eds), *The World We Have Gained*, Basil Blackwell, Oxford, 355–78.

Thompson, E. P. 1967: Time, work-discipline, and industrial capitalism. *Past and Present* 38, 56–97.

— —1968: *The Making of the English Working Class* (revised edn). Penguin, Harmondsworth.

Thorner, D., B. Kerblay and R. F. Smith (eds) 1966: *On the Theory of Peasant Economy*. Richard Irwin, Homewood, Ill.

Tilly, Louise A. 1985: Family, gender, and occupation in industrial France: past and present. In Alice S. Rossi (ed.), *Gender and the Life Course*, Aldine, New York, 193–212.

Tilly, Louise and Scott, Joan W. 1978: *Women, Work, and Family*. Holt, Rinehart and Winston, New York.

Todd, Emmanuel 1985: *The Explanation of Ideology: Family Structures and Social Systems*. Basil Blackwell, Oxford.

Trevelyan, G. M. 1945: *History of England* (3rd edn). Longmans, Green, London.

Trost, Jan 1977: The family life cycle: a problematic concept. In Jean Cuisinier (ed.), *The Family Life Cycle in European Societies*, Mouton, The Hague, 467–81.

Turnbull, Colin 1972: *The Mountain People*. Simon and Schuster, New York.

Ucko, Peter J. 1970: Penis sheaths: a comparative study. *Proceedings* of the Royal Anthropological Institute of Great Britain and Ireland for 1969.

US Department of Labor 1977: *U.S. Working Women: A Databook*. US Department of Labor, Washington.

Usher, Abbott Payson 1943: *The Early History of Deposit Banking in Mediterranean Europe*. Russell and Russell, New York.

Verdon, Michel 1980: Shaking off the domestic yoke, or the sociological significance of residence. *Comparative Studies in Society and History* 22(1), 109–32.

——1979: The stem family: toward a general theory. *Journal of Interdisciplinary History* 10(1), 87–105.

Vogt, Evon 1955: *Modern Homesteaders*. Harvard University Press, Cambridge, Mass.

Wall, Richard 1983: The household: demographic and economic change in England, 1650–1970. In R. Wall, J. Robin and P. Laslett (eds), *Family Forms in Historic Europe*, Cambridge University Press, Cambridge, 493–512.

——1986: Work, welfare and the family: an illustration of the adaptive family economy. In Lloyd Bonfield, Richard M. Smith and Keith Wrightson (eds), *The World We Have Gained*, Basil Blackwell, Oxford, 261–94.

Watkins, Susan Cotts 1986: Conclusions. In Ansley J. Coale and Susan C. Watkins (eds), *The Decline of Fertility in Europe*, Princeton University Press, Princeton NJ, 420–49.

Wells, Robert V. 1971: Demographic change and the life cycle of American families. *Journal of Interdisciplinary History* 2(2), 273–82.

Wheaton, Robert 1975: Family and kinship in western Europe: the problem of the joint family household. *Journal of Interdisciplinary History* 5(4), 601–28.

Whiteford, Linda M and Poland, Marilyn L. (eds) 1988: *New Approaches to Human Reproduction: Social and Ethical Dimensions*. Westview Press, Boulder.

Williamson, Oliver E. 1981: The modern corporation: origins, evolution, attributes. *Journal of Economic Literature* 19, 1537–68.

Wilson, Godfrey and Wilson, Monica 1945: *The Analysis of Social Change*. Cambridge University Press, Cambridge.

Wilson, Monica 1951: *Good Company: A Study of Nyakusa age-villages*. Oxford University Press, London.

Winch, Donald 1987: *Malthus*. Oxford University Press, Oxford.

Wolf, Eric 1966: *Peasants*. Prentice-Hall, Englewood Cliffs, NJ.

——1982: *Europe and the People without History*. University of California Press, Berkeley/Los Angeles.

Wolff, Henry W. 1919: *People's Banks: A Record of Social and Economic Success*. P. S. King, London.

Wolpe, Harold (ed.) 1980: *The Articulation of Modes of Production: Essays from 'Economy and Society'*. Routledge and Kegan Paul, London.

Wrigley, E. Anthony 1978: Reflections on the history of the family. In A. S. Rossi, J. Kagan and T. K. Hareven (eds), *The Family*, W. W. Norton, New York, 71–85.

Wrigley, E. A. and Schofield, R. S. 1981: *The Population History of England 1541–1871: A Reconstruction*. Edward Arnold, London.

Wynn, Margaret 1970: *Family Policy*. Michael Joseph, London.

Yanagisako, Sylvia J. 1979: Family and household: the analysis of domestic groups. *Annual Review of Anthropology* 8, 161–205.

Young, Michael and Willmott, Peter 1962: *Family and Kinship in East London* (2nd edn). Penguin, Harmondsworth.

Young, Michael W. 1971: *Fighting with Food: Leadership, Values and Social Control in a Massim Society*. Cambridge University Press, Cambridge.

Zacher, Hans F. 1988: Traditional solidarity and modern social security: harmony or conflict? In F. von Benda–Beckman et al. (eds), *Between Kinship and the State: Social Security and Law in Developing Countries*, Foris, Dordrecht, 21–38.

Zaretsky, Eli 1973: *Capitalism, the Family, and Personal Life*. Harper Colophon Books, Harper & Row, New York.

——1982: The place of the family in the origins of the welfare state. In B. Thorne and M. Yalon (eds), *Rethinking the Family*, Longman, New York, 188–224.

Zelizer, Viviana A. R. 1979: *Morals and Markets: The Development of Life Insurance in the United States*. Columbia University Press, New York.

——1985: Pricing the Priceless Child: The Changing Social Value of Children. Basic Books, New York.

Zuckerman, Michael 1975: Dr Spock: the confidence man. In C. E. Rosenberg (ed.), *The Family in History*, University of Pennsylvania Press, 179–207.

# Index

Vogt, Evon, 144, 218
voting, 119
  women, 119
Watt, James, 114, 188
wealth, 24–5, 32–3, 70, 85–91, 171
weaning, 6, 177
weaving, 111
Weber, Max, 152, 198
welfare policy, 37–8
welfare state, 110, 119, 168
West Africa, 80
West Virginia (USA), 177
wet nursing, 108
widow, 23, 186
  Ganda, 32, 36
  inheritance of, 57, 69
  pensioning, 90, 119, 189

Sotho, 48, 81
wife *see* conjugal relations
women *see separate subject headings*
wool, 108–9
working class, 14, 37–9, 47, 91, 92,
    94, 97, 100–1, 103, 104, 115–19,
    130–40, 164, 188
Wynn, Margaret, 37–8, 133–4, 173,
    178, 181, 193, 218

yeoman farmers, 109, 111
York (England), 37–9
Yugoslavia, 179

Zadruga (Serbia) 45, 169
Zelizer, Viviana, 64, 67, 178, 179,
    189, 191, 192, 218